The Body and the Text

The Body and the Text

Hélène Cixous, Reading and Teaching

edited by

Helen Wilcox, Keith McWatters, Ann Thompson and Linda R. Williams

 **HARVESTER WHEATSHEAF**

New York   London   Toronto   Sydney   Tokyo   Singapore

First published 1990 by
Harvester Wheatsheaf
66 Wood Lane End, Hemel Hempstead
Hertfordshire HP2 4RG
A division of
Simon & Schuster International Group

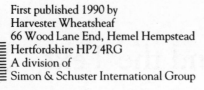

Typeset in 10½/12½ pt Goudy Old Style
by Keyboard Services, Luton, Beds

Printed and bound in Great Britain by
BPCC Wheatons Ltd, Exeter

British Library Cataloguing in Publication Data

The Body and the text,:Helene Cixous readings
and teaching.
   1. French literature. Cixous, Helene 1937–
  I. Wilcox, Helen
  848.91409

ISBN 0–7450–0821–6

1 2 3 4 5 94 93 92 91 90

Contents

Acknowledgements

The editors would like to thank Barbara Smith most warmly for her patient and good-humoured involvement in the administrative and secretarial tasks associated with both the original colloquium and this collection of papers which has resulted from it. They are also grateful to the French Cultural Counsellor, M. Guillemin, and the Service Culturel of the French Embassy, for their support for the colloquium, and to Jackie Jones of Harvester Wheatsheaf for her help in making the book a reality.

Part I

Hélène Cixous and
Etudes Féminines

Introduction

The essays in this collection all originated as papers for a colloquium held at Liverpool University in April 1989, at which the main speaker was the French feminist critic, novelist, dramatist and teacher, Hélène Cixous. The first section of this volume is therefore devoted to work by and about Cixous. The subsequent two sections move out to a broader feminist critical discussion of writing, gender and reading (issues which are, of course, constantly addressed in Cixous' writing), considering texts from French as well as English and American literature. The final section considers the wide-ranging practical implications of feminist criticism, and Cixous' work in particular, for the future teaching of literature.

The starting point for this volume, then, is a challenging essay by Hélène Cixous, entitled 'Difficult Joys', on the responsibilities and privileges of the writer. It is probably inappropriate to describe this fascinating and puzzling piece as an 'essay'; it is somewhere between autobiography, explication, meditation and prophecy. This is no ordinary literary criticism; it deals in metaphysical and poetic statements, such as, 'Death is implied in writing: the redeeming from death but also the giving of death' (page 18, below). As Sandra M. Gilbert wrote of Cixous' *Newly Born Woman*, reading her work is 'like going to sleep in one world and waking in another'.[1] The implication of a dream-like experience here is appropriate, for Cixous' writing has all the vision, strange assertiveness and apparent infinity of a dream. Her paper ends, deliberately, 'à suivre'; the debate remains open. Cixous herself, not surprisingly, believes in learning from the unconscious: 'our dreams are the greater poets' (page 22).

What is the subject of 'Difficult Joys'? It is nothing less than the 'world of books' and 'future of culture' (page 25). Cixous is concerned with the power of writing to transform mourning into joy, to merge violence and love. The discussion is rooted in texts – by Clarice Lispector, Mandelstam, Tsvetaeva, Rilke, Shakespeare – but moves swiftly from detail of wordplay to archetypes such as music and the sea. She gives extended consideration to the idea of writing as the crossing of boundaries, as 'circulation' (page 14); the writer is exile and other, but also the reconciler of opposites. Underlying this is always the matter of truth, authorship and gender, and the perplexing question of the 'I'. As Cixous disconcertingly comments, 'Of course I don't know who "I" am/is/are' (page 9).

Sarah Cornell's essay attempts to answer that question, on one level at least, by introducing readers to the biography and thought of Hélène

Cixous. The colloquium began with Cornell's talk, which was designed to give a foundation for those who are largely unfamiliar with Cixous as writer and teacher of *Etudes Féminines*. The paper by Nicole Ward Jouve vividly analyses the development from inner to outer theatre in Cixous' work, as she has moved from fiction and theory (the two are often inseparable) to writing for the stage in recent years. Ward Jouve considers Cixous' capacity to write 'in the present' (page 42) and to produce 'writing that is celebratory and poetic, . . . writing that is of woman for both men and women' (page 48). There is a hint here of a writing which is 'feminine' and yet beyond the limitations of gender. This complex interrelationship of 'feminine' and 'female', of culture, biology and language, is the subject of Judith Still's paper, which focuses particularly on the question of 'feminine economy' raised by Cixous' work. Still's approach is more overtly theoretical than that of the other papers in this section, and involves a careful examination of theories of masculine economy in order to clarify the possibility of a feminine version, whether 'theoretical extreme or poetic utopia' (page 58).

The four papers forming this section are startling in the variety of modes of writing which they offer the reader: inspirational grandeur, well-informed clarity, imaginative analysis, probing argument. Yet they are linked by common concerns, many of which are central features of Cixous' thought. They suggest, for example, the inseparability of reading and writing and, as Cornell puts it, the 'reciprocal replenishment' (page 32) given by the two activities. All the essays explore the idea of 'writing the body' and the nature of *écriture féminine*, which Still ends by defining as 'a writing shot through (like shot silk) with otherness' (page 57). They confront the difficult questions of biological and social 'femininity', and the use of the terms masculine and feminine to subvert rather than confirm a binary opposition. At the heart of all four papers, however different, is the perplexity of gender and the mystery of writing. As Ward Jouve suggests, 'you have to trust to language, its mobility, the spectrum of connotations that storm and sunshine can open in it, to show you the way' (page 43).

H.W.

NOTE

1. Sandra M. Gilbert, Introduction to Hélène Cixous and Catherine Clément, *The Newly Born Woman*, translated by Betsy Wing (Manchester: Manchester University Press, 1986), p. x.

Chapter 1

Difficult Joys

Hélène Cixous

I am going to tell you today about the things that are coming to my mind at the present time.* I myself was a bit surprised by what was coming out, which I think is the consequence of the particular historical year or time, not excluding the fact that for us in France it is '1789'. Therefore I'll entitle the whole thing 'The Writer's Rights'. But after having gone through my day-dreaming on the writer's rights, I thought that maybe I should have called it 'The Writer's Obligations or Duties'. There was in France in 1789 a big debate, during the debate on the Declaration of the Rights of Man and the Citizen, on Rights or Duties. Maybe these are two aspects of the same attitude. Another title that came was 'A Difficult Joy'. Let me try and tell you a few things about difficult joys in writing.

I have chosen to refer to some literary passages as a kind of soil in order to have a little thinking grow. The choice is something that is very close to my heart: a poem by Mandelstam, 'Verses on the Unknown Soldier'; a page from Clarice Lispector; a few pages of Tsvetaeva. I realise that my choice is actually of writers who are not very well known, and it is part of their destiny, part of fate, that it should be so, and part of the quality of their writing which is absolutely exceptional. It's probably the sign of their belonging to a certain country – the country of writers, the country of languages – to which we do have difficulties travelling. It's our work, our mission, all of us who are readers, to go to that country.

A few words on those writers: Mandelstam's poem was written in 1937. He died a year later, in Siberia, as an exile. He was a Russian poet who defined himself as belonging to 'civilisation' – that was his country – and he was condemned to exile and death for poems, for poetry. For me he is now (I may change my mind in ten years if I find somebody else) he is the greatest poet in that half century.

* When originally given, this paper was developed from bare notes written in French; the process of speaking it involved expansion and translation simultaneously. We hope that this printed version can still reflect the improvisatory freshness of the original.

As for Clarice Lispector, a Brazilian writer who died in 1977, for me, she is a kind of female Kafka. She's not a Kafka at all, she is not a dark philosopher, she is the 'yes' to his 'no', the life to his death, yet without excluding the presence of agony and death – attraction near the wild heart of life. She ranks with Kafka in the density and intensity of her thinking, because she is a thinking writer which is very rare. As for Tsvetaeva who was a contemporary and friend of Mandelstam, and also a very great poet, she wasn't exiled by the Soviets because she exiled herself, she emigrated. She wrote most of her poetry in exile in France (and other countries, but mostly in France) and unfortunately she decided – and she was encouraged – to go back to Russia in 1939, in order to suffer the war, and to be rejected from all kinds of places and institutions. She ended her life by committing suicide – she hanged herself in a tree. That was in 1941, she was 48 at that time, she was starving, she was alone on Earth, and she had no one to whom to write a letter any more – she chose that death as a way to that other world about which she had so often written. Lately, quite by chance, I came upon a long meditation of Thomas Bernhard (who has just died). He has written a lot about death by hanging, which struck me enormously because it was his own fantasy. He often thought of committing suicide in this way, and he even tried when he was a kid, he tells in his autobiography. And this hanging he links with *a piece of string*, with a link, the tie or untying, having a link with something which can be life or death.

So the first piece I am going to deal with is a page of Clarice Lispector, which is a kind of montage. At the top of the page is the title of her book, *The Hour of the Star*. As you see, the book has not *a* title but titles: The Hour of the Star, or The Blame is Mine, or The Hour of the Star, or Let Her Fend for Herself, or The Right to Cry, or Clarice Lispector (her own signature), or As for the Future, or Singing the Blues, or She Doesn't Know How to Shout, or A Sense of Loss, or Whistling in the Dark Wind, or I am Unable to Do Anything, or A Record of Preceding Events, or Tearful Tale of Cordel (which is a popular kind of ballad) or the Discreet Exit by the Back Door. So that's 'the title' of her book. And the main character of the story is called – rather, will be called towards the end of the book – Macabea, but actually it's a person who hasn't got a name for a long time, it's an almost nameless person, an unnameable, an 'almost', and the whole book deals with the difficulty of naming, of giving recognition to any thing or person or work. That is, it deals with the possibility or value of authority, or the legitimacy of the name, title or 'writership'.

Next, you have extracts from the first page of the book which is called 'Dedication of the Author' – followed by (*in truth Clarice Lispector*). Now that's the main problem that is going to be woven within this text, which is

A HORA
DA ESTRELA

A CULPA É MINHA
OU
A HORA DA ESTRELA
OU
ELA QUE SE ARRANGE
OU
O DIREITO AO GRITO

Clarice Lispector

.QUANTO AO FUTURO.
OU
LAMENTO DE UM BLUE
OU
ELA NÃO SABE GRITAR
OU
UMA SENSAÇÃO DE PERDA
OU
ASSOVIO NO VENTO ESCURO
OU
EU NÃO POSSO FAZER NADA
OU
REGISTRO DOS FATOS ANTECEDENTES
OU
HISTÓRIA LACRIMOGÊNICA DE CORDEL
OU
SAÍDA DISCRETA PELA PORTA DOS FUNDOS

The Blame is Mine — or The Hour of the Star — or Let Her Fend for Herself — or The Right to Protest — or Clarice Lispector — or As for the Future — or Singing the Blues — or She Doesn't Know How to Protest — or A Sense of Loss — or Whistling in the Dark Wind — or I Can Do Nothing — or A Record of Preceding Events — or A Tearful Tale — or A Discreet Exit by the Back Door. [1]

a very simple and at the same time extraordinarily small novel. 'Dedication of the author' – so here comes the author.

> And so I dedicate this thing to old Schumann and to his sweet Clara, who today are bones, poor us . . . I dedicate myself to the tempest of Beethoven. To the vibration of the neutral colours of Bach. To Chopin who softens my bones. To Stravinski who astonished me and with whom I flew in fire. To 'Death and Transfiguration' where Richard Strauss reveals to me a destiny? Above all, I dedicate myself to the eves of today and to today, to the transparent veil of Debussy, to Marlos Nobre, to Prokofiev, to Carl Orff and Schoenberg . . .
>
> I dedicate myself to the colour red, bright scarlet, like my blood of a fully-aged man, and so I dedicate myself to my blood. I dedicate myself above all to the gnomes, dwarfs, sylphids, nymphs that inhabit my life. I dedicate myself to the nostalgia for my old poverty, when everything was more sober and dignified and I had never eaten lobster.[2]

And during the whole of this small huge book, the author is going to be speaking with us, addressing the reader, having difficulties with himself (I'm not making a mistake) and wondering what to be an author is, although the author is, in truth, Clarice Lispector. So we as readers have to deal with that mystery of . . . I don't know what to call it, the precise definitions, I don't want to use the word gender, I don't want to use the word sex . . . But there is something that tells me that it must originally be from Clarice Lispector. The definition of the author remains undecided or at least the author is going to portray himself as a man. The author is a man, this man is 'in truth' Clarice Lispector.

I did need that passage in order to point to a very important problem for people who write and people who read, which is actually the possibility or the right of the writer to define him/his/her/oneself, to classify herself/myself/yourself. This is probably the problem that has come to the surface of our minds today, in our present time. Clarice Lispector is not a theorist, she's not trying to demonstrate anything or to illustrate anything – she just tries to cope with a very difficult situation, a dramatic situation – that is, how to deal with the character for whom she has written that book, whom she has loved, how to get into a close and at the same time careful relation with the character, Macabea, who is a woman – although she's not really a woman. She's a tiny bit of grass. She is almost nothing. She is such a slight person that she's almost invisible. This comes from her being at the limit of existence, because she is so poor, so famished. All the problems that Clarice Lispector has with her character mainly come from her wanting to be honest, wanting to be faithful, feeling that there are ethical problems in being a writer, even regarding the character she's inventing. And these ethical problems include particularly the problem of sexual definition. So I'm just laying that down, in order for us to know that somebody, a writer, has dealt with the problem, poetically not theoretically.

Just remember Macabea who, as I told you, is named very late in the book. Her name rings in a strange way; it *is* a signifier, it does mean something. Of course Clarice Lispector, or the author, do not say anything to us about the signifier: she is just Macabea. Maybe if she hadn't been called Macabea she would not have died; the text doesn't tell us anything about that. But the text tells us about her death; the text doesn't even tell us about her death, the text dies with her. Maybe she is killed by the writing, or maybe that is why the writing, from the beginning, refrains from advancing. The whole text is being refrained, reserved, as if Clarice Lispector, or the author, were afraid of what is imminent, and what is imminent is Macabea's death. But we don't know anything about it. Page by page the text moves toward her death, now and then guessing at it, now and then feeling that something horrible is going to happen on the next page; but it doesn't happen. And finally all of a sudden it happens, because the life of Macabea and the life of this book are one. So the book and Macabea die, and Clarice Lispector died two months later. How is it that she died two months later? We should put the question in another way – she wrote that book because she was dying. She reached the point when she felt she was going to die: she was very sick. So this is the book of a dying writer who deals with one of the most important problems in writing – the right of life, of death, on the characters, on oneself the writer, on the reader, on everybody we meet every day.

Now who is '*the writer in truth*'? Maybe we should always call the writer 'the writer in truth' or 'in untruth', but it's true that just using the word 'writer' is calling for the question of what is truth and how to decide about it. The truth of the writer, the identity of the writer, the authority of the writer, all these are matters that are always questionable. I am a writer who very often says 'I' and writes in the first person, but we all know that the first person is – though it's one of the most wonderful things in the world, it's a very happy thing to say 'I' – still very mysterious. Of course I don't know who 'I' am/is/are. The scope between the writer and truth, that opening, is probably where the writing slides by. What right has the writer – I should say, the author – to call herself/himself 'author'? What is the essential of the author? What is proper to the author?

I turn to Mandelstam because I prefer his definition in his extraordinary poem, 'The Unknown Soldier'. We all have an unknown soldier.

> Is it for this the skull grows wide
> And from temple to temple fills the brow,
> To stop the sockets of its eyes

From being filled with soldiery?
The skull grows wide from life,
From temple to temple to fill the brow;
It teases itself with the neatness of its seams,
Achieving clarity through comprehension's dome,
Bubbling with thought and dreaming of itself,
Cup of cups and fatherland's country
A cap picked out with star-spangled ribs –
Shakespeare's father – good fortune's cap. [3]

I'm sure you recognise the 'cup of cups', the 'skull of skulls' which comes from Hamlet and rolls down history into a Russian field of snow. As Mandelstam says, the skull is 'Shakespeare's father'. Who is father of the father? Maybe the Skull, Yorick, is Shakespeare's father. But at the same time the skull, which Mandelstam has picked up in his Russian hands as if he were a new Hamlet, is the cup which is full of all the poems in the world. And of course it's the unknown soldier's skull and cup. I realise that in the English translation we have 'from temple to temple' which is beautiful; I don't know what it is in Russian, I could check, but it works very well: it's a play on the signifier which, I feel, Mandelstam might have adopted. So that is the portrait of the poem and the poet: an unknown soldier who has been elected by the universal memory, because of his being unknown; but who, because of his (or her) being ourselves (whoever has a thought for the unknown soldier is the unknown soldier), is being kept as unique, as anonymous, and as carrying in his or her skull, millions. This unknown soldier has absolutely nothing that belongs to himself/herself, is without anything that can be called 'own' except the birthday date given later in the eighth stanza. That's the name of the unknown soldier, the 'year of his birth' which he whispers 'with bloodless lips'. This then is the discourse of the poet himself as unknown soldier, the dead among the dead, yet not only the dead among the dead, somebody who is being resurrected by poetry.

Brodsky, who is the inheritor of those great poets and also a Russian, who has escaped that type of painful death, writes apropos of Tsvetaeva: 'No matter how dramatic a person's direct experience is, it is always exceeded by the experience of an instrument. Yet a poet is a combination of an instrument and a human being in one person, with the former gradually taking over the latter. The sensation of this takeover is responsible for the timbre, the realisation of it for destiny.'[4] It's a poet speaking about poets (which is not exactly the same as a fiction writer) – a poet qualifying 'poet' in a musical way, not in a human way. Brodsky at one point quotes Akhmatova (another great Russian poet) saying that Marina Tsvetaeva 'begins a poem on a high C'.[5] Sometimes I have a kind of tender envy for a poet who can be described as beginning on a high C. That's the right of the poet, but it's also an indication of how we should read certain types of writing under the sign of music.

Who is the writer or the author of texts? I work by way of language, by voice, by music, not only work but am written by a certain type of language. Our Russian poets insist on the fact that they write but that they are also written by Russian, which I'm sure is absolutely true. It's true of all poets, that they are being written through by a certain type of tongue – particularly poets who write in the English language. That's why we have fewer great poets in French than in English, because our French tongue doesn't want to write poetically. But how do we define a writer? Who is the author of a poem that is written by a tongue? A sore point with everybody who reads is of course the problem of translation. It's true that it's a wonderful thing that books should be written in a foreign tongue; but it's a painful thing for all readers standing at the door of that tongue, except if we are inhabitants of this precise language.

We are strangers when we read a book, in every way; we are strangers too when we write a book, in every way. We write mostly in one language, which is pervaded with other languages. All writers in foreign languages and most writers who are really inspired by language or by linguistic elements, and have an ear for music, write as if they were riding in a chariot drawn by several horses, and those horses are different languages. I've realised that most writers I'm interested in are writers who ride several languages, and have either read other writers in the original language or weave their own originary tongue with foreign languages. Tsvetaeva, for instance, whose mother was German, was brought up in German and Russian equally; she could speak French as well and wrote in French as well. The opening of *Mother and Music*, a prose autobiographical text, is studded with French or other foreign words. The very first moments of consciousness and the very first lines of writing of Tsvetaeva are half-Russian, half-French and – if you'll allow a third half – half-German. This text tells of the birth of the writer, that is, of the coming to language and to writing of a very small girl, through the experience of language, but language that has immediately a double level – one refers only to signifiers, the second names notes of music. Just have a look at the first page:

> When, instead of the longed-for, predetermined, almost preordained son Alexander, all that was born was just me, mother, proudly choking back a sigh said: 'At least she'll be a musician.' And when my first, clearly meaningless and fully intelligible word, uttered before the age of one, turned out to be *'gamma'* 'scale', mother merely affirmed: 'I knew it all along,' and straight away started teaching me music, endlessly singing to me that very scale: '*Do*, Musya, *do*, and this is *re*, *do-re* . . .'. That *do-re* soon turn into a huge book, half as big as me – a 'koob'

as I said it, for the time being only into its, the 'koob's,' cover, but it turned into a gold of such strength and fearfulness piercing forth from that violet that still to this day in a certain reserved, isolated, Undinian place in my heart there is a fever of heat and fear, as if that murky gold, melted down, had settled at my heart's deepest depth and from there, at the slightest touch, would rise and suffuse my whole self right up to the edge of my eyes and burn out my tears. That's *do-re* (Dore), and *re-mi* is Remy, the boy Remy from *Sans famille*, a happy boy whom his nurse's wicked husband (*estropié*, with a precision-turned foot – *pied*), the cripple Père Barbarin, promptly turns into an unhappy one.[6]

That's the beginning of a long story which mixes family, mother, music, languages, musical notes, drawings, representations, boy and girl and 'Sans famille', with and without family. And the coming to language through that extremely rich collection of signifiers, coming from a foreign language.

I myself realise that I was born into languages, by a happy accident, in two different languages – then I was brought up with several languages being talked in my family house and the streets around me, which made for the fact that I've always lived French as one of those different foreign languages. Writing in a foreign language, playing a foreign instrument, is it possible? Of course you become familiar with it. But the most important thing is that you never become too familiar and you never come to the point when you can hear it speak to you and you think you speak it. Exile – real or imaginary exile – presides over the destiny of writers. Exile as one of the metaphors, one of the structures of depropriation. Tsvetaeva herself, although she was born in a wealthy family, was born an exile in her own family. Her mother was already half an exile. She didn't live it as something dramatic when she was a small kid, but it was inscribed in all her thinking and perceiving of the world. And then her whole career was that of exile afterwards. The same thing with Mandelstam and Clarice Lispector, and probably with all writers who belong to a certain type of writing – I don't say that all writers have to be exiles. But probably at one point, if they reach a certain kind of passion for writing, it is because there is a kind of exile implied in their biography.

Exile can be a metaphor. It was real, unfortunately – or fortunately – for all Russian writers; it was real for Clarice Lispector, whose parents were also Russian and who emigrated to Brazil. It can be double: for Tsvetaeva it was both real exile, and the exile she always felt as a woman. There is something of a foreignness, a feeling of not being accepted or of being unacceptable, which is particularly insistent when as a woman you suddenly get into that strange country of writing where most inhabitants are men and where the fate of women is still not settled. It would have been much worse fifty years ago, or twenty years ago, ten years ago and it may become worse in years ahead. So sometimes you are even a double exile, but I'm not going to be tragic about it because I think it is a source of creation and of symbolic wealth. Tsvetaeva formulated this in a very striking way in one of her most famous poems, 'The Poem of the End'. At one point she suddenly exclaims in a very harsh way, 'All poets are Jews' – but she doesn't even say 'Jews' she says 'Yids' – it's an insult, but of course in her mouth the tone of offence is reversing to the contrary. 'All poets are Yids.'[7] This small line of hers has been taken up by Celan in one of his most beautiful poems, 'On the side of the Occa' (the river in the birthplace of Tsvetaeva).[8] Celan writes this poem on poets and poetry and the difficulty of surviving the poetical condition, by dedicating the poem to Tsvetaeva. What does her line mean? Does it mean for instance that all poets belong to a special race, and again that this race should be 'the elected race'? Actually Tsvetaeva probably chose that kind of signifier – the Jewish one – because she was keenly aware of the metaphorical weight of the situation of the Jews in Russia at that time, and besides she had married a Jew. But she used other equivalents at other points, particularly one which is extraordinarily striking, that of 'Nigger'. This she used in relation to Pushkin – as she said, 'Pushkin was a "Nigger"', all poets were 'Niggers'.[9] Now all poets are also 'Jews' – that is, all poets are Others, they are 'The Others'. 'I am the other', 'I am a Jew'. I myself say that in a very special way: I should try and say 'I am a Jew' *although* I am Jewish. If I say 'I am a Jew', if you say 'I am a Jew', by saying it you say that you are the Other, you are, I am, without anything that I can call my own, except of course the limitless wealth of language and of words. What remains available to Jews, as Celan writes, is speech; they can speak. As for women, maybe they are double-Jews, or semi-Jews, I don't know exactly. But although Celan says that poets have no one to speak to, although he addresses some of his verses to No one, I don't think that women address their poems to 'No one' – I think there is a slight difference: when it comes to the point when there is really 'No one' to address a poem to, they die. Women speak to someone, even if someone is not there, in flesh and blood; they address someone, an ear, someone far away, but someone is there. It probably has to do with the structure of womanhood, that *utter* despair, absolute despair, is something that cannot be lived. In Tsvetaeva, within her – who had a very difficult relation with her mother, something more like hatred than like love, but of course one contains the other – you hear *the mother singing*; even if the mother is associated with death, even if she dies, even if she tried – or because she tried – to make her daughter a musician whereas she was born to be a poet. Or maybe she was born to be a poet only because of music. There is that voice always ringing, even if No one is left, in women's works.

Now let me talk about the 'real' genealogy of writers. As I said, I think exile makes one part of it, and another essential feature is *de-nationalisation*. I don't think that poets have the feeling that they do belong to one special nation, I think they belong to the internation of poets. We don't write letters any more, but twenty or thirty years ago one would still go on writing letters, entertaining correspondences which made for the vanishing of borders: mail would go round the surface of the earth and made it feel one country, and it actually at the same time dealt away with all limits, all borders, all separation. The definition of the author is linked with that circulation. It is me, I, within the other, the other within me, it's one gender going into the other, one language going through the other, life through death, or as Tsvetaeva wrote in a very beautiful poem to Rilke, her friend, one year turning into the other, the year '26 turning into the year '27, to celebrate Rilke's turning from one world to the other – Rilke died in December '26.[10] I should use the word *Wendung* – one of Rilke's favourite words.

One of the most important, most remarkable turnings or transitions or transits in writing is the one from one sex to the other – either imaginary or real, either for instance, the experience of going over from heterosexuality to homosexuality, or the one that Clarice Lispector tried to inscribe in *The Hour of the Star*, that extraordinary fact of her suddenly having to become a male writer, in order to be able to write on a particular character who is 'a woman'. Everything that has to do with 'trans', including translation, has to do with sexuality, and as difference.

What about the authors of the author, the real authors of the author? They belong to two different species – one, of course, the real biological parents, who immediately become imaginary, who are immediately trans-figured; the others are texts, other writers, other books. First what about parents? From whom do we descend? Tsvetaeva will tell us that she is the daughter of her mother. Oh, she has a father, he's very old; he is the founder of a museum. The father is a museum, the father is statues, the father is stone, plaster, white. The mother is music, the mother is piano. She's extremely repressive; she is the one who brings life and death into the life of Tsvetaeva, and she's also strangely associated with black, because she is always seen with her piano, a huge royal Becker which is a brilliant black. The mirror surface of the piano is going to be the first mirror for Tsvetaeva. She sees herself in the piano of her mother as a small Negro. So this is the real and imaginary origin of Tsvetaeva, and yet it's not the end of it: she will later have other parents, which will compose an extraordinary parentage for her, out of which she's going to write.

As for Clarice Lispector, apart from the fact that she was of Russian origin, there is a kind of drama which is a primary scene for her, which she has told us in a short story called 'Belonging'.[11] In that story she writes about the trouble she has in '*Pertencer*'. She has never belonged; she has never been able to belong to anybody or to anyone – it's a very violent text. She writes that she's alone in the world, and she publishes that text in the *Journal of Brazil*, which has 2 million readers – so she tells 2 million readers, 'I am completely alone, and I don't belong to anybody or any place', except to Brazilian literature. Why? Because when she was going to be born her mother was sick and everybody in the family believed in a superstitious way that by being born she would heal her mother and bring her own mother to life. She was supposed to be the baby who was going to be the mother of the mother. Unfortunately her mother was not cured and died very soon after, so that Clarice Lispector was born in a way without a mother, and with a guilt: that she hadn't been able to save her mother. The guilt has a reverse side: it is her mother who has abandoned her and killed her. The close relation between mother and child, or let's say mother and daughter – but mother as mother of the daughter and daughter as mother of the mother – should work both ways in order to give life. But everything starts with the cradle, and everything we can hope for is that the cradle shouldn't be at the same time a grave, which it is very often. It was so for Tsvetaeva, it was so for Clarice Lispector. Hence their writing will go from cradle to grave, or from grave to cradle – these are the same types of places, of birth actually. You could say the same with Genet . . .

Thus the personality of the writer is composed of a large family of living and dead persons, sometimes with the majority of that family composed of 'women', sometimes composed of men. Now if you're a woman writer and you're mostly composed of men, then you've got a problem. Personally I myself am issued out of a family mostly composed of women, and of course I didn't do it on purpose! I might have been completely composed of men.

What about the texts that are the parents of the writer? We are made by what we read – writing starts with reading. Of course there are writers who don't read: there are writers who say that they don't read and who lie; there are writers who say that they don't read and say the truth. I personally am interested in writers who read. There's something very moving, very necessary, in writers who read. Tsvetaeva is a reader, Mandelstam is a reader, Kafka is a reader; Clarice Lispector is not a reader. She says that she doesn't read – and I don't believe her: it's very important for her not to have a parent, even in books.

Now what they read, and the way it works inside their writing, is of course decisive for everything that comes later. Tsvetaeva started with Pushkin – which most Russian writers did, but the way they do it is of course very different in each case: you read different parts of the writer, and even different parts of the body of the writer, because writers have bodies. Tsvetaeva starts with two 'augural signs'. The first is that her mother expected a son who would be called Alexander. If we're not Russian we don't even realise the importance of that prediction of the mother: Pushkin's first name is indeed Alexander. Tsvetaeva was completely impregnated with Pushkin; was she going to be a 'male' writer? The Pushkin theme becomes more and more complex. In her wonderful book *My Pushkin*, you have all the secrets of writing, the secrets of a great writer. It's almost a recipe for the origin of writing – except that when you want to write you've got to find your own recipe. So here writing starts *with a book*: 'It begins like a chapter in that novel, that indispensable tabletop reference work of all our mothers and grandmothers – *Jane Eyre*'. Not of our fathers – it begins with mothers and grandmothers.

> The secret of the red room.
> In the red room was a secret cabinet.

A secret within a secret, a room within a room, a cave within a cave. (I won't call it a uterus.)

> But before the secret cabinet there was something else, there was the picture in mother's room – *The Duel*.
> Snow, black, sapling branches, two black people are supporting a third under his arms, taking him to a sled – and still one more man, a different one, walks away, his back turned. The one they are taking away – is Pushkin, the one walking away – is d'Anthès. D'Anthès called out Pushkin to a duel, that is, he lured him out into the snow and there among the black leafless saplings, he killed him.[12]

This description of the duel is the embryo of the whole world of Tsvetaeva. It starts with a picture which is black and white, the colours of Tsvetaeva, and the picture has a legend: 'The first thing that I learned about Pushkin is that they killed him'. So it starts 1. with Pushkin, and 2. his first definition is that they killed him. 'Then I learned that Pushkin is a poet – and d'Anthès – a Frenchman.' These are two nationalities – French and poet. The poet is the killed one and he is killed in a very special way: he is killed in his stomach.

> From Pushkin's duel a certain self was born in me, *the sister*. I'll go even further – in the word 'stomach' there is something sacred for me – even a simple 'my stomach hurts' floods me with a wave of trembling compassion that rules out all humour. With that shot they wounded all of us in the stomach.

You lose everything in the English translation here. In French and Russian the stomach is also the *womb*. Actually Tsvetaeva was born out of the womb of Pushkin – the woman womb of Pushkin. Although he is an Alexander, he is also a woman, and the whole story of Pushkin as it is created here is going to be woven with mother, music, the womb, the stomach and the first poems. Pushkin is writing within Tsvetaeva all the time. She has translated Pushkin into French; the whole system of ties and of inheritence goes the way of that poetic flesh. Pushkin becomes a kind of included inner contemporary of Tsvetaeva, the way everything we read becomes part of our writing (everything we read and love of course; everything we suffer with, everything we identify with).

The texts we read are also writers; but those who read us or those whom we address are also part of the writer. Tsvetaeva is the champion of that kind of writing; when she wrote letters to Pasternak and Rilke, her others, her letters were really worked upon and actually these letters were inspired by the persons and writings of the addressees. She would ask Rilke, 'Write to me', or 'Write me my own letters'. It all works, as Rilke would say, as if there were only one poet. And this poet is a combination of many poets. Actually Rilke addressed a poem, dedicated a poem in three languages, to Tsvetaeva. He wrote it in German, he wrote it in Russian and in French:

A Marina Ivanovna Tsvétaïeva

Wir rühren uns, womit? Mit Flügelschlägen,
mit Fernen selber rühren wir uns an.
Ein Dichter einzig lebt, und dann und wann
Kommt, der ihn trägt, dem der ihn trug, entgegen.

Касаемся друг друга. Чем ? Крылами.
Издалека свое ведем родство.
Поэт-*один*. И *тот*, кто нес его
встречается с несущим временами.

Nous nous touchons, comment? Par des coups d'aile,
par les distances mêmes nous nous effleurons.
Un poète seul vit, et quelquefois
vient qui le porte au-devant de *qui* le porta.[13]

RAINER MARIA RILKE
mai 1926

I'll translate it broadly in English: 'We touch one another how? By wind strokes, by the very distances we touch and brush. One poet only lives, and sometimes there comes the poet who brings him, bears him, comes towards him.' Of course I'm sorry it's written all in the masculine.

I shall now tell you the story of the first poem written by Tsvetaeva – it's to be found at the end of *My Pushkin*. It's the first time she has reached the sea – she has been dreaming about it. (She belongs to a continental part of the country.) The family had been promised a visit to the sea as a result of the mother dying of TB. So the sea, the mother, death, and poetry, expectation, are associated. Now, for little Tsvetaeva 'To the Sea' was only the title of the poem by Pushkin – so when the mother said, 'We're going to the sea', it sounded for her as 'We're going to the poem'. So there she went to the poem; she went to the poem when she went to the sea. The sea wasn't there; when she arrived the sea wasn't there, it was far away. So the poem was far away too, yet the poem was there. The poem of Pushkin was there because Tsvetaeva the little girl had carried the poem of Pushkin which is called 'To the Sea' with her. She knew it by heart – she had it in her heart – and when she tried to meet the sea, which wasn't there, at least she could meet one small stone that was left by the sea, and on a huge rock she started writing the poem of Pushkin called 'The Sea'. That's how she tells about her first experience of writing; the girl writes on the rock that has been left naked by the sea, the poem of Pushkin: 'Farewell free element': 'And suddenly turning my back to it' (that is to the sea that isn't there) she tells; 'I arrived with a fragment of slate on the rock.' (That is her first book):

> 'Farewell free element . . .'
> The poem is long and I started high up as far as my hand could reach, but the poem I know from experience, is so long that no rock would suffice. And there isn't another one just as good nearby, not one. And I keep on reducing and reducing the letters. I squeeze and squeeze the lines and the last ones are already big writing, and I know that the wave will come and not let me write to the end, and then the wish won't come true. What wish? Oh, to the sea. But does that mean that there's no wish any more? But all the same? Even without the wish I must write to the end before the wave comes, write everything to the end before the wave and the wave is already coming, and I just have enough time left to sign, Alexander Sergeyevich Pushkin. And everything is washed away as if licked by tongue. And again I'm all wet. And again there is the flat slate, but now it is black like that granite.[14]

So that's the first poem by Tsvetaeva, signed Alexander Pushkin on a rock washed away by the sea – a metaphor of writing. The text itself works in reality exactly like that rock: it keeps and doesn't keep, it is both the keeper and the gravekeeper, it is both gravekeeper and the grave.

Now a few reflections about violence and writing. Let me first say that I am speaking mostly, in that particular chapter, of fiction that has an autobiographical starting point. Writing is very violent. Death is implied in writing: the redeeming from death but also the giving of death. When you write, there are two types of people you deal with. You write – Tsvetaeva, or Clarice Lispector – with people or on people or on characters; there are those whom you never speak about because you forget them or because you don't want them to appear, or because you repress them. There are those who are alive and because they are alive you can't speak about them. Actually in books you only speak about dead people. Note the ambivalence:

writing both buries and evokes; it's in the text that dead people or forgotten people can come back, be recalled, and find a kind of resurrection. That's why Virgil as a metaphor is so important for poets – you find him everywhere, in Mandelstam, in Dante of course, in Thomas Bernhard, in Broch, all of them are haunted by Virgil because Virgil is the poet who decided that the poet should go in the realm of the dead – and come back. Writing is a going to the realm of the dead, but we're not always aware of it. Why is it that we mainly speak about the dead? Because writing is violent. Writing is supposed (I think so at least) to try and say the truth – it's a desperate deep poet's truth. And truth is always violent; it is a synonym of violence. Therefore you can't say the truth except in a posthumous voice, either because you are dead or the others are dead. And at the same time – it's paradoxical – if you don't speak about people then they're dead, then they disappear. Writing is writing about or above or on or alongside death – my death or your death, it's the same. Besides, it's only with the dead that we are free, to love them and to hate them. I can even love people whom I would not have loved if they were alive, or if I were alive. I know that I can love Clarice Lispector, without any problems, although I also know at the same time that if she were alive and I met her I probably wouldn't love her and she probably wouldn't love me – which means that we are complex people. Part of us is dedicated to love and the other part is not dedicated to love.

One of the most important pieces of poetry in my life of writing – I realised that a long time ago – is Shakespeare's Ariel's song:

> Full fathom five thy father lies,
>   Of his bones are coral made;
> Those are pearls that were his eyes;
>   Nothing of him that doth fade,
> But doth suffer a sea-change
> Into something rich and strange. [15]

You're lucky to have that in your English memory as a treasure. It's one of those keys to writing, writing as the key to death – with father or mother, with the sea, and transfiguration, with the transposition of dead parent into beautiful metaphor, with the becoming jewel signifiers of the dead person, with the economy of suffering and transformation of mourning into a strange joy – that's writing. Actually you write thanks to death, against death, beginning with death, and at the price of death; at the price, sometimes, of the person who has given us writing by refusing us writing – for example, Tsvetaeva's mother who didn't want her daughter to write. Thomas Bernhard is explicit about that. He also was supposed to become a musician, he was taught the violin in reality. He writes about it too, and he tells us in some of his books how he became a writer. He became a writer because his grandfather was a writer who didn't want his grandson to become a writer. Bernhard loved his grandfather and he started writing the moment his grandfather died. For him writing was a substitute, but a devouring one. He says, 'I started writing hundreds and hundreds and hundreds of poems; I existed only when I was writing. My grandfather, the poet, had died, now I had the right to write. I would use the whole world by transforming it into poems.'[16] The mystery is, how, out of so much death comes life. It's the same mystery for us in daily life. Of course writing is a disapproval of death, even if it's a using of death, turning death into, as Shakespeare says, a 'sea-change'. In ordinary life, running round and round, we don't have time to think about death because we don't have time to write; if we had time to write we'd have time to think about death – it's the same thing. Writing is dying; it's being born and dying.

When you start writing I think you very soon come to the point where you have to think about death. About the mystery of death, about our mortality, about the fact that we are strange things, we are completely alive and we know that there is some border there, the real limit. We know that people have departed, as all languages say (they always call that 'departed') – and we know that those people who have departed are in advance, they know things that we don't know, we can even be jealous of them, as Genet was. He was madly in love with those people who had been sentenced to death, because they knew something, that he didn't know yet, of that mystery, which is one of our riches.

If we do want to write we have to deal with the best and also with the worst. The best and the worst actually come into contact; the best and the worst – the best is happiness (it's very difficult, I don't even know whether we can define happiness, whether we ever reach it) and the worst, will be, is, death in life. When we come to writing, we come to that point when we have to be completely and violently true, about everything that we don't take time or don't have the courage to deal with in ordinary life. Should we call it transgression? I don't know. It's really forbidden in our usual life to speak about what can hurt; we're organised not to hurt people. We're organised in order to live socially, not to be excessive, not to do things the way Clarice Lispector does – for instance, violently, calmly, proclaim to 2 million readers that she's alone. She's not mad, when she does that: she wants to shake people, and to wake them up to their own loneliness. She hurts them by saying that; when you say to 2 million readers, 'I am alone', it's a way of spitting in their face, since they think that they're with you. It's really a kind of cruel way of reaching towards the other, of shouting very quietly. It may look arrogant, it may sound selfish; actually it's a kind of 'Why?' It's completely sincere but it's also a way of trying to make the readers come to their own point of truth. But as you know, we don't have the right to do that, it sounds aggressive. It is aggressive. We don't have the right to complain truthfully; we don't have the right to die for love, or we don't have the right to proclaim hatred and demonstrate it. It is only possible in a very special place which is the theatre. When you write for the theatre you have a kind of special right, a strange right, which is utterly reserved for the stage. You can be a criminal, you can be passionately in love, you can be Antony or Cleopatra, you can lose the whole world for a kiss, everything is possible. I don't say that it's allowed but it becomes possible. How is it that what is impossible when we write a piece of fiction today, or when we write in the first person, we can do on the stage? Of course it's a matter of distance from the stage: although it's very near, it's very far. We don't identify in the same way. There is a kind of convention, which makes us believe that the people on the stage who say 'I', who are all first persons, are not first persons but third persons. They appear, although they say 'I', as 'she' or 'he', but not 'me' – which is the reason why, I feel, some people write for the theatre, because they can be extremely violent and at the same time, not very violent. The stage is eventually less violent than fiction writing. And it can give very strange half satisfactions. And in fiction? You can also write on crime and you can also act as a criminal, but I don't think that you can do that easily today. One could do that in the classical novels in the nineteenth century. Dostoevsky wrote in this way, about criminals, but it was in another perspective and it was a kind of theatrical writing, actually, with a distance. Our own cruelty, our own violence, we don't know how to practise it in writing. That is why I have a lot of admiration for people like Clarice Lispector, who can be very violent, or for Thomas Bernhard, who is extraordinarily violent and who has hurt everybody around. Bernhard dares not lie; what people never dare say he dares say openly and directly. He took risks. When you do, you must have courage because what you will get back in answer will be hatred. It's very difficult for a writer to accept hatred. I keep wondering how he did it, knowing that he was going to pay for it: as you know he died early, which was what he had looked for. If you say the truth, then you must be ready to be killed for that.

Yet he was a man. I can't imagine that a woman could ever be granted the right to write the way Bernhard wrote, unfortunately. It's really a matter of right, it's really a matter of state of culture, of development of civilisation. A woman who would write as violently, as openly as Bernhard, I mean – she wouldn't write, she wouldn't be published – she would immediately be called hysterical. Whereas Bernhard was called a writer.

Yet it's the only way, the only direction one should take, the only thing which is worth writing – violently and truthfully. Actually we all know about that because we all have an experience of that kind of writing, even if we haven't completely achieved it, and that happens in our dreams. We have a kind of writing which is night writing; our dreams are absolutely shameless. We should write as we dream; we should even try and write, we should all do it for ourselves, it's very healthy, because it's the only place where we never lie. At night we don't lie. Now if we think that our whole lives are built on lying – they are strange buildings – we should try and write as our dreams teach us; shamelessly, fearlessly, and by facing what is inside every human being – sheer violence, disgust, terror, shit, invention, poetry. Our dreams are the greater poets; if we could only write as our dreams, we'd be great poets. In our dreams we are criminals; we kill, and we kill with a lot of enjoyment. But we are also the happiest people on earth; we make love as we never make love in life. So at least let's not forget that we have secret authors hidden in our unconscious – and try to go to school at night.

Writing should dedicate itself to the truth which is violent. What would the truth be, what would violence be, for a woman writer? First of all, there are situations that are common to both sexes and then women writers have exactly the same problems as men. It's as difficult for a man as for a woman to deal with the truth of our cruelty or of our anger, of our incapacity to be fair or just, or of our general cowardice.

Coming here, I was thinking (in a humble way because I'm not at all authorised to have any opinion) I was thinking of the drama of Liverpool now, and that obviously the attitude of the city of Liverpool, I felt when arriving here, is one of grief and communion, mourning.[17] What would a writer think about what has happened here? It's now being suffered through. Apart from it being a tragic event, it is also a metaphor for what happens to us everyday, that is, we are killed and we kill and then we look for the criminal and we reject the guilt, and the more urgent the situation the more we look for a scapegoat before we look for the one who is really responsible.

There was another event which struck me, very deeply, this week, that is, Hitler's birthday. In France we heard statistics which have made me sick: they said 50 per cent of the Germans now approve of Hitler and consider him to be a great statesman. I felt extremely worried, not about Nazism, but for humankind, because of the way we are always the same. We can absorb evil – and make it a part of us. Last night I watched television here.[18] I saw a long television programme on Hitler. It was ambivalent, very powerful; Hitler is coming back very strongly, Hitler that is a metaphor for everything evil. That television programme was a kind of unconscious celebration of evil. Actually, we don't even realise that, we do it, we ourselves.

Later again I watched television, this time it was a programme on beautiful gardens; and I felt full of gratitude for the English people, and for this country where you still can have honourable television programmes on gardens that are accompanied by a commentary in a civilised voice.

Now why do I say that? Because that's part of the scene on which a writer writes today. Maybe I didn't sound very happy yesterday. You mustn't believe that, I'm very happy but I'm very strongly aware that we now live in a time which we don't call war (because we've heard about another war which was concrete, visible) but which is indeed a time of war against culture, against thinking, against poetry, and against women, not simply against women as only the half of the world which is oppressed, but also as what they can represent as keepers of a certain culture.

Now what would the truth worth fighting for be if you're a woman writer? First of all Truth, generally speaking. Working poetically, that is, truthfully on a language is something that is less and less acceptable in the world of publication, in the world of mass media. All people who write know about it. I suppose people who read, and who are really the army, the peaceful army that is there to defend the values of writing, are not as aware as writers of what is happening to writing; because readers don't have directly to face all of the different publishing institutions. Now simply writing, writing poetically, treating language as one of the most important things in the world, today sounds mad. Yet for human beings it is the first most important thing. I realise that humanity is becoming less and less human. Fighting for the life and freedom of language is becoming rare and more and more difficult. That's something that we share with men. But again, writing as a woman is perhaps the more dangerous position now.

What about what I call 'the quarrel', of sexual difference in writing. It is not simple, it's not men against women, it's one economy versus the other. I don't believe in rigid positions or categories, or oppositions. I don't think that women are sheerly women and men, men. I believe that women have enemies within the world of women and that they often are themselves their own enemies. Sometimes it has to do with the difficulty for a woman to affirm her powerfulness in front of those for whom she feels responsible, that is, somehow a woman is always bound to be a mother. Listening to the lecture this morning, I was thinking, unfortunately it's true that we have to work on papers that will be entitled mother-and-daughter, mother-and-son, and so on.[19]

Could we think in other terms? Can a mother write as a mother? Do we have mothers writing? Why doesn't a mother write as a mother? The sacrifice of the mother – the silence of the mother. Of course you can write the fiction of a mother. You can even write *As I Lay Dying*, but it's a fiction. Reality is different. Maybe mothers should write the truth about being mothered – that is, make open, show the family scene, the family drama. I don't think it's ever been unveiled, we haven't got enough genius to be able to cope with a scene which is extremely contradictory, where everybody actually suffers. Writing the relation of the mother with the son, how is it possible to do it? It would suppose that both are equal, that mother and son are equals in strength, in rightness, in capacity for suffering and enjoyment. This rarely happens in life. When you are in a couple, whatever it is, mother and son, lover and lover, there lurks a kind of war which is veiled. We, as mothers, have to work on the situation all the time in order not to let the other kill us, we as lovers. We, as sons, don't know what we do. We don't even know we are blind. Very clever, very human people probably succeed in making life out of that initial situation of war but this needs a lot of patience and a lot of silence. The speaking of the situation happens only exceptionally, the coming to language and consciousness.

In any kind of couple – married couple or lovers, two women or two men – one element will be at the place of the mother, whatever the sex of the person is, at the place of the person who wants to give life, of the good mother, who doesn't want to prevent the other from progressing, who doesn't want to hurt the other, and I think that in the majority of cases women are in the situation where they have to accept and help the other as being potentially castrated. The classical example: a woman who doesn't create because the husband is (supposedly) a creator, or because he is a creator. Or a woman who creates (Tsvetaeva) and who nurses her husband–son. But we can have the reverse situation: the man being the mother and the woman being the son.

We live in a time when everything that is given us to see on different screens is always a lie, a political – televised – time. We can of course play with that and remain at that level of relation to the world which is a comedy, and even enjoy it. I personally can't accept it because I know that every kind of lie leads to 'Hitler'. 'Hitler' is a metaphor. Any kind of small compromise is already the largest compromise. Life today is largely tragic except that we are not victims the way in some countries people are really in jail and really forbidden to write or to have a piece of paper, but since we have the right to write then we should write thinking that others haven't got the right to write. Why don't we always do it? We are cowards. We are cowards in every way.

When there was all that Rushdie business, in France, people who should have been immediately active (after all, he was somebody who belonged to their own sphere), intellectuals, writers, etc., took a long time reacting because they were afraid.[20] Actually, it was really *the* choice, the choice of the whole of life, the choice you had in 1940–3. Would you be a 'Resistant' in France or not, that is, would you survive without honour or would you take the risk of death and at least keep your honour?

It's always the same question, but for the writer it ought to be the first question. There is indeed the physical fear, of being killed; then there is a subtler fear. It's the fear of being excluded, of being rejected, marginalised, forgotten, buried alive, and this is very painful to cope with.

The state of my feelings today is merciless, it's merciless to everybody including myself, but it's not without hope. As I said yesterday, I believe that women don't know *total* despair. They know about despair that brings us back to hope. Actually the fact that we are here together is a joy for me. I don't know what you think or who you are, but I already know that you have come all the way to a university – even if you don't completely believe in the world of books or in the future of culture, you do believe in it since you're here. Every time I see a meeting of people who have read a book, and who speak about it, whatever they say, I'm happy because I know that whether they know it or not, they belong to that good army we need.

I believe in what we call in French *quand même*, the however, the nevertheless, or the still, because there are readers, because there are writers. For me joy is always linked to the possibility of sharing in a work of art. Texts come to us, your text, my text, it's true celebration, why not use the word.

I live in this world as it is and in the other world where things are written; and that world where things are written, has a kind of strange landscape or shape – as if it were made of one huge cosmic book, made of all the books I love and who speak to me and who come to me from all countries, languages, centuries.

I feel the joy Tsvetaeva felt when she was waiting for Rilke to send her a book of his verse, and she would say to him, 'I'm waiting for your books as for the storm which is going to break and to tell my heart, to operate on my heart as surgery'.[21] She uses the word surgery and she says it's not a metaphor because all poems cut through the heart. Whether I want it or not, whether I expect it or not. All authors and all readers have experienced being wounded by the coming of the text, being wounded by wonder because the joy that a text inflicts hurts. Why does it hurt? When it comes to us, first of all it tears the night and the lie in which we usually live; it hurts to see the truth but it is of course a joy.

Here is what Kafka wrote in 1904:

> I believe that we should only read those books which bite us and stab us. If the book that we read doesn't wake us up with a big knock on the skull, why should we read it? So that it should make us happy? By God, we can be happy without those books or we can even write those books that make us happy if we need them. But we need, what we don't have, what we need, are the books which work upon us as a terrible event, as a stroke of happiness which hurts us, as the death of one whom we love more than ourselves would hurt us, as when we were lost in forests without human beings around, as suicide. Books must be the axe to break the frozen sea within us, that's what I believe. [22]

I'm interested in readers. It's true that we need the books that wake us up from among the dead. Waking up from among the dead is the greatest joy in the world. It happens several times in life but it also hurts because we also experience the death of a former life. There is no writing without reading. Writing is actually a kind of alliance between writer and reader. The reader within myself and the reader outside. Readers don't realise enough how much they are implied in the writing, how much they are at work, how much they write. They give rebirth. The person who receives is the giver. The person who sends away can only send if she or he believes that there will be somebody else, somewhere else in another time, to receive. When you send the bottle to the sea, as all poets do, there is the sea. You believe that reading will happen and the sea, which so often in that metaphor – almost a cliché – appears as the country of humankind, which comes in place of the receiver, the sea is already the matter or the way that will give birth to reading. You throw it into the sea of time.

When you write actually, although it's a little mad, it is because obscurely, you are situated in that very strange space/time of generations. In itself, writing is a kind of reversible motherhood. The writer will have children and those children will be mother to the writer. That is the secret meaning of the word 'contemporary'.

When I write, I read–write, I know that the works of others are being resurrected in translation. When I write, I rewrite; of course I write my own work, but my own work is already a gathering of other works. An answer; if I write, it's because I have received a letter. My writing is the letter that answers the letter I've received, and the correspondence goes on.

Now to finish on that note, I'll quote Clarice Lispector's foreword to *The Passion According to G.H.*, one of her most beautiful books. She addresses the book to possible readers and she says:

> This book is like a book, like others but I would be satisfied if it were read only by persons who have their souls already well-shaped. Those persons who know that the approach of everything can only be done progressively and painfully and must very often go through the contrary of what is being approached. Those persons will

understand very slowly that this book doesn't take anything away from anybody. To me, for example, the character of G.H. has by and by given a difficult joy but this joy has a name and it's Joy.[23]

The Passion According to G.H. is a difficult book. It's painful to read, it's a joy to read and that's why it's called Passion. A woman's passion.

About writing as a woman: in Paris we have had a colloquium of women writers coming from several countries, the Soviet Union, The United States, France, and the general issue was 'women writers'. There were very strong cultural differences expressed. Most French writers said that they weren't writing as women, which was a paradox since they were attending a symposium of women writers.

Let me make a few remarks. First of all, writers are free, they are what they are, who they are and no one can reproach anyone for anything, either for being a woman or for not being a woman. There are different types of writing or approaches to writing. *Personally*, when I write fiction, I write with my body. My body is active, there is no interruption between the work that my body is actually performing and what is going to happen on the page. I write very near my body and my pulsions. This doesn't mean that everybody does it the same way nor does this mean that it should be done. There are texts that are made of flesh. When you read these texts, you receive them as such. You feel the rhythm of the body, you feel the breathing and you make love with these texts. We meet texts in different scenes – at school, in a café, etc. We can read in our room, or in our bed, either we're very close to the book or we don't like it; when we do, obviously we have a kind of carnal, fleshly, bodily relation with the book. But the moment we suddenly start speaking about reading in public rooms, then we change our attitudes. We don't know how to say that we've eaten a book, that we've stroked a book, that the book has made us have an orgasm, or that it has hurt us or that I have cried. It's forbidden.

Now there is one category of text that obviously causes joy and damage directly to our flesh and blood soul. And there are texts that are written at a remote distance, that are not made of flesh, that are made of style, of structure, or sometimes narratives. This doesn't mean that they are a lesser literature or a greater literature. They don't touch us in the same way. We don't enjoy in the same way, we don't enjoy with the same part of our being. The classical novel most often belongs to that other more distant type of writing.

Poetry of course, is very near the pulsions, as is music. When you write for the theatre and create characters, your position as a writer is totally different from that of a fiction writer. You must on the contrary suspend yourself and your body because it is the other who must be there completely and so you experience disappearance, your own complete disappearance. What happens? It's something very difficult to speak about. If you are somebody who is used to having that companion, the body, disappearing is something difficult to achieve and extremely painful. What remains of yourself in the play, is the pain, probably the pain remains and is somehow reinscribed in the characters.

Of course truth is not a totalising concept.[24] When I equated truth and life, it was a kind of intellectual violence. I meant that without truth you live only a kind of crippled life. Truth is the matrix for what I would call life, that is life worth living. I am, again, referring to intimate relations between human beings. Because we want to avoid the difficulties of the exchanges, most of the time we simplify relations and we think of love as a whole, love as a sphere that is full of love. That's not true of course. Love is full of separation, full of anguish. We may have times when we feel betrayed by our friends, or we betray our friends – and it may be wrong or right, never mind – realising that in the greatest passion, the greatest love, there is something that can be harmful for the other, that there is pride and humbleness, that it is very difficult to be humble, that maybe it's the most desirable thing in the world and in the moment you desire to be humble you are already full of pride. All those very acute inscriptions of the reality of our behaviour are what we never accept facing because we are afraid of ruptures and don't take the time. I meant most of the time we don't live, we exist. We call that living but it's not true. We exist or we survive. Living is a battle. It changes all the time. Living according to changes is also something that belongs to that work of truth that I believe in. But again let me say that when I speak in this way, I hope you don't feel that I am moralising in any way, *because I first address myself to myself.*

I, for instance, have to do with my own stories, 'comedies', which is very complicated because I am more a coward in personal relations than in social or political relations. I'm afraid not of dying but I'm afraid of hurting and of being hurt. I'm more afraid of waging a war against somebody I know than against the state. This is a normal moral problem in my daily life. It becomes a very important problem when you write because when you write you are responsible. When you write you are sowing and you don't know where it's going to grow. Besides, writing has a special status: it's both repressed, rejected, despised, particularly by money powers and power powers, but at the same time it has a huge hidden influence which we can never measure. There is something very tricky with writing. The moment there is an author in the place there is a kind of air of authority that blows, it's like a kind of poisoned air. The author has no authority and yet the author has authority. We are structured in such a way, that is a phallic way, we have such a relation to narcissim that we can't help as readers, giving a kind of leadership to the writer. Now if the writer is not conscious, it's really dangerous: he/she/we can become phallocratic – that is the snare.

How to deal with that? Beware of writers. A writer should be very careful to say 'I'. Read, for instance, Tsvetaeva's small prose essays. She attacks, ruthlessly, critics, poets, the USSR. She is absolutely fearless, but she says 'I', she always speaks only in her own name. She doesn't take responsibility for the whole world and she always specifies very precisely what her place is, where she speaks from, whom she addresses, because she doesn't consider herself as representative of every poet or every woman. This honest precaution is necessary.

Beware of the writer (male or female). The beginning of the history of a writer is not motherhood. Writers begin as sons, male or female, but later they may become mothers when they come to think about what writing is. When you start writing usually, you don't think in those terms because you are so nervous. The craft is so difficult to master that you only think in terms of the language, of the page, of the sentence. You don't think in terms of the ethics of writing. Later, when you start thinking in terms of the ethics of writing and reading, then you may become a mother whether you are a man or a woman. (But in our time it's mostly women who are driven by experience to think ethically.) And then you know that you are going to give birth to all kinds of persons and effects of identification. Whether you like it or not. You will be echoed, imitated (or rejected), overrated (or underrated), given undue importance – for, after all, as Thomas Bernhard once wrote, what is so mysterious in artists? We listen to them more attentively, and eventually, the day comes (may it come!) when we readers realise we have stuffed them full with our hopes, illusions, and our own ideal greatness.

Let's not forget the mysterious, grave, humorous cycle, where we readers are authors of the writers, we writers are both engendering and engendered . . . *à suivre*.

NOTES

1. Clarice Lispector, *The Hour of the Star*, translation by Sarah Cornell, Joao Camillo Penna and Catherine Franke of *A Hora da Estrela*, edited by Jose Olympico (Rio de Janeiro, 1976), p. 7.
2. Lispector, *ibid.*, p. 13.
3. Mandelstam, 'Verses on the Unknown Soldier', *Ossip Mandelstam: 50 Poems* (New York: Persea Books, 1977), pp. 93–4.

4. Joseph Brodsky, 'A Poet and Prose', *Less than One* (Harmondsworth: Penguin Books, 1987), p. 183.
5. Brodsky, *ibid.*, p. 182.
6. Tsvetaeva, 'Mother and Music', *Marina Tsvetaeva: A captive spirit*, translated by J. Mary King (London: Virago, 1983), p. 273.
7. Tsvetaeva, 'The Poem of the End', translation by Hélène Cixous, *Le Poème de la montagne, le poème de la fin* (Lausanne: L'âge d'homme, 1984), p. 61.
8. Paul Celan, 'Und mit dem Buch of Tarussa', *La Rose de personne* (Paris: Le Nouveau Commerce, 1979), p. 30.
9. Tsvetaeva, 'My Pushkin', *Marina Tsvetaeva: A captive spirit*, p. 321.
10. *Correspondence à trois: Pasternak, Rilke, Tsvetaeva* (Paris: Gallimard, 1983), p. 282.
11. Lispector, 'Belonging' ('*Pertencer*'), translated by Hélène Cixous, *A Descoberta do Mundo* (Rio de Janeiro: Nova Fronteira, 1984), p. 151.
12. Tsvetaeva, 'My Pushkin', p. 319.
13. Rilke, 'A Marina Tsvetaeva', *Correspondence à trois*, p. 9.
14. Tsvetaeva, 'My Pushkin', p. 360.
15. Shakespeare, *The Tempest*, I, 2, 397–402.
16. Thomas Bernhard, *Die Kälte* (Residenz Verlag: Salzburg and Vienna, 1981).
17. Hélène Cixous was speaking in Liverpool one week after the Hillsborough Stadium disaster in which nearly a hundred Liverpool football supporters were crushed to death.
18. The paper was given in two conference sessions on consecutive days; the first session closed at the pause on page 22.
19. Naomi Segal, 'Patrilinear and Matrilinear'; see page 131 in Part III below.
20. The publication of Salman Rushdie's novel *The Satanic Verses* – a work regarded by some Muslims as blasphemous – led to death threats which forced the writer into hiding.
21. *Correspondance à trois*, p. 96.
22. Franz Kafka, Lettre à Polack, *Correspondance* (Paris: Gallimard, Bibliothéque de la Pléiade, 1984), p. 575.
23. Lispector, *A Paixao secundo G. H.* (Rio de Janeiro: Nova Fronteira, 1979), p. 5.
24. From this point onwards, Cixous was responding to questions from the audience and developing a discussion.

Chapter 2

Hélène Cixous and
les Etudes Féminines

Sarah Cornell

This is an attempt to give a brief summary of Hélène Cixous' works and introduce the Centre d'Etudes Féminines at the Université de Paris VIII. I am well aware that this kind of presentation may run the risk of over-simplifying, reducing and/or overlooking certain elements. However, I hope that it can be useful to those who are not too familiar with Hélène Cixous' writing and research.

Hélène Cixous was born in Oran, Algeria, in 1937. Her mother is German and so her mother tongue was German. Her mother is of European Jewish descent with family roots in Germany, Austria and Czechoslovakia. Her father spoke French and was of Mediterranean Jewish descent. His family came from Spain, Morocco and Algeria. Hélène Cixous' mother was a midwife and her father was a doctor. She grew up in Algeria and lived there until 1955 when she left for France. Her family background, her birthplace, and the subsequent loss of or separation from her birthplace, are determining factors in her writing.

Hélène Cixous developed an ear for language at a very early age because there was German and French at home and Arabic and Spanish were spoken in the streets. As a result of this polyglot environment, she had an early exposure and sensitivity to the musicality of various spoken lan-guages. This primitive musical quality of the language is what she will later name 'the song of the mother', i.e. the voice of the mother that the small child hears as music before the intervention of the symbolic order and access to language as organised discourse. This early musical ear for language favoured the development of a poetic ear for language in writing later on.

From childhood, Hélène Cixous lived with, and was directly confronted by, the upheavals of history. Her mother fled the rise of Nazism in Germany in 1933. Afterwards, there were the repercussions of the Second World War in Algeria, where her father was forbidden to practise medicine by the

Vichy government. Then before and during the Algerian war, she witnessed and lived the effects of the oppression of the Arabs by the French, the racism of the Jews regarding the Arabs, and the anti-semitism of the Arabs. As Hélène Cixous has said, one of her primal scenes was 'to discover anti-semitism in the kindergarten'.

In the middle of such turbulent surroundings, Hélène Cixous discovered another universe and happiness in books. They took her above and beyond the violence and suffering around her and she quickly became an avid reader. Among the writers who have deeply influenced her works are Kafka, Shakespeare, Dostoevsky, Joyce, Freud, Kleist, Celan, Mandelstam, Akhmatova, Tsvetaeva and Clarice Lispector.

The flowing relationship between reading and writing has been an important theme in Hélène Cixous' writing as well as in her university research. The exchange between reading and writing is seen as a continuous process of reciprocal replenishment.

PARADISE LOST

Hélène Cixous' birthplace, Oran, Algeria, became a metaphor for Paradise Lost. Writing provided the means of regaining, reconquering and reconstituting the loss of paradise. As a Jew, she found herself exiled from her place of birth because of the Algerian War. Exile was one of the founding themes of her thought and written works, beginning with her doctoral thesis entitled 'The Exile of James Joyce, or the Art of Replacement'.

A second fundamental loss, the death of her father, engendered her fictional writing. It was the subject of her first 'novel', *Dedans* (*Inside*), published in 1969.[1]

From the outset, writing serves as a necessary means of repairing the separation from a place or a person caused either by exile or death. Writing does the work of bereavement, of reconstituting the loss, and of keeping the memory of the precarious.

THE COMPLETE WORKS

Hélène Cixous has writen over thirty major texts as well as numerous articles and short pieces. Her works are of great diversity, ranging from fictional texts, poetical and theoretical essays, to theatrical plays. To facilitate this introduction to Hélène Cixous' writing, I would like to outline some of the specific characteristics of the fictional works.

First of all, an essential trait of the fiction is the emphasis on the inscription of the unconscious through the intricate poetic work of the signifiers.

Secondly, the fictional pieces generally have a free form which defies the laws of literary genre. More specifically, most of the texts could not be classified as what we would call 'novels'.

I should also point out that the position and the state of the author are quite distinctive. The author claims no appropriating authorship or ownership to the text. The poetic text is given to the writer, is received by the writer, as a stroke or a blow (*un coup*). The author writes in a state of narcissistic porosity, in a state of selflessness (*démoïsation*) which leaves room for the other to enter.

Moreover, in nearly all the fictional texts, there are no 'characters' as we might find in traditional novels. What we find instead might be partial sketches of a character, or certain aspects of femininity. And what about men? The fiction also inscribes the presence of the father, the brother, the lover. Certain texts emanate from the paternal figure and reinscribe him. Others work on the Oedipal fantasy. Whereas in the fictional work women have the majority, in the theatrical pieces this is no longer true. The principal characters in the plays are men. This is a sign of historical times and presents a contradiction that Hélène Cixous works upon and elaborates.

It is also important to note that the fiction contains no realism. It has a more universal or epic dimension. Many of the texts plunge, with intense questioning, into the conflicts of the unconscious. The question leads, begins the quest, and becomes the means of exit from scenes of encirclement, anxiety or uncertainty hidden in the unconscious. The text is a means of travel, it makes its way (*il fait un cheminement*). It explores, meditates upon, and works through questions like: 'Where to live? Where are we in reality?' (*Le Prénom de Dieu*)[2]; 'Who am (I)?/Who do (I) follow?' ('Qui? Suis?') in *Illa*[3]; 'And now, your life, where now . . . ?' (*Anankè*)[4]. Hélène Cixous' writing traces paths of learning and the itinerary of a woman's life experiences. Another specificity of the fiction concerns the enunciating subject. The narrating 'I' may be several. There is no closed oneness of the subject. The speaking voice may at times be the mother, at times the daughter, at times the grandmother, etc.

PRINCIPAL THEMES

Some of the recurrent themes are love, hope, belief, confidence and the vision of life as a struggle against death and the effects of death. The fiction often deals with the question of overcoming restrictive limits and the constraints of the forbidden, safeguarding the precarious and keeping the memory. The texts often evoke themes of abundance, continuity and giving. Her writing inscribes 'trans': transformation, transition, transfer, transportation and transposition.

Most recently, Hélène Cixous has been actively writing for the theatre with two plays produced by the Théâtre du Soleil, staged by Ariane Mouchkine, *The Terrible but Unfinished Story of Norodom Sihanouk, King of Cambodia*[5] in 1985 and *The Indiad or the India of Their Dreams*[6] in 1987. The plays attempt to explore the epic dimensions of contemporary history. The theatre gave Hélène Cixous the opportunity to begin work on the creation of theatrical characters. The effects of her theatrical work on her fictional work are reflected in her most recent book, *Manne aux Mandelstams aux Mandelas*, where for the first time characters appear in a fictional text.[7]

LES ETUDES FEMININES

In 1974, Hélène Cixous instituted the first and only French doctoral degree in *Etudes Féminines* at the Université de Paris VIII at Vincennes. Since then, she has directed the Centre d'Etudes Féminines at the University of Paris VIII which has now been moved from Vincennes to St Denis. The centre is inter-disciplinary and works in conjunction with le Collège International de Philosophie in Paris and with numerous universities in Europe and North America. There are courses offered at the Centre in literature, history, sociology and psychoanalysis. In English, we would probably call this Centre a 'Women's Studies Centre' and we would be using a more generic term that could englobe both Feminist Studies and Feminine Studies.

For us, there is no binary opposition between Feminist Studies and Feminine Studies. They are two fields of research that supplement each other. For example, in the Centre, the courses in sociology and history are more oriented towards the feminist aspects of Women's Studies. Obviously, all the participants in the Centre understand the importance of the Women's Movement.

But what about Feminine Studies? How can we qualify the specificity of *Etudes Féminines*? What is this notion of 'the feminine'? In our work, the concept of 'the feminine' stems from a very precise context. In Hélène Cixous' research seminar entitled 'The Poetics of Sexual Difference', we study the relationship between writing and sexual difference. We seek to find the inscription of sexual difference in the poetic text. Hélène Cixous has developed this question of writing and sexual difference over the past few years and I will try to set forth the main points of this research.

In 1975, Hélène Cixous published two theoretical works which are both translated into English: 'Le Rire de la Méduse' ('The Laugh of the Medusa')[8] and *La Jeune née* (*The Newly Born Woman*)[9]. These two texts expose and explore the difficulties that confront women and keep them away from their own femininity. More specifically, in both texts, there is a call to writing, a pressing invitation to women to 'write themselves':

> A feminine text cannot not be more than subversive: if it writes itself it is in volcanic heaving of the old 'real' property crust. In ceaseless displacement. She must write herself because, when the time comes for her liberation, it is the invention of a new, insurgent writing that will allow her to put the breaks and indispensable changes into effect in her history. At first, individually, on two inseparable levels: woman, writing herself, will go back to this body that has been worse than confiscated, a body replaced with a disturbing stranger, sick or dead, who so often is a bad influence, the cause and place of inhibitions. By censuring the body, breath and speech are censored at the same time.
>
> To write – the act that will 'realize' the uncensored relationship of woman to her sexuality, to her woman-being giving her back access to her own forces; that will return her goods, her pleasures, her organs, her vast bodily territories kept under seal; that will tear her out of the superegoed structure where the same position of guilt is always reserved for her (guilty of everything, every time: of having desires, of not having any; of being frigid, of being 'too' hot; of not being both at once; of being too much of a mother and not enough; of nurturing and of not nurturing . . .). Write yourself: your body must make itself heard. Then the huge resources of the unconscious will burst out. Finally the inexhaustible feminine Imaginary is going to be deployed.[10]

Writing is an act of liberation from social censorship and personal inhibitions. The poetic text is the privileged place of inscription of the 'feminine' Imaginary and unconscious. Parallel to the practice of writing 'the feminine', I attempt in my research seminar to read the traces of 'the feminine'. But once again, what is this 'feminine practice of writing'? How can it be defined? Hélène Cixous responds to this question in pointing out that the idea of a 'feminine' practice of writing resists enclosure in restrictive conceptual frameworks:

> At the present time, defining a feminine practice of writing is impossible with an impossibility that will continue; for this practice will never be able to be theorized, enclosed, coded, which does not mean it does not exist. But it will always exceed the discourse governing the phallocentric system; it takes place and will take place somewhere other than in the territories subordinated to philosophical–theoretical domination. It will not let itself think except through subjects that break automatic functions, border runners never subjugated by any authority. But one can begin to speak. Begin to point out some effects, some elements of the unconscious drives, some relations of the feminine Imaginary to the Real, to writing.[11]

Since this idea of 'feminine writing' began to circulate in 1975, there has been a number of distortions and misunderstandings concerning the true meaning of this theory. In an interview with Verena Conley in 1984, Hélène Cixous attempted to guide her readers clear of some of the misconceptions that had cropped up over the years:

> The preliminary question is that of a 'feminine writing', itself a dangerous and stylish expression full of traps, which leads to all kinds of confusions. True, it is simple to say 'feminine writing'. The use of the word 'feminine' – I believe I have discussed it at length elsewhere – is one of the curses of our times. First of all, words like 'masculine' and 'feminine' that circulate everywhere and that are completely distorted by everyday usage, – words which refer, of course, to a classical vision of sexual opposition between men and women – are our burden, that is what burdens us. As I often said, my work in fact aims at getting rid of words like 'feminine' and 'masculine', 'femininity' and 'masculinity', even 'man' and 'woman', which designate that which cannot be classified inside of a signifier except by force and violence and which goes beyond it in any case. So it is true that when one says 'feminine writing', one could almost think in terms of graphology. One could say, it is the writing of an elegant woman, she is this or that. That is obviously not what is at stake. Instead of saying feminine writing or masculine writing, I ended up by saying a writing said to be feminine or masculine, in order to mark the distance. In my seminar, rather than taking this elementary precaution, I speak of a decipherable libidinal femininity which can be read in a writing produced by a male or a female. The qualifier masculine or feminine which I use for better or for worse comes from the Freudian territory.[12]

Hélène Cixous speaks of a 'decipherable libidinal femininity'. What is meant by 'libidinal femininity'? The word 'libidinal', just like the terms, 'masculine' and 'feminine', originates from what Hélène Cixous calls the 'Freudian territory'. Sometimes we hear objections raised when we make reference to Freud and even more so when we actually make use of the theoretical instruments he has given us. As we all know, Freud was misogynous and he was a phallocrat, unconsciously, of course. However, it would be to our own disadvantage to deny the importance of some of his research: he discovered the unconscious, the importance of sexuality in life, and the work that goes on in dreams. He gave recognition to the importance of sexual life in the psychological, intellectual and social determination of a subject.

In spite of all the credit we can attribute to Freud, we are not going to take for granted everything he had to say so far as 'the feminine' is concerned. Freud was a man of his Victorian times, he knew about social and cultural 'feminine', but he did not know about libidinal 'feminine'. For example, Freud says that normal libidinal femininity is organised by penis envy, which we know is not true.

The social and cultural 'feminine', as it is used in everyday language, does indeed have a negative connotation. How can we account for this? It is simply because 'femininity' at this level designates the woman as the man wishes her to be. It never has anything to do with the femininity of the woman lived by the woman. Social femininity has always been defined by masculine fantasies.

To clarify what we mean by the 'libidinal feminine', as opposed to the 'social or cultural feminine', we make use of the expression 'libidinal economy', that is, the economy of sexual life. Libidinal refers to the system of sexual experiences that Freud discovered and studied, and to the system of energy of the body which may be pulsional. It has to do with the drive of the body and soul towards something. It has to do with the economy of desire. The adjective 'libidinal' is derived from the noun 'libido', which describes the system of exchange between the individual and other individuals and the world in terms of investment, disinvestment, displacement, etc. One of Hélène Cixous' principal theoretical points deals with libidinal economy and with the question of the difference in libidinal economies. This is where we come back to the question of sexual difference when we speak in terms of 'feminine' libidinal economy and 'masculine' libidinal economy.

When we speak of 'feminine' and 'masculine' in this context, we are speaking in terms of difference and equality and not in terms of binary opposition nor hierarchy. Nor are we necessarily referring to social sexes or to human anatomy. The male-defined world puts difference on the scale of hierarchy. If the hierarchical values imposed by a social and cultural context defined by the patriarchy are interiorised, then in fact it is very difficult to think in terms of difference. We are not speaking about opposition, not about the war of the sexes. We are talking about equal and different. If 'equal' becomes an equivalent to 'the same', then those who are different are excluded.

This is the threshold of our work. These libidinal economies are distinguished by adjectives (masculine and feminine), but these adjectives do not refer, in a closed and censoring manner, to men and women. However, for cultural and social reasons, it would probably be more current to find something defined as a 'masculine libidinal economy' in male individuals than in female individuals. Inversely, it would probably be more current to find something defined as a 'feminine libidinal economy' in female individuals than in male individuals. But this is a matter of culture.

While recognising the fact that the use of the words 'masculine' and 'feminine' can be misleading, we cannot replace them with words like 'blue' or 'green' because 'masculine' and 'feminine' come from the Freudian terminology used to describe the theory of the child's originary bisexuality. Freud defines a certain period in childhood when there is a bisexual potential. There is a latent double sexuality in the child which gives the potentiality, the virtuality, of masculine and feminine economies. Then as the child grows up and learns to identify with adult models there can be a relative erasure of one economy and reinforcement of the other.

How can we try to specify some of the traits of these libidinal economies? Hélène Cixous describes a feminine libidinal economy as one which

> has a more supple relation to property, which can stand separation and detachment, which signifies it can also stand freedom – for instance, the other's freedom . . . It's an economy that tolerates the movements of the other, that tolerates the comings and goings. [13]

The feminine libidinal economy is more on the side of expense, of a certain way of accepting the part of life which is uncertain, of enjoying possibility, of risking investments, a kind of openness. The feminine libidinal economy might be freer than the masculine libidinal economy which would refer to something like conservation, centralisation, or capitalisation, subject to reappropriation and controlled within limits. All of this could come from a fixation on the phallus. What interests us most specifically in Hélène Cixous' seminar about 'The Poetics of Sexual Difference' is the inscription of these libidinal economies in artistic practice, and more precisely in poetic writing.

While society runs on an 'apparent' separation of the sexes, in poetics originary bisexuality is not necessarily repressed. The poetic management of this bisexuality in art can be conflictual, but it finds sublimation in artistic inscription. One could find traces of both economies in a same writing, or in a same practice. For example, in a text entitled 'Tancredi Continues', translated into English in the collection *Writing Differences*, Hélène Cixous writes about sexual hesitation in music, in Rossini's 'Tancredi' opera. [14] She contends that artistic practice, be it poetic or musical, can only exist if there is a liberation from the law (that makes the law, and, in particular, makes the law of genders).

In poetic writing, as in music, this originary bisexuality, or this sexual indecisiveness, can express itself freely. There is uncertainty, crossing, blending, interweaving of the two libidinal economies. There is no constraint or restriction that forcibly imposes a binary attribution or distinction of gender. What can we find inscribed in the language of the poetic text? We can find traces of sexual difference, of the unconscious, of the body, and of sexual pleasure. We can learn to hear the unconscious that resides in any conscious discourse. In working with the signifiers, we can listen to the sounds of the unconscious.

The body is linked to the unconscious. It is not separated from the soul. It is dreamed and spoken. It produces signs. When one speaks, or writes, or sings, one does so from the body. The body feels and expresses joy, anxiety, suffering and sexual pleasure. Sexual pleasure is the least constrained, the least bridled manifestation of the body. 'Feminine' sexual pleasure (*la jouissance feminine*) is overflowing, undecided, decentralised and not caught up in the masculine castration scene, and is not threatened by impotency. The body lets desires pass through and this desire creates images, fantasies and figures. Feminine desire is flowing, so we often find images of the spring, of liquid, of water. This does not mean that a woman cannot feel castrated insofar as she may be structured phallically. Castration exists for women too, since it is imaginary.

For the cultural and social reasons mentioned above, Hélène Cixous says that, generally, the poetic inscription of a feminine libidinal economy is rare at the present time.

> The problem is not with men: one finds a great deal of femininity in men, the problem is with the women who have produced, who have written, because culturally, they have been subjected to the obligations of masculinization in order to hoist themselves on the scene of socio-political legitimacy. With the result that most of the texts by women up to our time have been terribly marked by the 'masculine' economy.[15]

However, the works of Clarice Lispector, a twentieth century Brazilian writer, give a good example of the textual inscription of a feminine libidinal economy. Moreover, although Hélène Cixous does not say so herself, we can also consider her own works as an example of 'feminine' writing.

To provide poetic examples of the masculine libidinal economy, Hélène Cixous cites the writing of Kafka and Blanchot. In *Writing Differences*, she states that their writing is 'at the mercy of scenes of castration' and gives 'rise to forms which are dry, stripped bare, marked by the negative'. She also speaks of other 'men writers', such as Kleist, Genet or Shakespeare, whose texts show a great deal 'of femininity, of being capable of the other. And they give rise to forms of economies that are open, expansive, generous, daring.'[16]

In conclusion, I would simply like to add that in spite of the present effort to clarify any misconstrued ideas about the notion of the 'feminine', as we have endeavoured to define it, we should not forget that Hélène Cixous is first and foremost a poetic writer. As a writer, she claims the poet's right to say what she feels to be true:

> 'An economy said to be F.', 'an economy said to be M.' – why distinguish between them? Why keep words which are so entirely treacherous, fearful, and warmongering? This is where all the traps are set. I give myself a poet's right, otherwise I would not dare to speak. The right of poets is to say something and then to say, believe it if you want to, but believe it weeping; or else to erase it, as Genet does, by saying that all truths are false, that only false truths are true, etc.[17]

NOTES

1. Hélène Cixous, *Dedans* (Paris: Editions Bernard Grasset, 1969).
2. Hélène Cixous, *Le Prénom de Dieu* (Paris: Editions Bernard Grasset, 1967), p. 122.
3. Hélène Cixous, *Illa* (Paris: Editions des femmes, 1980), p. 7.
4. Hélène Cixous, *Anankè* (Paris: Editions des femmes, 1979), p. 9.
5. Hélène Cixous, *L'Histoire terrible mais inachevée de Norodom Sihanouk, roi du Cambodge'* (Paris: Théâtre du Soleil, 1985).
6. Hélène Cixous, *L'Indiade ou l'Inde de leurs rêves* (Paris: Théâtre du Soleil, 1987).
7. Hélène Cixous, *Manne aux Mandelstams aux Mandelas* (Paris: Editions des femmes, 1988).
8. Hélène Cixous, 'Le Rire de la Méduse' (Paris: L'Arc, 1975).
9. Hélène Cixous and Catherine Clément, *La Jeune née* (Paris: Union Générale d'Editions, 10/18, 1975).
10. Hélène Cixous, *The Newly Born Woman*, translated by Betsy Wing (Minneapolis: University of Minnesota Press, 1986), p. 97.
11. *Ibid.*, p. 92.
12. Verena Andernatt Conley, *Hélène Cixous: Writing the feminine* (Lincoln, Nebraska and London: University of Nebraska Press, 1984), p. 129.
13. *Ibid.*, p. 137.
14. Hélène Cixous, 'Tancredi Continues', translated by Ann Liddle and Susan Sellers in *Writing Differences: Readings from the seminar of Hélène Cixous*, edited by Susan Sellers (Milton Keynes: Open University Press, 1988), pp. 37–53.
15. *Ibid.*, p. 25.
16. *Ibid.*, p. 25.
17. *Ibid.*, p. 15.

Chapter 3

Hélène Cixous

From inner theatre to world theatre *

Nicole Ward Jouve

The crippling combination of hubris and self-doubt in my make-up makes me want to do the big thing: produce an account of the whole of Hélène Cixous' work. Immediately I want to say that this is of course impossible, and in any case I am not up to it. Set your target too far. Fail to reach it. Crucify yourself with your failure. A characteristic female manoeuvre and one that Hélène Cixous herself has steadily avoided. Indeed, her whole work urges us to avoid it. Do not dream, the retreat. Act. Go through the gate. Do not hang around it, fashioning ghostly guardians out of your dreams and fears.

My purpose is to speak of a larger Hélène Cixous than is normally discussed in Great Britain. The translation process implies untold selections, omissions, enlargements, that have as much to do with the translating culture, its needs and projections, as they have with the writing that is being translated. Only seven or eight out of forty-odd texts by Hélène Cixous exist in English: *Angst*, *Portrait de Dora*, *To Live the Orange*, *Inside*, *The Newly Born Woman*, and a few essays, 'The Laugh of the Medusa', 'Castration or decapitation', the pieces in Susan Sellers' *Writing Differences*.[1] Among these, the theoretical essays have been the object of the more intense scrutiny, and have been more influential than the so-called creative prose. I say 'so-called', being at a loss for a word to apply to drama and fictions that are poetic, meditative, critical and sometimes autobiographical; and because the so-called theory is written creatively. Indeed, *La Venue à l'écriture* is more directly autobiographical than any of the first-person fiction, and arguably as imaginative. But in Anglo-Saxon terms the theoretical Cixous has prevailed and been perceived as the proponent of a practice called *l'écriture féminine*, the defender of a *fémininité*

* This paper also appears in Nicole Ward Jouve's collection of essays, *White Woman Speaks with Forked Tongue: Criticism as autobiography* (London: Routledge, 1990), and is included here by permission of the publishers.

that has to do with *jouissance* and body language. It is assumed that, as she herself is a practitioner of *l'écriture féminine*, her practice as it were illustrates her theory; that her writing is difficult, and need only be taken into account by the Francophone specialists; and that the writing, as well as the theoretical positions, is homogeneous, unchanging over time. A monolith is thus engineered, placed on the horizon of foreign theory, its clay feet dangerously planted in the marshy ground of experimental writing. Will the water seepage melt those feet, will the idol tumble of its own accord – or will it be toppled by the lances of Anglo-American pragmatists Quixotic enough to charge it?

This, though unfair, is not meant to be negative: if translation is always a betrayal (*traduction/trahison*, as Risset says), it is a necessary betrayal, and a productive one. If each language, each culture, distorts the foreign that it takes into its midst, it is because it is different: it also casts new lights on it, gives it new life, is fertilised by it. And so it is with Cixous. It is Great Britain, not France, that has centred a colloquium in Liverpool on her work and practice, that has paid tribute to her. What I have said of the Anglo-American Cixous is not meant as an attack on a generous and enthusiastic readership. It is meant to serve as a backcloth to the other Cixous, the one that my position as a bilingual reader and friend, one with a foot planted in France and the other in England, makes me perceive.

How to convey that perception?

Being simple (especially when your tongue so instinctively forks) is the most difficult thing, the most important thing. It means striving to grasp the thing that stares you in the eye and which you cannot, will not, see. Making the two prongs of that damned tongue for once act as one channel. Gathering the bridles of all the horses that are galloping through you at any minute and making them run together, as Plato's coachman does the black and the white horse in Phædo's fable of the well-regulated soul.

Here goes.

Hélène Cixous always writes in the present.

There are two ways of writing in the present.

It can be argued that any text is in the present. In *Writing Degree Zero* Roland Barthes has described the prevailing mode of fiction, the preterite, as a disguised, idyllic and bracketed present. You could also say that any of the futuristic modes of science fiction, or the present or future or conditional tenses of Nouveau Roman or post-modernist fiction, include an element of the present: partly because, as Barthes and Sartre have first shown, reading is always done in the present, and any text addresses itself to the reading-in-the-present of its prospective readers.[2] Partly also because, whether you're writing a historical novel or a utopia, the process of writing itself means you're summoning what is in you as you write, which is often only brought to the fore as it is being written.

But there is another way of writing in the present, which is, as it were, writing blind. Writing as a process of projection and discovery. Not writing out of an intention or as a *projet*, nor as mimesis, nor reportage, nor to tell a story. Writing as surprise. To find out what you do not know but somehow know that you know. I can find no better example of this than Clarice Lispector's *The Apple in the Dark*.[3] I think that Hélène Cixous was dazzled by Lispector's gift of a truly refreshing fruit of knowledge, as she tells in *To Live the Orange*, because she had found that here was a woman superbly practising what she herself had in a multitude of ways striven to do for years.[4] 'Ten years to wring from my body the strength to take another step,' *Angst* says.[5] Such writing keeps crossing the gate of the Law, from Kafka's fable as described in *The Newly Born Woman*.[6] Our fear of going through is what keeps the gate up, and each step requires that the fear be conquered. Risk and surprise are continuously involved. Nothing to help you before or behind. Each step is costly, from word to word, sentence to sentence, book to book, and the unpredictability of Hélène Cixous' as of Clarice Lispector's writing is the mark of this. The sequence is engendered by the attempt, is born out of what precedes, but you had not seen that it could; it comes as a surprise. You have to trust to language, its mobility, the spectrum of connotations that storm and sunshine can open in it, to show you the way. 'Elle ne plante pas, elle fraie' (She does not plant, she opens a path). You might say that, unlike man the agriculturalist, who sows *logos spermaticos*, the hunter-gatherer-woman-who-writes and her sentence open paths for others, and other sentences, to follow.[7] They do not deplete the woods, use up the earth, yet there is abundance in the process. And each new moment involves beginning again. Such writing is hard to read, hard to translate. I see nothing wrong with reading it bit by bit, as you read poetry. Antoinette Fouque used to say that women need new forms of literacy: they need to learn to read without such reliance on habit and memory, for the weight of a cultural past that has almost always placed them in inferior positions makes habit and memory dangerous tools for women.

Such writing is in the field of paradox (though it doesn't seek paradox for its own sake, indeed confesses itself suspicious of it). Contradicting what I have just said, Cixous' writing, however much in the present mode, shows both sequence and progress: looks to the past, and to the future. It is sequential in that the fiction at least shares in the diary-writer's compulsive need to record every single stage being passed through. It also has the inner logic of a psychoanalytic cure, but one that is home-made. It progresses from an obsessive innerness (*viz* titles like *Les Commencements, Neutre, Dedans, Souffles, La* and so on) to the elaborate construction of a confident identity. The voice gradually becomes open to others, as co-writers of the text, as people to love, as characters (*Illa* – Latin for 'that one there', takes over from *La*). Until self is no longer central, and theatre begins. Theatre is selflessness incarnate. Cixous' theatre has evolved from the domestic though mythological dramas of Dora and Oedipus, to political plays on a huge scale, concerned with Cambodia and the partition of India. The titles alone express this evolution from self to the world. The preoccupation with identity of *Portrait de Dora* and *Le Nom d'Oedipe* give way to the Shakespearian-sounding *L'Histoire terrible mais inachevée de Norodom Sihanouk, roi du Cambodge* and the epic *L'Indiade*. Private, leads to public. Inner, to outer. The link is made. It is unbroken.

The fictions written up to 1978 (up to *Préparatifs de noces au-delà de l'abîme* and *To Live the Orange*) proceed in a painstaking way towards more integrated selfhood, better self-knowledge. The thing-that-writes is in a sense the thing-that-is-being-written. The material is psychic (conscious/ unconscious) and cultural (made up of mythologies, the political, etc.). The method is often associational, as with psychoanalysis. The meanings dormant in etymologies, sounds, permutations of letters, slips of the tongue, are given creative importance. All forms of subjecthood are used – *je, tu, elle, elles, vous, nous*: the whole scale. The archetypal, the relation to the Other, are all at work in a textuality that is woman-centred, not just because the sexuality at work is that of a woman, but because the enterprise is political. The body-that-writes is retrieving woman from age-old constructs.

In Valéry's 'La Pythie', for example, a Pythoness goes through appalling throes, is flooded by darkness before the god can speak with her voice. The female body has to go dormant, lose consciousness before it can be possessed by 'Saint Langage', 'le dieu dans la chair égare' (the god who has wandered into female flesh): before the 'August Voice' which is at once the voice of the poet (always male) and a disembodied voice, the voice of the 'caves and woods', can speak. The female body speaks without knowing that it speaks.

This account of creativity repeats the situation of (male) doctor versus (female) hysterical patient. Indeed, as the links between *The Newly Born Woman* and *Portrait de Dora* show, it is no accident that Cixous, a writer attempting to create a genuinely female voice, should have had to traverse hysteria, and the Dora case in particular. Writing a body-that-writes, and knows that it writes, calling a fiction *La* in reply to Lacan who had just said that you cannot write *La femme* without crossing *La*, is conquering ground, not just for the writer Cixous, but potentially for all women who write.

Recent psychoanalysis has shed interesting light on the relation between hysteria and knowledge. Peter Lomas argues that the psychotherapist has to recognise that the hysterical symptoms are both a search for a socially acceptable breathing-space and a highly-condensed autobiography. The hysteric, burdened by emotional trauma, refers to it so as to 'disown the disturbing implications' of the bodily message, but yet to express 'that which is not known or socially acknowledged'. The bodily symptoms (the oppressed chest, the aching throat, the paralysed tongue – my own halting start) convey 'information about a problem, the desire to solve it, and the fear of facing it': but not 'knowledge' (which would include some conscious volition and awareness).[8] Though the term 'body language' is used to describe these symptoms, they are not language but 'iconic signs'. The task of the psychoanalyst, Szasz says, 'is to foster the self-reflective attitude in the patient towards his [her?] own body signs in order to facilitate their translation into verbal symbols'.[9] Art is precisely the domain in which symptoms can be translated into symbols. The creative imagination has the power to breach the impossible gap – to step across the gate. Writing can act as the psychoanalyst holding up a mirror to the self so that it can perceive its own bodily symptoms, the voices of the 'caves and woods' in us, that want to speak but do not know how to, and that need the self-reflectiveness to become transformed into symbols. They also need creative playing, need speculation for the transformation to occur, as Winnicott has shown.[10]

It seems to me that this is precisely what happens in Cixous' fictions, at least between the early 1970s and *Préparatifs de noces au delà de l'abîme*. Writing installs a scene in which the narrative voice is at the same time patient, mirror and analyst. Part and parcel of the process of self-discovery which I described earlier as a continous present is the creative play, the punning, the 'let's have another go at this', 'try it this way', 'what if . . .?' which according to Winnicott opens up images to interpretation and multiplicity. Identity becomes constructed through repeated acts of identification. The hysteric, the great figure of the repressed and alienated woman, ceases to be divorced from her own knowledge, only able to make sense through iconic signs.

Body language does not mean writing in milk instead of ink, developing a writerly stammer or talking non-stop about *jouissance*, significant as all these might be as symptoms. It means constructing verbal symbolisations that enable the writing self to know what she knows only in the depths. To experience profound pleasure in being able to say 'I' or '*La*'. That is why it seems to me so daft – I can think of no better word – to talk as Toril Moi does of Cixous as somehow stuck in some pre-Oedipal Imaginary state, or as gathering 'all the contradictions within the plenitude of the Imaginary'.[11] The whole problem, instead, is how to make that repressed Imaginary find ways of reaching forms of symbolisation. Eventually, because self has reached self-knowledge and self-love, which is the basis of all love, the world opens up. The multiple voices that contribute to the single text are recognised as multiple in *Limonade tout était si infini*. Love appears, timidly in *Préparatifs . . .*, powerfully in *Le Livre de Promethea*. The thieves of language, Cixous and the women who have become sources of inspiration to her and are sung by her texts, reclaim a woman's voice.

Three women in particular play Promethean roles in Cixous' mythologies. First, in the late 1970s and early 1980s, Antoinette Fouque with the Editions des femmes, her publishers and collaborators in what was then felt to be a joint venture. Then, from 1978 onwards, Clarice Lispector, the giver of the orange, showing the way to the lost springs of the self: 'I wandered ten glacial years in over-published solitude, without seeing a single human woman's face, the Sun had retired . . . and behold, it was Clarice, the writing'.[12] And then, from about 1985 on, the collaboration with Ariane Mouchkine and the Théâtre du Soleil opens out Cixous' writing to yet another form of body language. It is through the bodies of the actors, their long training, inspired from the theatres of the East, in mime, dancing, meditation, make-up, costume, that the text now speaks, is communicated. Performance is a live present in which the body is more complete than in the written text, since it is there as flesh, spectacle, music, movement, speech. Through theatre, the voice that was once threatened by hysteria, that had to articulate itself out of its inward-looking state, becomes many voices talking to many. From the self-knowledge grown out of a long struggle against the forces of death in the body, in the psyche, is born the capacity to imagine and body forth the struggle between the forces of life and the forces of death at large in the world. The two major plays to date, done by the Théâtre du Soleil, the play on Cambodia and the play on India, are about how the forces of war and hate prevailed over the forces of life and love: how Cambodia turned from the gentle Khmer kingdom into a place of fanatical holocaust, sucked as it was into the East–West maelstrom of the Vietnam war; how India became partitioned at independence, how flesh was torn from flesh, land from land. They tread a fine line between fidelity to history, recreation of the facts as they can be known, and a re-reading of the facts in the name of the 'impossible': Gandhi, being Khmer. Forces which might have prevailed, to which theatre gives form.

L'Indiade, the epic of India, of a fratricidal war, avoidable perhaps like the war between Greece and Troy, is subtitled *L'Inde de leurs rêves*. There might have been – Gandhi and Nehru dreamt of – an unpartitioned India. The play explores what complex forces, political, tribal, religious, international, psychological, made for division; it embodies them in symbolic characters as once the symptoms of the hysterical body were made conscious through verbal symbolisation. In other words, the drama, however grand and public, is born out of, is continuous with, the work of self-discovery and healing of the fiction. This is writing which aims at producing at least the dramatic dream of a cure: discovering a principle of life, of healing, in the very process of showing how hate and death prevailed. Utopian perhaps, but more than utopian, in that it does not bring news from nowhere. It brings, together with news from the actual Cambodia and the actual India, news of what might have been, what should be, what could and can be if each of us was to work in and around ourselves to make those life-forces prevail which the writing, the theatre, bring into symbolic existence.

Another progress, almost mystical, runs throughout Cixous' work alongside the personal and political progress, the progress from inner to outer theatre I have just tried to describe. Taken over time and from book to book, the writing has the character of a *Divine Comedy*, a long journey through the Other World.

Strikingly like Dante, the fictions traverse a variegated hell, and ascend a mount of healing if not a mount of Purgatory (the wedding beyond the abyss, the gift and curative power of the orange). A variety of figures (Kafka, Lispector) are there as guides. Then, at the top of the mount, very much as in Dante, Eden is reached. A state of innocence which is art, not ignorance. The taste of the fruit, which has the freshness of childhood tastes: *With, ou l'art de l'innocence; Limonade tout était si infini*. Here the resemblance to *The Divine Comedy* ends. Cixous' recent writing does not reach out towards the spheres of paradise beyond the Earthly Paradise. It chooses to return to earth, more precisely to history, bringing back as gifts what it has glimpsed of paradise: the possibility of a better world.

The last book I have read, *Manne aux Mandelstams aux Mandelas*, has a title that says it all. It attempts to make the imaginative gift of loving poetry, food from heaven, Manna, to two couples who in reality, having suffered all the agonies of the desert, exile, separation, imprisonment, are beyond retrieval. No one can alter the fate of the Russian poet Mandelstam, dead in Siberia in 1938 for his opposition to Stalin. No one can give back to Nelson and Winnie Mandela the life they might have had as a couple, had they not been partitioned by apartheid. Only Manna from heaven, the gift of a writing inspired by and continuous with the love of the two wives, Nadedja Mandelstam and Winnie Mandela, the gift of a writing that is celebratory and poetic and never tries to exploit the tragedy of its characters for its own purposes, writing that is of woman for both men and women, can make the 'impossible', like Gandhi, 'smile upon' them. And upon us.

NOTES

1. Susan Sellers, *Writing Differences: Readings from the seminar of Hélène Cixous* (Milton Keynes: Open University Press, and New York: St. Martin's Press, 1988).
2. Roland Barthes, *Writing Degree Zero*, translated by Annette Lavers and Colin Smith (Boston: Beacon Press, 1970), (initially published Paris: Gonthier, 1964); and Sartre, *What is Literature?*, translated by Bernard Frechtman (New York: Harper and Row, 1965), especially Chapters 2 and 3.
3. *The Apple In the Dark* (London: Virago, 1985).
4. *Vivre l'orange/To Live the Orange* (Paris: Editions des femmes, 1978).
5. *Angst*, translated by Jo Levy (London: Calder, 1985), p. 190.
6. *The Newly Born Woman*, translated by Betsy Wing (Minneapolis: University of Minnesota Press, 1986), pp. 101–3.
7. See Christine Battersby's most interesting discussion of theories of the genius as male throughout the ages, in *Gender and Genius: Towards a feminist aesthetics* (London: The Women's Press, 1989).
8. Peter Lomas, *True and False Experience: The case for a personal psychotherapy* (London: Allen Lane, 1973), p. 117 and p. 120.
9. Thomas Szasz, *The Myth of Mental Illness* (New York: Harper and Row, 1974, and London, Toronto, Sydney and New York: Granada, Paladin Books), pp. 226–42, and D. W. Winnicott, *The Maturational Processes and the Facilitating Environment; Studies in the theory of emotional development* (London: Hogarth Press, 1965), and *Playing and Reality* (Harmondsworth: Penguin, 1974), Chapter 2.
10. I am deeply grateful to Marie Addyman for having drawn my attention to this particular line of thinking in her PhD thesis, 'The character of hysteria in Shakespeare's England' (York, 1989). Chapter 4 is the one from which I have drawn. I quote this most relevant passage: '[For] Donald Winnicott, fantasy is, like brute fact for Coleridge, entirely fixed and dead. As the factual world is an inflexible state of affairs in which the person moves passively and uncreatively, not seeing action therein as the possibility of self-expression; so the non-functioning, split-off part is given over to the dead process of fantasising – apart, unproductive, something which "happens immediately, except that it does not happen at all", and is therefore unavailable for interpretation, identification and authentic existence in reality. Conversion symbolisation, like a record stuck in a groove, corresponds to the fantasying process . . . Quite contrary is the activity of the imagination in which, instead of dislocation, "conflict and coalition" within the person, subjectivity and objectivity come together as the realm of urgent and immediate possibility, of "what if . . . ?", to enrich life. In Winnicott's vocabulary, this is creative playing . . . for we are again talking about the artistic process'. *Ibid.*, p. 92.
11. *Sexual/Textual Politics* (London and New York: Methuen, 1985), p. 121.
12. *To Live the Orange*, p. 48.

Chapter 4

A Feminine Economy

Some preliminary thoughts

Judith Still

I want to approach (and I will have time only to approach, certainly not develop, let alone resolve) a series of issues raised for me by the ambiguous French adjective *féminin(e)*, which translates into English *either* as what might be a cultural description 'feminine' *or* – more problematically – as a bodily description 'female'.[1] The issues raised are as follows:

1. The significance of defining that adjective in terms of what that defini-tion implies about the relationship between the material (by which I mean the historical, the economic, the political and so on) and the qualities evoked by *féminin(e)*. Are these feminine qualities independent of other material factors – or do they interact with them? The body, male or female, is sometimes presented as independent of other factors – as though we could at least rely on the fact that all females have wombs and vaginas and then elaborate a theory based on that fact. Yet there are a number of problems with this 'commonsense' simplicity. For a start, male and female biology is a continuum rather than an opposition even if there may be some clustering around the polarities. Again, very many aspects of the body (such as size, hair texture and colour, and so on) do vary as a result of social factors such as diet or fashion, which may be class- or race-related. More radically, chemical and surgical intervention mean that almost any physical characteristic can be altered, and some-times the health of the body as a whole requires such alteration (such as hysterectomies performed because of cancer of the womb). Most impor-tantly, it is our relationship to our bodies which is crucial, rather than any physical detail in itself.[2] I would like to introduce various differences – not only racial difference, which involves the body to some extent, but also class difference, which today is more readily perceived as a function of political economy rather than as an innate given, although history informs us that such a perception is far from inevitable.

49

2. The particular cases of *économie féminine* and *écriture féminine* – what these terms mean and what that implies for the meaning of the feminine. Although the *féminin(e)* is often taken to imply a resistance to theory, it seems to me that its very power has been precisely in the domain opened up by post-structuralist (post-Lacanian) theory – theory which does not exclude many of theory's traditional others (poetry, mysticism and so on). Hence my theoretical interrogation.[3]
3. Whether there could be problems with privileging qualities attributed to *féminin(e)* – either because this is establishing a hierarchy, or because of something about the qualities themselves.
4. Finally, the relationship of (woman) reader to (woman's) text – and how that shadows the relationship of feminine reader to feminine writing.[4]

First of all, I want to raise the question of history, of the economic, the socio-political, and so on. Feminist research in general has often been accused of being ahistorical, of trying to fit a grid of assumptions which, if it applies at all, applies to one particular historical/geographical moment, to a wide range of times and places where it is quite inappropriate – for example, castigating someone for his or her unenlightened views on women when those views were relatively emancipatory in that particular socio-historical context.[5] The kind of work associated with Hélène Cixous has attracted from anti-feminists and also some feminists the criticism that it is so ahistorical as to rely upon eternal essences (essences which some see as biologically determined).[6] Quotations such as 'la différence c'est au niveau de la jouissance' (*La Jeune née*, p. 151; hereafter *JN*), translated as 'the difference, in my opinion', becomes most clearly perceived on the level of *jouissance*' (*The Newly Born Woman*, p. 82; hereafter *NBW*)[7] are, taken in isolation, provocative, but Cixous does go on to modify this bald assertion, explaining how the 'économie pulsionelle d'une femme' (translated as 'a woman's instinctual economy', *NBW*, p. 82) is affected by the political economy and by various ideological state apparatuses such as the education system:

> Nothing allows us to rule out the possibility of radical transformation of behaviours, mentalities, roles, political economy – whose effects on libidinal economy are unthinkable – today. Let us simultaneously imagine a general change in all the structures of training, education, supervision – hence in the structures of reproduction of ideological results. And let us imagine a real liberation of sexuality, that is to say, a transformation of each one's relationship to his or her body (and to the other body), an approximation to the vast, material, organic, sensuous universe that we are. This cannot be accomplished, of course, without political transformations that are equally radical. (Imagine!) Then 'femininity' and 'masculinity' would inscribe quite differently their effects of difference, their economy, their relationship to expenditure, to lack, to the gift. (*NBW*, p. 83)

Cixous' choice of terms suggests an engagement with the work of Louis Althusser on 'Ideological State Apparatuses' (ISA).[8] The ISA contribute to the reproduction of capitalist relations of production. I think that this is a crucial issue, and one which is of course related to the question of how differences other than sexual difference (such as class and race differences) intermesh with sexual difference.

Another way of phrasing this problem is to say: can we usefully talk about 'women', or more controversially 'woman'? Is a biological definition a sufficient bond such that the term 'women' can function in non-tautological statements without greater precision of, say, time and place being necessary in terms of accuracy? If we do need to be more specific, then, in pragmatic terms, how specific is useful? Any generalisation (even 'female polytechnic lecturers in 1980s London') is to some extent a betrayal and inaccurate, but nothing could be said (there would be no language) if we ever reached the discrete unit – a unit which would be less than *one* woman in physical terms since within the space, the matter of flesh and bones, defined as *a* woman there are in fact *many*.

Within the writing and speech of Cixous there is, I would suggest, a tension (a creative tension because of the way it challenges us) between what appear as ahistorical references to *woman* (for instance, on pregnancy: 'How could the woman, who has experienced the not-me within me, not have a particular relationship to the written?', *NBW*, p. 90), and statements in which the historical is admitted (as in the quotation above from *NBW*, p. 83). The term 'woman' raises the twin spectres of ahistoricism and biologism. It would have to be – and could be – explained (via an act of interpretation – at once creation and destruction) that 'woman' is a construction or a fiction – certainly not fixed for all time. As I have already said, I want to focus on the adjective *féminin(e)* which is perhaps slightly easier, but, if in any way elucidated, sheds light on the general issues. It is perhaps slightly easier in that (especially in English) we are more used to the idea that *femininity* is something which is constructed and defined differently at different historical moments (in different environments), and that the collection of attributes which may be associated with the feminine at any given moment can be attributed to some biological males and not all biological females. Cixous points out that it was largely men who first theorised *une économie autre*, and that these were (therefore) men who allowed expression to their femininity, their homosexuality: 'It is men who have inscribed, described, theorized the paradoxical logic of an economy without reserve. This is not contradictory; it brings us back to asking about their femininity' (*NBW*, p. 86). Nevertheless, slippage into essentialism or biologism is a constant – and necessary – danger. Necessary because of our desire to speak about women (and I want to leave that statement wilfully unglossed for the present). Analysis in terms of other (say, class and race) differences alongside sexual difference helps because, for example, the question of a biological support for difference is raised in quite another way with respect to race and is again displaced in the case of class. The displacements allow our perspective to vary.

I am going to look briefly at the examples of *économie masculine*, *économie féminine* and *écriture féminine* in that order. I am going to look first at the question of economies both because I see it as fundamental and because the term 'economy' outside feminism also arouses controversies over history and historical periodisation, for instance, divisions between (and within) pre-capitalist and capitalist regimes, controversies which relate to the interpretation of gift exchange. Cixous suggests in *The Newly Born Woman* that at the moment, and for some time, there have existed simultaneously two distinct economies – but that such a situation is not innate or essential but rather subject to change: 'All the difference determining history's movement as property's movement is articulated between two economies that are defined in relation to the problematic of the gift' (*NBW*, p. 80). I shall briefly consider what is meant by (a masculine) economy since feminine economy seems to be defined by its difference from, its otherness to, that familiar point of reference (rather as 'primitive' economies are defined with respect to capitalism). The masculine economy, also known as 'l'Empire du Propre' (*JN*, p. 144, translated by Wing as 'the Empire of the Self-Same', but by Toril Moi as 'the Realm of the Proper'), is an economy of appropriation which I think we could usefully relate to that economy which is the subject of (neo-classical) economics. Economics as a discipline can be crudely divided into the neo-classical and the Marxist – a crucial part of the distinction between these two kinds of economics is that the neo-classical is ahistorical (i.e. universal) whereas the Marxist (historical materialist) mode of analysis insists that the economy described normatively and ideologically by neo-classicists is specific to the capitalist mode of production. Pierre Bourdieu writes, in *Algérie 60*:

> It is the universalisation of a specific class of preferences which is at the root of that justificatory and moralising discourse which transforms what are the objective constraints of *one* economy into universal precepts concerning morality, foresight, denial or saving yesterday, credit, expenditure and pleasure today. Unbeknownst to itself the science of economics, which is still 'the most moral of the human sciences', frequently participates in that discourse.[9]

The neo-classical economy presupposes some kind of allocation of property rights (mine and thine) and assumes that individuals behave rationally. Rational behaviour is that which is calculated to bring about desired outcomes, the calculation is done on the basis of mathematical probabilities using as much data as it has been economic to acquire (another calculation). The desired outcome is maximum profit (profit defined as revenue minus expenditure), in other words the accumulation of property, or 'more is better' as economists will summarise the law. Hence investment, the temporary relinquishing of property, follows from the calculation that in the longer term more property will accrue to the investing individual, which will compensate for the short-term diminished consumption possibilities. This economic behaviour need not of course be confined to finance/business, but occurs in many situations, so we are told. Emotional relationships can be perceived in terms of investments (e.g. of time, emotional energy, material goods) in the expectation of finally profiting from that investment – increased pleasure, ego massaging, whatever. Cixous gives the example of Don Juan as a figure who treats personal relationships economically.

That kind of extension of economic behaviour to situations beyond the profit-maximising equation of the capitalist, leads on to the question of the analysis of behaviour in pre-capitalist societies. Economic behaviour in, say, love affairs today could be hard to avoid due to the training we have all received in economic calculation because of our socio-historical environment. That is to say, capitalism affects (and is affected by) many domains outside production. But is economic behaviour universal as some theorists would suggest, affecting not only all exchanges in capitalist systems (bad enough), but also all possible exchanges between human beings throughout time? Or is uneconomic behaviour (say, *une économie féminine*) to be found *somewhere*, and if so could it exist, even vestigially, under our present social and economic system?

Analysis of uneconomic (or 'otherly' economic) behaviour has usually taken the form of a study of gifts. (I refer to work by Lévi-Strauss, Bourdieu, Bataille, Derrida and Lyotard as well as work by women on some kind of feminine economy.) One of the most famous studies of gift exchange in different cultures, both classical and so-called primitive, was by the social anthropologist Marcel Mauss.[10] Some theorists (including neo-classical economists) would maintain that gift exchange amongst the tribes which he studied is simply a different *form* of economic transaction from, say, a sale or a loan, but involves identical content in terms of the calculation on the part of the individuals concerned (rational maximisation) – that it would be 'a gift-that-takes', (NBW, p. 87), i.e. that a gift is only given in the rational expectation that there will be a return; social codes ensure that a donor does not lose out although the profit may take many different forms.[11] Indeed much of the evidence Mauss presents reinforces this hypothesis; he suggests that *potlatch*[12], for example, is like warfare in a different guise (we may feel, of course, that it is a far preferable guise), that the motivating emotions are ones of desire for power, fear of losing power and hostility towards rivals in generosity:

> We intend in this book to isolate one important set of phenomena: namely, prestations which are in theory voluntary, disinterested and spontaneous, but are in fact obligatory and interested. The form usually taken is that of the gift generously offered; but the accompanying behaviour is formal pretence and social deception, while the transaction itself is based on obligation and economic self-interest. (*The Gift*, p. 1)

Other theorists argue that nevertheless there is a difference in that gift exchange in pre-capitalist societies is incommensurable with rational profit maximisation; Pierre Bourdieu writing on pre-colonial structures in Algeria insists on the importance of the temporal separation of gift and repayment and of the absence of precise calculation:

> Is generous exchange anything other than the spreading out into a succession of different moments in time of a transaction which the rational contract squeezes into an instant? It is precisely thanks to that intervening interval of time that the gift can seem to the observer like an obligatory step in a continuous series of gifts and return gifts, while it is actually experienced as a disinterested and thoughtful act. Is it not the case that the worst offence you can commit is returning a gift immediately or reciprocating with an identical offering? As long as the return gift is deferred each act of giving can be understood as an absolute beginning and *not* as the obligatory continuation of an exchange process. (*Algérie 60*, p. 35)

Mauss' analysis is useful in the theorisation of a feminine economy only insofar as it provides a salutary warning that the form of gift-exchange may conceal 'obligation and economic self-interest'. If we studied Bourdieu's hypothesis concerning pre-capitalist Algeria, what effect would that have on our 'feminine economy'? It seems to me that his work raises some relevant points, for example, the question of the observing eye which perceives the familiar structure of obligation or self-interest in all that it surveys. Bourdieu points to some possibilities of interposing a *different* structure via the questions of temporal and spatial deferral, of fragmentation, and of non-quantification. The temporal and spatial deferral means that it is unclear when, where and by whom a gift would be returned; the fragmentation suggests more radically that any return is out of the question, that is to say, that there are only gifts and no return gifts. Non-quantification could mean no more than that exchange is approximate rather than the precise transactions which are enabled by currency; however, it could also imply a more radical refusal to calculate. However, Bourdieu's writings on the Algerian situation in particular also ring certain alarm bells for feminists. He presents feudal domesticity in a somewhat idealised fashion (for instance, pp. 111–12). Feminists have long argued that men's exploitation of women's unpaid domestic labour should not be confused with the notion of feminine generosity. Another practical point is the consideration that men's generosity may be enabled by the exploitation of women.

In *Economie libidinale*, Jean-François Lyotard takes a rather different approach, and one which could be more significant for our question of *une économie féminine*. He argues that theories (or myths) of Before Capitalism are utopic fantasies which serve to keep capitalism 'pure' – pure rationality, pure calculation, etc., whether you love it or you hate it (more likely both):

> When Baudrillard says: '*There is no mode of production nor indeed production* in primitive societies, there is *no dialectic* in primitive societies, there is *no unconscious* in primitive societies', we reply: there's no such thing as a primitive society.
>
> First of all, from a methodological point of view (yes, I'm afraid so. . .), that gift and return gift society plays the role in Baudrillard's thinking of a (lost, of course) reference, of an (unlocatable) alibi for his critique of capital. Baudrillard doesn't want to hear talk of nature or naturalness. How is it that he doesn't see that the whole problematic of the gift, of symbolic exchange as he gets it from Mauss, with or without Bataille's, Caillois's or Lacan's additions and rewritings, belongs in its entirety to western imperialism and racism – that it's still ethnology's noble savage, somewhat libidinalised, which is passed down to him along with that concept?[13]

In fact, he says, no economy is completely *propre*:

> ALL POLITICAL ECONOMIES ARE LIBIDINAL
> Here's the first thing that makes us say: there's no such thing as a primitive society, i.e. there's no exterior reference, not even an immanent one, where the division between what is part of capital (or political economy) and what is part of subversion (or libidinal economy) can always be cleanly and properly made; where desire is clearly readable, where its *own proper economy [économie propre]* is not muddied. (*Economie libidinale*, p. 133)

This kind of shattering of the monolithic enemy could be read optimistically (that generous alternatives could be fostered here and now), although it is often received as a pessimistic message (that there is no alternative). Many societies or situations within a society have been interpreted as gift-exchange when that gift-exchange is not importantly different from what I have been calling a masculine economy or capitalism. But if Lyotard is understood to be arguing that there is no possibility of distinguishing between capitalism and a gift economy (rather than the more limited point that neither is absolutely exterior to the other), then his conclusion would be that there is no such thing as a feminine economy. I would like, however, to argue that even if there is no such thing nor any such place as a feminine economy, there is an ethical, political and theoretical point to retaining that utopic horizon.

Georges Bataille argued that expenditure (of the self) without reserve (which can be related to Cixous's 'economic sans réserves', (*JN*, p. 160)

'economy without reserve', (*NBW*, p. 86)) can escape economic calculation. Interestingly, Jacques Derrida's analysis of his work does not – as
popular deconstruction might expect – take the form of detecting mysticism,
a desire for presence or plenitude in Bataille's laughter or his sovereign
sacrifice, even if Bataille's transgression (like any other transgression) is said
to confirm and conserve to some extent that which it transgresses. Derrida
says of Hegel:

> the phenomenology . . . corresponds to a restricted economy: restricted to
> commercial values . . ., limited to the meaning and the established value of
> objects and to their *circulation*. The *circularity* of absolute knowledge could
> dominate, could comprehend only this circulation, only the *circuit of reproductive
> consumption*.[14]

On the other hand, he says of Bataille:

> Sovereignty certainly makes itself independent through the putting at stake of life;
> it is attached to nothing and conserves nothing. But, differing from Hegelian
> mastery, it does not even want to maintain itself, collect itself, or collect the profits
> from itself or from its own risk, it 'cannot even be defined as a possession' . . .
> sovereignty *does not govern itself*. And does not govern in general: it governs neither
> others, nor things, nor discourses in order to produce meaning. . . . it must expend
> itself without reserve, lose itself, lose consciousness, lose all memory of itself and
> all the interiority of itself; as opposed to *Erinnerung*, as opposed to the avarice
> which assimilates meaning, it must *practice forgetting*, the *aktive Vergesslichkeit* of
> which Nietzsche speaks, and as the ultimate subversion of mastery, it must no
> longer seek to be recognized. ('From Restricted to General Economy', pp. 264–5)

What about a feminine economy? Are the accounts of gift-exchange in
pre-capitalist societies of any relevance, or is feminine generosity another,
even less calculated kind of gift? How does it relate then to Bataille's
staking of life itself? Cixous suggests that there is no absolute *don gratuit*, yet
that there can be a gift which does not involve a profitable (supplementary)
return:

> All the difference lies in the why and how of the gift, in the values that the gesture
> of giving affirms, causes to circulate; in the type of profit the giver draws from the
> gift and the use to which he or she puts it . . . She is able not to return to herself,
> never settling down, pouring out, going everywhere to the other. (*NBW*, p. 87)

Bataille's *dépense* is an erotic and death-defying one – Cixous' lyric
celebration of Antony and Cleopatra or Achilles and Penthesilea reminds
me of that, but a feminine economy would surely involve a maternal-loving
component which is notoriously absent from Bataille, who is too close to
Sade.[15]

Ecriture féminine is related to the idea of an *économie féminine* in that both
display a different relation to 'the other'. Whereas a masculine economy
requires strict delineation of property (from the ownership of one's body

onwards to the ownership of the fruits of one's labour and so on), a feminine economy is one (of proximity) of taking the other into oneself and being taken into the other also. A feminine economy is about mutual knowing and knowing again (re-cognition in those senses only). *Ecriture féminine* therefore should be a writing shot through (like shot silk) with otherness. Does this require it to be 'difficult' (since we are trained in conservative forms), modernist, expressionist, James-Joyce writing? If so, much contemporary women's writing (especially black women's writing) fails.[16]

Categorisation, whether deriving from pretensions to scientific rigour, from claims to an aesthetic sensibility, or from the espousal of political priorities, inevitably involves establishing some kind of hierarchy – whether explicit or implicit. Cixous' 'Castration or decapitation' suggests that this kind of activity is part of *l'Empire du Propre*.[17] But 'feminist' criticism usually has explicit political priorities, and very often measures texts against a previously-established ideal model, or, at the very least, has a check list of criteria by which it can award points to (and take them off) the text under scrutiny. The work of earlier feminist writers, such as that of Simone de Beauvoir, is often judged, and found lacking, by recent feminist readers – on the grounds, for example, that it is too dependent on male criteria (form and content).[18] But a founding Mother can be excused on account of the times in which she was writing. Someone writing in the 1980s has no such historical escape route.

I wish to argue against always reading in terms of measuring against a standard and in favour of reading in a motherly, creative fashion. That is to say that not only should 'creative' writing be open to the other, but that reading should be too. In a sense this is only to reiterate the point that reading is writing as writing is reading. Cixous' own readings and writings often demonstrate this point. However, she is also associated with the assertion that *écriture féminine* is to be found in very few places. I do not wish to deny the necessary aggressive elements in mothering, reading or creating! I simply wish to privilege (of course!) the reconstructive over the critical, the generous over the calculated. I would argue (following the theoretical hints by Cixous) that the *féminin(e)* is not chosen for us, as Annie Leclerc suggests when she says we are wombs/vaginas/breasts, end of argument. Leclerc should be supplemented with Christine Delphy's analysis.[19] Femininity is not a fixed content which females can only accept or deny (and to which males have no access), but a complex construct involving many 'others' to that which presents itself as universal 'man' – a construct which is influenced by (though not absolutely determined by) relations of production, ideological state apparatuses and the like. Before there is a radical change in the political economy, we can foster the feminines (at the same time as we take our place within the masculine) in different ways. That *économie féminine* which is a theoretical extreme or poetic utopia can still inform our practice, showing that the (masculine) economy of rational (i.e. calculated) profit maximisation is not universal and inevitable in all spheres of exchange. As readers and teachers – both positions of would-be mastery – the feminine economy of generosity, as opposed to a Hegelian seeking of recognition (*reconnaissance* – also gratitude), can influence our practice. A search for feminines in texts can be a celebration of what we find as well as an analysis of the interplay of all the various differences; it need not involve a marking down of those works judged as insufficiently feminine nor a fetishisation of any one particular mode of discourse or practice.

NOTES

I should like to thank the Nottingham Critical Theory Group's 'Research in Progress' Seminar for comments on an earlier draft of this paper.

1. In English-language writing the distinction is often made between questions of gender ('feminine') and questions of sex ('female'). Yet that distinction, which can be a useful tool for one stage of analysis, is not clear cut since our (relation to our) sex is always to some extent constructed by our gender. The adjective *féminin(e)* has become a topic of debate in a new way due to the work of certain contemporary French women writers; the key text to which I shall refer is Hélène Cixous and Catherine Clément, *La Jeune née* (Paris: Union Générale d'Editions, 1975), translated by Betsy Wing as *The Newly Born Woman* (Manchester: Manchester University Press, 1986). Cixous' sense of '*féminin(e)*' is inspired by psychoanalysis – this of course does not resolve the question even in interpreting her work, of the long debates about the psychoanalytical use of the term *phallus* and its relationship to the penis.

2. *Herculine Barbin* (edited by Michel Foucault, translated by Richard McDougall (New York: Random House, 1980)) is just one text which brings home the argument that sexual biology is a continuum even though society has a very problematic relationship to that fact. It also suggests the part that law and medicine play in constructing gendered identity.

3. This is in no way ruled out by Cixous; for example, see her exchange with Clément where she asserts that 'masculine' forms need not be abandoned: 'I use rhetorical discourse, the discourse of mastery, orally, for example, with my students, and obviously I do it on purpose; it is a refusal on my part to leave organized discourse entirely in men's power.' (*NBW*, p. 136)

4. I have discussed these issues in relationship to one particular novel by an Algerian woman writer, Djanet Lachmet, *Le Cow-boy* (Paris: Belfond, 1983, translated by Judith Still as *Lallia*, Manchester: Carcanet, 1987) in 'Body and Culture: The representation of sexual, racial and class differences in Lachmet's *Le Cow-boy*' in

Contemporary French Women's Fiction: Feminist perspectives, edited by M. Atack
and P. Powrie, Manchester: Manchester University Press, forthcoming. *Le Cow-
boy* raises important issues to do with women, the construction of a gendered
subject and the contradictions which attack that would-be coherent construction.
I don't know whether it could be termed *écriture féminine*. Lachmet's work 'fits' the
mould in the way in which it weaves together women's stories, dreams, generosity,
love and suffering, but, in formal terms, it is not a radical postmodern text, as are
some of Cixous' own pieces. What might it imply to judge that Lachmet's work fails
to fit the bill of *écriture féminine*?

5. There are problems with using the term 'feminist' in the context of French writers,
   because of the contamination with *féministe* in French which has a rather narrower
   range of connotations than 'feminist', and is often used (pejoratively) to refer to a
   primarily middle-class reformist movement which is willing to work entirely within
   existing male-dominated structures in order to achieve small improvements in
   the lot of some women. Since the English term encompasses a very broad range
   of positions and is usually only employed pejoratively by those who are opposed
   to any improvements in women's situation, I shall adopt it with no further
   demurral.

6. See, for example, Toril Moi, *Sexual/Textual Politics* (London: Methuen, 1985),
   pp. 110–13.

7. I have quoted the French as well as the English to suggest that the translation
   is already an interpretation – and one which softens the impact of the statement.

8. See Louis Althusser, 'Ideology and Ideological State Apparatuses (Notes towards
   an Investigation)' in *Lenin and Philosophy and Other Essays* translated by Ben
   Brewster (London: New Left Books, 1971), pp. 121–73.

9. *Algérie 60* (Paris: Minuit, 1977), p. 8. Where there is no reference to a published
   translation I have translated quotations myself.

10. See Marcel Mauss, *The Gift*, translated by Ian Cunnison (London: Routledge and
    Kegan Paul, 1969).

11. Over recent years neo-classical economics has devoted much time to the question
    of 'rational expectations' in recognition of the argument that it is implausible
    to assume that economic agents have perfect knowledge. However, the theoreti-
    cal result of assuming rational expectations on the part of all economic agents
    does not differ greatly from assuming perfect knowledge, since (via a more com-
    plex mathematical process) rational expectations are deemed to be on average
    right.

    Cixous refers less to the economic context in the commercial sense than in the
    psychoanalytic sense. She argues that psychoanalysis describes the traditional man
    who wants to 'gain more masculinity: plus-value of virility, authority, power,
    money or pleasure, all of which reenforce his phallocentric narcissism at the same
    time' (*NBW*, p. 87). I would translate 'plus-value' (*JN*, p. 161) as 'surplus value'
    since that term is used in Marxist contexts and such a translation would bring out
    Cixous' analogy between two kinds of *homo economicus*: capitalist man described by
    Marx and psychoanalytic man described by Freud.

12. Mauss tells us that *potlatch* is a Chinook word which meant originally 'to nourish' or
    'to consume' (*The Gift*, p. 4); it is used to describe festivals when chiefs compete by
    offering ever more sumptuous gifts to other nobles, sometimes going so far as to des-
    troy accumulated possessions in order to eclipse a rival. The original meaning is a
    reminder that one of the primary gifts is that of food, and its history reminds us that
    nourishment can become or be perceived as aggressive, for example in the child's
    fantasies concerning its mother's gift of milk. Just as an *économie féminine* can be

found in *écriture féminine*, so fighting with gifts also occurs textually – in agonistic intertextual relations; see my 'From Eliot's "raw bone" to Gyges' ring: Two modes of intertextuality', *Paragraph*, vol. 1, 1983, 44–59.
13. Jean-François Lyotard, *Economie libidinale* (Paris: Minuit, 1974), p. 130. References are to Baudrillard, *Le Miroir de la production*.
14. Jacques Derrida, 'From Restricted to General Economy: A Hegelianism without reserve' (an essay on Bataille) in *Writing and Difference*, translated by Alan Bass (London: Routledge and Kegan Paul, 1978), p. 271. I have changed the translation of *maîtrise* from 'lordship' to 'mastery' in the following quotation.
15. Writing of the Hegelian need for recognition, and noting how masculine desire requires the sense of conquest (of rape), Cixous asks: 'Why did this comedy, whose final act is the master's flirtation with death, make Bataille laugh so hard, as he amused himself by pushing Hegel to the edge of the abyss that a civilized man keeps himself from falling into? This abyss that functions as a metaphor both of death and of the feminine sex' (*NBW*, p. 80).
16. Here I am thinking in particular of institutional questions such as access to education and (colonial) education in a language other than the mother tongue. These questions relate to class as well as race.
17. 'Castration or decapitation', translated by Annette Kuhn, *Signs*, vol. 7, no. 1, 1981.
18. See, for example, Mary Evans, *Simone de Beauvoir: A Feminist Mandarin* (London: Tavistock, 1985); Judith Okely, *Simone de Beauvoir: A re-reading* (London: Virago, 1986); T. Moi, 'She came to stay' review of Evans and Okely, *Paragraph*, vol. 8, 1986, 110–20.
19. See A. Leclerc, *Parole de femme* (Paris: Livre de Poche, 1974); some extracts have been translated in *New French Feminisms* edited by Elaine Marks and Isabelle de Courtivron (Hemel Hempstead: Harvester Wheatsheaf, 1980), and in *French Connections* edited by Claire Duchen (London: Hutchinson, 1987). C. Delphy's critique of Leclerc is in 'Protofeminism and antifeminism' in *Close to Home: A materialist analysis of women's oppression*, translated and edited by Diana Leonard (London: Hutchinson, 1984).

Part II

Women Writing

Introduction

One of the interesting things about this book is the way that the essays in it will not sit neatly in place. They keep spilling into the terrain of their neighbouring sections, moving around in their implications and subject, and each piece reads as if it could also fit snugly elsewhere in our volume. With my editor's hat on I couldn't help but feel that this made them very badly behaved essays. It makes a job easier if you can somewhere draw a definite line and pragmatically put things in their place. But our writers are much more interested in opening up these 'easy' processes, of naming and placing and establishing boundaries. I confess to feeling that I was violating something by placing them in an order, because even though they were written and redrafted in relative isolation (the writers are certainly geographically distanced), there is a debate and communication going on among them, as they refer backwards and forwards to each other through a network of questions, conjectures, responses. These five pieces, like the whole volume, cannot be read in a linear or teleological fashion, and the resulting double-movement enacts in one form a problematisation of the way we read from 'a' to 'b'.

So here at point 'a' of this section, it is perhaps more appropriate to begin by invoking a text which is discussed at its end by Françoise Defromont; Virginia Woolf's *A Room of One's Own*:

> The title women and fiction might mean . . . women and what they are like, or it might mean women and the fiction that they write; or it might mean women and the fiction that is written about them, or it might mean that somehow all three are inextricably mixed together . . . But when I began to consider the subject in this last way, which seemed the most interesting, I soon saw that it had one fatal drawback. I should never be able to come to a conclusion.[1]

The question of women writing is the oblique starting point for each of the pieces collected here. It is, of course, not an easy question to articulate, perhaps because it is unanswerable. It has been addressed in diverse forms: involving problems of the identity of the writer and the role or risk of anonymity, the relationship between writing and the body, writing as subversion. Faced with the title 'Women Writing', any of our writers could offer a similar range of 'mights' as Woolf's. Susan Wiseman, in her discussion of Susan Sontag, Hélène Cixous, and the role of the intellectual, fixes more openly on 'the question of writing under the sign of gender', which can involve 'attempting to subvert or eschew that sign' (page 108).

One debate which continues to be opened up is that of the 'nature' of *écriture féminine*, feminine writing which is not the same as women's writing. It is writing which inscribes itself through an affirmation of the feminine body, and yet it is not exclusively female; for Cixous, men can produce *écriture féminine*. It is evocative, necessarily indefinite, playful. As Phil Powrie writes in his discussion of Chantal Chawaf, *écriture féminine* is 'a question needling through patriarchal language like lacework', which 'allows the body to breathe' (page 85). This is beautifully and positively realised by Françoise Defromont, for whom *écriture féminine* is language in a process of becoming, 'flowing thinking' rather than 'thought', the liquid gold half seen in a fish's movement rather than 'a nugget of pure truth'. It is an embrace between one's body and 'thinking it out', an 'erotic ravishment' which 'produces an endless syntactic and lexical turmoil at the very moment of the ecstatic embrace between words and the body' (page 122). Crucially for Defromont, *écriture féminine* subverts through metaphor ('metaphors give flesh to thought') the boundaries between poetry and theory.

For Shirley Foster *écriture féminine* both opens up the possibility of speaking 'otherwise' (evoking Xavière Gauthier's notion of 'the unsaid or non-sense') just as it paradoxically closes it down, since writing is also for Foster definition, naming, and an act which 'identifies' the writing self: 'the theory [of *écriture féminine*] can only be notional since to define is to enclose, codify, and thus reinstate the dominant linguistic system' (page 67). Foster also opens up another facet of our title, since for her 'Women Writing' also importantly evokes the writing which women produce, and the self which is produced through writing, its anxious identity and instability. What is for Foster important, then, about Christina Rossetti and Emily Dickinson as *women* writers is in a sense the way that they negotiate being *masculine* writers: 'their defiance is voiced not from within the female Imaginary but from within the male Symbolic' (page 68). They subvert by deploying irony and parody, so that humour becomes a political weapon. In a different way the question of political strategy emerges in Phil Powie's engagement with the work of Chawaf (particularly *Le Soleil at la terre*), to discuss the political criticisms of biologism and essentialism which have been levelled against *écriture féminine* recently.

Perhaps, then, one of the strengths of this group of essays, and the sense in which they are pushing the debate around *écriture féminine* one stage further into the 1990s, is the way that they avoid deifying or protecting essential ideals of femininity, or the space of writing as sacred or paradoxically inarticulate. Just as in her opening piece Hélène Cixous explores 'difficult joys', so the terrain of women writing which these writers cover and recover is one often barbed with hard questions and painful possibilities. Anne Green's analysis of the role of anonymity in writing and the production of a writer's identity, shows through a discussion of the work of Madame de Lafayette that the act of writing is both one of power and of risk. 'The act of creation creates hostages to fortune' (page 95): bodies, texts and their written embrace.

L.W.

NOTE

1. Virginia Woolf, *A Room of One's Own* (St Albans: Granada, 1977), p. 5.

Chapter 5

Speaking Beyond Patriarchy

The female voice in Emily Dickinson and Christina Rossetti

Shirley Foster

Feminist theory over the last two decades has made us familiar with the idea of 'woman' as constructed by patriarchal ideologies. We have been made aware of how images of femininity derive from notions of female subordination, such as non-being, service and sacrifice, selflessness, and resignation to loss and non-fulfilment, with womanhood itself predicated in terms of relativity and 'otherness'. Hélène Cixous argues the existence of a set of binary and hierarchised gender-defining oppositions which place female on the negative or inactive side – so woman symbolises the passive, the concave, the supporting, and the containing, part of a conceptual scheme entirely privileging the male. In men's eyes, Cixous continues, women are the non-social, non-political, non-human half of the living structure; hence, repressed in order to ensure the functioning of the masculine system, they have to acknowledge their fate as 'loss', burial, and relegation to the shadow thrown on them by patriarchy.[1] This representation of woman as nobody, reduced wholly to the position of 'other', is taken up by other feminist critics: Luce Irigaray, for example, in 'Ce Sexe qui n'est pas un', states that woman has been thus placed in a situation 'where she can experience herself only fragmentarily as waste or excess in the little structured margins of a dominant ideology, this mirror entrusted by the (masculine) "subject" with the task of reflecting and redoubling himself'.[2]

Intrinsic to these concepts is woman's relation to language, and French feminist critics in particular have pointed to its role in structuring the nature of female subjectivity. Lacanian theory is a central element in their analysis. Lacan posits that the child moves from the Imaginary (perceptual, pre-verbal) state to the Symbolic (the state in which the self is perceived as separate, and the individual enters language, an order of abstraction and structuring). But, as these critics argue, for women the Symbolic means awareness of the self as a subject constituted through an alien – because logocentric and phallocentric – discourse, which depends on pre-ordered naming and categorisation. Entry into this state thus destines woman to a position in which she is linguistically marginalised, rendered inactive or mute in speech as well as in social signification. The only way to overcome this verbal suppression is to speak through a language not dominated by the phallus, making affirmation, as Cixous puts it, 'somewhere other than in silence, the place reserved for her in and through the Symbolic'.[3]

This theory of female discourse or 'voice' is descriptive and prescriptive, both discovering a style specific to women (*l'écriture féminine*) and suggesting how it may be implemented ('write the body'); in either aspect, the theory can only be notional since to define is to enclose, codify, and thus reinstate the dominant linguistic system. Various characteristics are, however, foregrounded as a means of distinguishing an essentially feminine articulation. So Irigaray says that the speaking female self is incoherent, its meaning fluid, its words never fixed or immobilised; it refuses exact definitions, and is multiple and diffuse in its thought. Xavière Gauthier argues that woman's voice is heard through blanks, gaps, spaces, silences, the holes in the discourse, a praxis conditioned and underlaid by rupture and fragmentation.[4] Cixous, too, sees a feminine style as venturing to the brink 'where writing, freed from law, unencumbered by moderation, exceeds phallic authority'; the text is turbulent, non-unified, analogous to flying or diving.[5]

The concept of the female voice speaking in its own non-alienating language in order to subvert an oppressive system has been taken up by much current feminist criticism, Anglo-American and French, and has been applied to nineteenth-century as well as twentieth-century writers. The two Victorian women poets who I shall discuss here, Emily Dickinson and Christina Rossetti, are particularly appropriate subjects for such an analysis. Their personal circumstances are in themselves significant in this regard. Both were writing at a time when patriarchal ideologies weighed especially heavy on women, sexually and socially, producing in those who were writers a double sense of 'difference' as secondary beings and as 'abnormal' creators. For both, too, the question of personal identity was of crucial importance: Dickinson chose to remain sealed in social isolation, but was discouraged from public literary self-revelation by male judgement; Rossetti was idolised by stiflingly adoring brothers who fixed her in an angelic iconography that sought to confine her to a saintly otherness.[6] The poets' awareness of the fissured female ego, conscious of its own individuality but powerless to articulate this directly, is expressed in their pervasive concern with self-definition and the problems of 'speaking'.

Several recent studies of these poets have examined the elements in their work which challenge the ideologies their age imposed on them. Such studies have discovered a questioning feminine voice that displays the characteristics I have outlined. Attention has been called to the fragmentation, disruption, and hiatuses in Dickinson's poems, as well as to her apparent refusal to proceed along 'normal' lines of reasoning, as evidence of her feminine style. Cora Kaplan allies Rossetti with her in this respect, noting that both writers use synecdoche and metonymy to create 'gaps' in their poetry, creating deliberately distorted or unclear images. Kaplan also argues that Rossetti exploits fantasy in order to explore and interrogate her own psychic state – a 'feminine' mode which exempts her from the demands of clarity and permits multiple meanings.[7] According to this critical view, then, Dickinson and Rossetti articulate their sense of unease with prevailing constructs of womanhood by overturning 'normal' (i.e. masculine) discourse, this verifying Gauthier's claim that women can speak 'otherwise' only in the unsaid or non-sense.[8]

While admitting that this gender-specific style can be seen as subversive, most of their critics also claim that neither poet is iconoclastic because she does not clearly refute contemporary images of femininity, and indeed seems to have considerably internalised them. Kaplan, and Gilbert and Gubar, for example, argue that to a large extent Rossetti's work confirms the traditional Victorian view of woman as passive and self-negating, embodying renunciation as the highest female virtue. Gilbert and Gubar also suggest that Dickinson articulates notions of female insignificance and destitution in order to circumvent the problem of unfeminine self-assertiveness or to create a set of self-protective masks.[9] I would like to argue, however, that this very articulation of contemporary ideology is the means by which Dickinson and Rossetti most profoundly challenge it. In much of their work, both poets, rather than employing a style which, in order to express a sense of 'difference', separates itself from the prevailing discourse in its specific femininity, attacks the patriarchal from within, temporarily taking on the dominant voice which they wish to undermine. Their linguistic methodology is controlled and strategically structured, and exploits the relationship between the signifier and the signified, between apparent and actual meaning. In other words, their defiance is voiced not from within the female Imaginary but from within the male Symbolic, even while it seeks to overthrow the latter's constructs and assumptions.

To express their resistance to an imposed 'femininity', Dickinson and Rossetti act out certain roles in their poetry, male-derived conceptions of womanhood which they proceed to demolish; apparently acceding to the patriarchal ideologies, they subvert them by a tactic of irony which may be considered 'feminine' insofar as it depends on a collusion between woman writer and woman reader, a shared awareness of the formulaic and insidiously powerful nature of such sexual constructs. Throughout their work, they represent femaleness in terms of loss, disappointment, endurance, estrangement, and feelings of non-identity, often associated with a male Other for whom they yearn without hope of reciprocation. Such representation should not be seen wholly as role-playing. Much of Rossetti's verse seems to express a genuine and painful sense of impotence and self-distrust, while many of Dickinson's poems, with their emphasis on female smallness, their pleading tone, and their acceptance of obscurity and non-fulfilment, suggest at least partial internalisation of the ideological mandates of the period. But it seems to me that frequently, in rehearsing these gender identifiers, both poets are consciously adopting – even parodying – them in order to express their own scepticism about them, and implicitly to assert their own sense of selfhood.

Dickinson's poetry is more familiar to us today than is Rossetti's, and its ironic reversals make more initial impact than the subdued meditativeness of much of the latter's work. Two of Dickinson's poems, especially relevant here because they explore the issue of female creativity, well illustrate how her irony operates. In each case, Dickinson articulates the ideology of the dominant (patriarchal) order so as to produce a profound disidentification with it. The first, 'Sang from the Heart, Sire' (Johnson, 1059), deliberately adopts a self-deprecating humility: the speaker, a dying bird, addresses a Divine superior, apologising for the deficiencies of its 'awkward' and 'faltering' song, tainted by the blood which indicates the singer's imminent death. By analogy, the bird becomes the woman poet, excusing herself to a male authority whom, she senses, is unsympathetic towards her utterance and who therefore must be placated. The suspicion that this intensely devaluing self-estimation (a familiar feminine strategy to deal with anticipated hostile criticism) is in fact a mock apologia is confirmed by the last stanza:

> Pause in your Liturgies —
> Wait in your Chorals —
> While I repeat your
> Hallowed name —

Ostensibly, this clinches the hierarchy of all-wise superior and meek subordinate which the poem sets up. In reality, the isolation of the term of address in the final line suggests a far more sardonic attitude to the sanctity of masculine judgement and approbation than at first seems the case. This is not an appeal for concession or forbearance, but a sarcastic deconstruction of self-absorbing male egotism.

A second poem (1088), which more directly links verbal utterance with the expression of self-identity, further suggests Dickinson's resistance to the male Logos, while apparently acceding to a Divinely-ordained suppression of the female voice:

> Ended, ere it begun —
> The title was scarcely told
> When the Preface perished from Consciousness
> The story, unrevealed —
>
> Had it been mine, to print!
> Had it been yours, to read!
> That it was not Our privilege
> The interdict of God —

On one level, the poem is about an abortive relationship between the narrator and a potential lover, but the extended literary metaphor implies an additional metaphoric meaning. The woman's writing is killed at its inception because it is forced into the world of the Symbolic where it becomes subject to totalitarian control (hence 'Consciousness' becomes here a negative term). It is destined to be silenced because a supreme authority has found it unworthy of publication. Again, the ironic tone, highlighted here by the juxtaposition of 'privilege' and 'interdict', belies the apparent acceptance of patriarchal judgement; as in the previous poem, a counter-force of opposition is set up in the terms of the orthodox image of submissive womanhood on which it is based.

Sometimes Dickinson's subversion operates in a more directly humorous way. In her well-known 'I'm Nobody' (288), for example, she takes up the idea of the 'non-being' of woman and turns it into a declaration of self-significance, by debunking the commonly-held notion of 'being somebody':

> I'm Nobody! Who are you?
> Are you — Nobody — Too?
> Then there's a pair of us!
> Don't tell! they'd advertise — you know!
>
> How dreary — to be — Somebody!
> How public — like a Frog —
> To tell one's name — the livelong June —
> To an admiring Bog!

This is surely to be read as a positive statement about the sanctity and strength of the private self, not, as Gilbert and Gubar see it, a retreat into defensiveness.[10] A similar strategy is enacted in 'A solemn thing — it was' (271), where Dickinson begins by valorising the traditional concept of woman – diminutive, virginal, veiled in 'blameless mystery', and self-depracating – and ends by challenging the power which has tried to force her to internalise these images:

And then — the size of this 'small' life —
The Sages — call it small —
Swelled — like Horizons — in my vest —
And I sneered — softly — 'small'!

Here she directly overturns the self-abnegation with which the poem opens, and in asserting her own importance, makes clear her scorn for traditionally incontrovertible male wisdom.

It is impossible to deal adequately with the range and variety of Dickinson's verse in such a short space, but before turning to Rossetti, it is worth looking briefly at two more of her poems, also from the early 1860s. The first, 'Except to Heaven' (154), offers the familiar representation of woman as of no account or influence. Ostensibly, the poem is about a small flower, presumably a daisy, but it is also implicitly about female self-definition, with the added irony that one of Dickinson's own names for herself was Daisy. In the first two stanzas, each statement made is apparently an admission of 'non-being' or insignificance: the woman is 'nought', 'lone', 'superfluous', 'provincial', 'unnoticed'. But the syntactical inversion in lines 1–3 and 5–6, in which the conditional 'Except' is repeated four times, actually foregrounds the positive assertion, undercutting the self-obliterating identifications which follow. Only in male eyes (as opposed to Heaven's Angels', and nature's – hardly trivial adjudicators) is she seen as such, in fact. The final three lines – 'Yet take her from the Lawn / And somebody has lost the face / That made Existence — Home!' – both confirm the narrator's sense of personal importance and look quizzically at masculine views of womanhood. For man, Dickinson suggests, woman has merely negative meaning: non-existent outside a domestic context, she attains significance only when absent from it – a double indictment of patriarchal attitudes.

'Although I put away his life' (366) extends the idea of female insignificance, subverting through irony the notion of service. The speaker begins by declaring her own unworthiness to be associated with the all-powerful 'he', but goes on to say that had they been united she would have enacted a traditional female role, soothing, serving, amusing, and obeying him, rather than indulging in other more idle pleasures. Then in the sixth stanza, her tone becomes more sinister as she envisages the time when 'Your Servant, Sir, will weary – / The Surgeon will not come', and he will suffer neglect and destitution. At this point, she proposes, she will appear as his guardian angel, brightening up his life again and thus restoring herself in his favour:

That I may take that promise
To Paradise, with me —
To teach the Angels, avarice,
You, Sir, taught first – to me.

Dickinson's iconoclasm fully asserts itself in the word 'avarice'. On one level, this indicates in a spiritual sense the degree of the speaker's voracious desire for approbation and redemption, finally satisfied in a paradigmatically heavenly context. But on another level, it is associated with materialistic greed and the outer male world of business and commerce, by which the speaker herself has been corrupted through contact with her adored master. From being the meek, yearning spirit at the beginning of the poem, she becomes the avenging demon, carrying this corruption into the next world and extending its influence there. Here, as in all the poems I have discussed, Dickinson is using her 'female voice' to challenge male orthodoxies, but rather than speaking through the gaps or incoherencies of 'feminine' creativity, she carefully and deliberately dismantles patriarchal discourse from within its own terms of reference.

Rossetti's feminine discourse operates in a more specifically Christian context, a spiritual/gender hierarchy in which woman is accorded a place of angelic endurance and saintly self-abnegation, and in which the displacement of female selfhood is valorised by submission to a mastering Divinity. Though undoubtedly a more convinced 'believer' than Dickinson, she, like the latter, is by no means uncritical of the notion of Divine omnipotence, and it is misleading to 'place' her work solely, as some anthologies have done, in the genre of 'religious poetry'. As Nina Auerbach has argued, while never totally separating herself from the angelic image imposed on her in her own life, Rossetti used her ironic poetic voice to assert her own more radical perspective on a world which she felt had betrayed her.[11] So, in many of her poems, she expresses self-abasement, self-pity, even self-hatred, states of being which are apparently transcended not by personal will but by a vision of spiritual redemption and transformation. The vision, though, is undercut by a sceptical awareness of the nature and efficacy of this redemption.

In 'An Old-World Thicket', one of Rossetti's fantasy/allegory poems, the narrator describes a dream-like experience in which she finds herself in a natural paradise, a pre-lapsarian, pre-symbolic state (the female Imaginary), where all creation exists in total harmony, speaking its own language and fulfilling its own purposes. She, however is alienated from this paradise, fearful, and conscious of her own deprivation and non-fulfilment ('Each sore defeat of my defeated life / Faced and outfaced me in that bitter hour'). Her anguish is exacerbated by her sense of hopelessness:

> For all that was but showed what all was not
> But gave clear proof of what might never be;
> Making more destitute my poverty,
> And yet more blank my lot

The syntactical convolutions and paradoxes of the first two lines of this stanza stress her feeling of eternal separation from the means of self-satisfaction. In such a condition, she begins to interpret her surroundings in terms of her own despair – the whole universe seems to weep with her. But instead of seeking humility, 'My heart then rose a rebel against light'; and even while recognising the uselessness of 'such revolt . . . / That kicks and breaks itself against the bolt / Of an imprisoning fate', she continues her angry chafing. Finally, she falls into a state of nihilistic despair, 'Birthless and deathless, void of start or stop, / Void of repentance, void of hope and fear, / Of possibility, alternative', compounded by self-pity. At this point, the poem takes a sudden turn. The speaker is roused by the sight of a flock of sheep, bathed in golden evening light, peacefully filing westwards through the trees, led by a 'patriarchal ram with tinkling bell'. Since, on one reading, she is currently in a state of spiritual errancy, the image, with its Biblical overtones, obviously suggests the way of salvation for the fallen soul; she too must join the 'homeward flock', self-forgetfully following their patient and calm progress 'toward the sunset and their rest'.

But this interpretation fails to take account of the more subversive suggestiveness of this concluding image. In the first place, even though the word 'patriarchal' does not have the same implications for Rossetti that it does for us today, even here it contains slightly sinister undertones of control and enforced subordination. Moreover, not only is the vision too 'easy', too unexplained (we are reminded of a similarly unconvincing visionary solution at the end of Tennyson's 'The Two Voices'), but there are basic questions which remain unanswered in the poem. On an alternative reading, the speaker is in a state of psychic division or disharmony, separated from her 'natural' self by an alien and phallocentric order. Can, the poem asks, this rift be healed by the controlling hand of male authority? Are the pains of female estrangement really so simply and definitely overcome?

Similar questions are raised in 'Twice' and 'An "Immurata" Sister'. The former reminds us of Dickinson's 'Ended, ere it begun' in its treatment of female linguistic and emotional suppression by a patriarchal authority. The speaker describes how, conscious of her own verbal deficiencies ('a woman's words are weak') she offers her heart to an earthly lover who calmly rejects it – 'With a friendly smile, / With a critical eye you scanned, / Then set it down'. Left desolate, broken-spirited, but unprotesting at the

male judgement, she then humbly offers it to God, asking that it may be
purged of its unworthiness. Thus revived by the Divine power who accepts
the offering, 'I shall not die, but live'; cleansed of earthly 'dross' and
apparently secure in her h(e)aven, she will have the power of utterance
restored to her. The last line of the poem, however, suddenly topples the
assurance: I will sing again, says the narrator, 'But shall not question
much'. The strongly ironic overtones of 'not . . . much' subverts the
apparent pleading self-abasement which she has articulated. Read 'slant',
this is no more an expression of humility than is Dickinson's 'While I repeat
your / Hallowed name', but is an assertion of a new feminine voice which
enables the speaker to criticise her subordinate position, as much as she
chooses.

'An "Immurata" Sister' is more startling in its conclusion. It presents a
chilling picture of the nun/woman, stultified and nullified in her enclosed
order, with only death to look forward to. As a woman who 'feels' (opposed
to men who 'work and think' – the pronouncement of this conventional
dichotomy itself has a sardonic ring), the speaker declares:

> I should be glad to die,
> And cease from impotence of zeal,
> And cease from hope, and cease from dread,
> And cease from yearnings without gain,

She sees herself as an 'empty I' in an 'empty world'. The poem is not only an
attack on the futility and psychic destructiveness of the female monastic
life, but also symbolises the feelings of entrapment felt by all women (again
we are reminded of Tennyson, this time of 'Mariana'). Here too, however,
there is an ironic discrepancy between the apparent and the covert
signification of the 'solution'. Death for the nun means salvation, restoration via the sanctifying fire of martyrdom:

> Sparks fly upward toward their fount of fire,
> Kindling, flashing, hovering: –
> Kindle, flash, my soul; mount higher and higher,
> Thou whole burnt-offering!

But for the feeling woman the apotheosis is far less redemptive. Her
selfhood is sacrificed to the flames of authority in a gesture which dooms her
to the loss of vital individuality and to the acceptance of annihilation. As
in 'An Old-World Thicket', too, the vision seems curiously detached from
the rest of the poem, suggesting an 'imposed' salvation which has no
connection with the woman's real needs and desires.

'To What Purpose is this Waste?', another of Rossetti's dream poems,
explores the notion of female 'use' by drawing on the Biblical account of

the disciples' self-righteous condemnation of Mary Magdalen for 'wasting' costly ointment on Christ. The poem opens with the narrator asking why hidden treasures of nature are destined to remain unexposed to human eye – 'What waste / of good, where no man dwells!'. The examples given – lily, blushing rose, tiny mouse, and precious pearl – are all traditional images of womanhood, and even though the narrator does not directly identify herself with them, she is clearly also implicitly concerned with unfulfilled or wasted female potential. Her questionings are answered by 'secret whisperings' in a dream which explain to her that such obscured or underrated worth is part of a wider scheme, acknowledged in the spiritual world. Not only is such obscurity a protection from possible violation by 'human hands' (there is an obvious echo of Gray's 'Elegy' here), but the notion of service is emphasised: the hidden stream will refresh birds and squirrels, and the oak 'deep in the forest's heart' will provide shelter for mice. Moreover, the accusation of humanity's sinfulness in venturing to criticise God's purpose in this respect is reinforced by the extended image of the 'lily blossoming unseen', strongly reminiscent of much Pre-Raphaelite iconography – in particular of Rossetti's own portraiture by her brother Dante Gabriel in *The Girlhood of Mary Virgin* (1848–9) and *Ecce Ancilla Domini* (1849–50) – and emblematising the sacred perfection of womanhood:

> the fair blossom lifted up
> On its one stately stem of green
> Is type of her the Undefiled,
> Arrayed in white, whose eyes are mild
> As a white dove's, whose garment is
> Blood-cleansed from all impurities
>   And earthly taints,
> Her robe the righteousness of Saints.[12]

It would be blasphemy to criticise such blessed humility.

The poem has a conventionally pious ending, reproving earth for the faithlessness which Christ will find on it when he returns. But beneath this overt 'message' we can again detect dissent. The heavenly scheme which gives meaning to the apparent anomalies is revealed by 'utter love' whose 'force' 'silence[s]' all objections and which hence implicitly fixes womanhood in an ideology of unseen and unacknowledged beneficence, ordered by the Divine will. The poem, then, expresses a 'covered' but none the less acute awareness of the tyranny of female sanctification; Christ may have chided the disciples for failing to recognise the blessedness of Mary Magdalen's action, but, as Rossetti's sub-text hints, the feminine ideal thus elevated is inescapably encapsulated in adoring self-sacrifice. As well as suggesting that such a notion of womanhood merely reinforces the patriarchal status quo of female powerlessness and suppression, Rossetti daringly suggests that Christ's valuation of women rested on these same patriarchal and negating concepts.

Rossetti, therefore, like Dickinson, invites alternative readings of her poems, readings which subvert their ostensible meanings. She too speaks through patriarchal discourse and structures, working within them in order to undermine them, rather than setting up an alternative 'feminine' voice of incoherence and disorder. Her ironies and deliberate ambiguities are less pointed than Dickinson's, but she still questions the images of womanhood imposed on her by her own society. Both women challenge orthodoxies in ways whose subtleties simultaneously belie and promote their iconoclasm.

NOTES

1. Cixous makes these points most forcibly in 'Sorties', in *La Jeune née* (1975), reprinted, and translated by Betsy Wing, in Hélène Cixous and Catherine Clément, *The Newly Born Woman*, Theory and history of literature vol. 24 (Manchester: Manchester University Press, 1987), pp. 63–132.
2. Luce Irigaray, 'Ce sexe qui n'en est pas un' (1977), in Elaine Marks and Isabelle de Courtivron (eds.), *New French Feminisms* (Hemel Hempstead: Harvester Wheatsheaf, 1980), p. 104.
3. 'Sorties', *The Newly Born Woman*, p. 93.
4. 'Ce sexe qui n'en est pas un', *New French Feminisms*, p. 103; Xavière Gauthier, 'Existe-t-il une écriture de femme?' (1974), p. 164.
5. 'Sorties', *The Newly Born Woman*, p. 86.
6. With each poet, masculine authoritarianism had a notable effect on the transmission of her poetic creativity from the private to the public sphere. Dickinson, having sent some of her poems to Thomas Wentworth Higginson for comment in 1862, decided to keep her subsequent work to herself after his negative and patronising reply; except for a handful of poems, her enormous output was published only posthumously, a complete edition not appearing until 1955. While much of Rossetti's work appeared in her lifetime, her brother William Michael issued a posthumous volume of her work, *New Poems*, in 1896, in which his editing skills were directed towards stressing its devotional nature, in some cases by altering the poems to make them more saintly still.
7. Cora Kaplan, 'The Indefinite Disclosed: Christina Rossetti and Emily Dickinson', in Mary Jacobus (ed.), *Women Writing and Writing About Women* (London: Croom Helm, 1979), pp. 61–79.
8. 'Existe-t-il une écriture de femme?', *New French Feminisms*, p. 163.
9. Sandra Gilbert and Susan Gubar, *The Madwoman in the Attic* (New Haven: Yale University Press, 1979), pp. 581–650. Isabel Armstrong also explores the notions of 'lack', non-being and oppression in language to be found in Rossetti's poetry, in 'Christina Rossetti: Diary of a feminist reading', in Sue Roe (ed.), *Women Reading Women's Writing* (Hemel Hempstead: Harvester Wheatsheaf, 1987), pp. 117–37.
10. *The Madwoman in the Attic*, p. 554.

11. Nina Auerbach, *Woman and the Demon: The life of a Victorian myth* (Cambridge, Mass.: Harvard University Press, 1982), pp. 115–17.
12. In both these paintings, the figure of an angel holds a single-stemmed lily before a meek, passive, almost fearful-looking young Virgin. Rossetti stressed that *The Girlhood of Mary Virgin* represented 'a symbol of female excellence. The Virgin being taken as its highest type' (quoted in *The Pre-Raphaelites*, London and Harmondsworth: The Tate Gallery/Penguin Books, p. 65).

Chapter 6

Myth versus Allegory

The problematisation of narrative in Chantal Chawaf's
Le Soleil et la terre

Phil Powrie

The 1970s were very much the decade of *écriture féminine* – one thinks of
Annie Leclerc's *Parole de femme*, for example, which vulgarised to some
extent the seminal work of Cixous in that decade.[1] The 1980s, however,
have seen a decline of interest in *écriture féminine*, if not a critique, which
usually centres on what is considered to be a politically flawed essentialism,
or biologism. For Moi, Cixous' work is 'marred as much by its lack of
reference to recognizable social structures as by its biologism.'[2] A second
area of critique for Moi is Cixous' attempt to deconstruct patriarchal logic.
Moi finds it difficult to accept the coexistence of Cixous' deconstructive
discourse with the metaphysical implications of her mythological/elemental
imagery. For Moi, this contradiction can only be resolved 'within the
secure haven of the Imaginary', in other words, Cixous' texts cannot
operate the liberation of the reader, since they are an escape from the
Symbolic Order.[3] Her texts function rather as a sort of utopian ghetto,
stimulating perhaps, but a ghetto nevertheless.

This chapter is a reaction to those criticisms, but I shall be focusing on a
writer less well known than Cixous. Like Cixous, Chantal Chawaf has
been writing consistently during the two decades in question, and, like
Cixous, publishing her first, as well as a more recent novel, with Edition
des femmes.[4] Unlike Cixous, however, Chawaf has never achieved the
status of theoretican of *écriture féminine*, despite the occasional pronouncement, and a style of writing which is explicitly in that tradition.[5] I shall be
reacting to the criticism levelled at Cixous by focusing on a text published
by Chawaf in 1977 which was considered popular enough to find its way
into the Livre de Poche collection.[6] I shall be explaining why I think
Chawaf's text is a good example of *écriture féminine*, and trying to counter
Moi's criticism of its liberating function within patriarchal discourse.

Le Soleil et la terre has a loose narrative base. A mother and child have taken refuge from a war raging outside their home in a country resembling Algeria. There are a few flashbacks to the relationship between the female protagonist and the conscripted father of her child, but apart from this, there are no 'events'. The text merely describes the mother–daughter and mother–lover relationships, the war raging outside and the narrator's reaction to them, in a repetitively florid manner. A superficial reading suggests that an oversimplified metaphorical scheme is operating through the text, with key images organised along gender lines. The male is equated with the sun, desert, military uniform, blood; the female with the earth, home, lace, milk.

This is clear in the first chapter which juxtaposes fictional epigraphs which recount the bloody deeds of Assyrian kings with long passages which dwell on things domestic. Here, for example, is the opening of the text:

> They killed fifty thousand in a few months. 'In my 30th campaign, while I was in the town of Kalakh, I put Assur, the great Tartan [*sic*] of my army, at the head of my troops; he crossed the Zab and advanced towards the town of Khubusku; he advanced into the lands of Madakhir and he imposed tributes on the towns which belonged to its territories. He advanced towards the towns under the power of Udaki, king of the lands of Van. Udaki of Van feared the strength of my wrath, he abandoned his capital Zirtu, he took flight to save his life. I pursued him and I took cattle, sheep, innumerable treasures. I laid waste to his towns, I razed them to the ground, I put them to the flame.'
>
> SALMAN-ASAR.
> ANNALS OF THE ASSYRIAN KINGS.
>
> The veil was embroidered to cover a breast. It's my bedroom. A room where I like to watch the confused shapes of my daydreams clothe themselves, watch them wander amongst the trinkets, amongst the linen. It's my bedroom of dusty mirrors and baubles. The lacework which decorates it belonged to my grandmothers because today such fine work is no longer made. The light embroidered with rosettes and reflections looks like a lace foundation or a network of tulle. And I pass through it fairylike without making any holes in it, without tearing it. (*ST*, pp. 7–8)

I have quoted at length to give some idea of Chawaf's style, which constantly opposes male violence with female softness. The soldiers march purposefully on, razing towns, interested only in rape and pillage, and public names, whereas the female protagonist inhabits a private, domestic sphere, whose inhabitants are nameless, surrounded by precious objects preciously preserved, and delicate materials, dreaming.

The text thus explores the arrogation of power by men, symbolically by images of male violence (rape, warfare), and the passive resistance of domestic women to that power. It would be a mistake, however, to see in this text an image-ridden *reductio ad absurdum* of the war of the sexes, as the title of the novel itself might lead one to assume. Leaving aside for the moment the ironic exaggeration of such clichés, this is firstly because, like Cixous' work, Chawaf's texts are a patchwork of discourses.

The three most prominent discourses are the mythopoeic, the allegorical and the political. There are others, of course, such as the short-lived pseudo-historical discourse of the four epigraphs in the first chapter, or the more pervasive domestic discourse, with which it was juxtaposed in the example given above, and which I shall be returning to.

I mean by 'political' discourse passages where the text discusses the implications of male violence, rather than simply describing it in symbolic networks. For example:

> What can you expect from a society of machines? What can you expect from man when he is diminished? Exploited? Reduced to economic profit? What can you expect from an individual freedom which is conformist and harmless? What can you expect from destitution? What can you expect from war? poverty? the risk of nuclear disaster? (*ST*, p. 151)

Similar apostrophes are scattered throughout the text.

The allegorical discourse is associated with maleness, as is made clear in the following passage:

> Mouth to mouth, I drew the wine, I drank, and his golden throat filled me with what named the Father.
> I was thirsty.
> A scholar, a lord, a profile sharply drawn and severe, a descendant of heroic swordsmen, a man embroidered by the silken braid-maker, a son whose fathers clothed in purple-black and gold were portrayed for posterity.
> 'I have made you mine.'
> His illustrious name made him proud, imbued in his birth and his rank, and even in the way he held his head he wanted to show that he had breeding and despite myself, I admired him enough to idealize him in an allegory where, seated in the place of honour, he represented the values of mind over nature, mind as domination and I was afraid of him.
>
> The goldsmith, the Braid-maker, the Celebrant, the First Crown, the Sun, the Minister marks the contour of the planets and the mountains with a golden ribbon and strews the sky with window-roses and the sky is bathed in the light of this braided glory and the Braid-maker links his knot-worked embroideries together to make a solid body and he turns the earthly sky into an eternal sky whose golden silks project rays for the golden symbol to sit in glory, Thought. (*ST*, p. 41)

Religious metaphors are combined with military metaphors in this passage, so that the gold braid of military uniform is associated with the gold braid of the chasuble; and these are, finally, themselves metaphors for an overarching philosophical metaphor, that of logical thought.

Opposed to this discourse is the mythopoeic discourse of goddesses, as opposed to gods, as for example in the following passage, where the

daughter is celebrated and transfigured by a halo of pantheistic myth which
links her to Ceres, goddess of fertility:

> Her hair streams with the blondness of a corn broth . . . I like it when a plait
> undoes itself . . . when her blondness is the blondness of four sorts of corn . . . I
> brush her beautiful hair once more, meadows, forests, springs, and the hairbrush
> scatters the clouds of her long hair and the moonshine is reflected in her hair as if
> on the water of a lake. (*ST*, pp. 81–2)

We now have all the elements we need to counter Moi's critique of
Cixous' discourse, and which could equally well be levelled at Chawaf's,
i.e. biologism and utopian ghettoisation.

To consider biologism first, it is clear from the few extracts I have quoted
that Chawaf's text relies heavily not simply on the naming, but on the
praise of the repressed female body. As she puts it in one of her few
theoretical texts, to write as a woman is to write (with) the body (*écrire au
féminin* is *écrire corporellement*); for her writing is the place 'where the
artificial division between mind and body is abolished'.[7] This statement
would seem to justify the rather simplistic metaphorical opposition
between male/female which underlies the above extracts, and which is
equally characteristic of Cixous's work.[8]

But in the same text, Chawaf writes about domestic labour, talking of the
need to 'displace this anciently feminine place and to make domestic labour
linguistic' ('E', p. 77). For her, this textual operation represents a liberation
whereby 'woman frees herself from domestic tasks and starts to speak woman,
whereas the housewife silenced woman' ('E', p. 77). The displacement of
which she speaks strikes me as a subversive strategy, echoed by Hélène
Cixous when, talking of women as guardians of culture, she says that
'nothing is more poetical than a cookbook'.[9] Effectively, Chawaf is taking
traditional female tasks and exploring their linguistic connotations, exploding the clichés which they represent by disregarding their social implications
so as to concentrate on the materiality of language: 'I like to restore materiality to words, orality, because I can feel that words pass through your
mouth like food' ('E', p. 74). Similarly, her novel's reliance on a simplistic
opposition between masculine and feminine values could be considered an
ironic strategy, as I suggested earlier, which explodes myths by exaggerating
them. We might well feel, then, that Chawaf's writing is essentially deconstructive in its essentialism, i.e. her biologism is an ironic strategy calculated
to explode clichés rather than maintain them.

What of Moi's second criticism, utopian ghettoisation? On a first
reading, the narrative of *Le Soleil et la terre* suggests explicitly that the male
and female world-views are totally divergent, and that women feel as
though they inhabit a different world:

> It is mostly in my daughter that I get to the core of my identity, . . . I identify
> myself with my sex and . . . my female organs discover their woman's powers,
> bringing fertility to the work of the world and defending life and love and child-
> hood, and, . . . running parallel to the exhausted societies which make us suffer so
> much, I can feel the strong unbroken flow of a world working towards harmony, a
> world in harmony with the animal, gazeous, vegetable, human, mineral elements
> of life. (*ST*, p. 95)

But it is not to this very literal level that Moi's criticism refers. Her
criticism of Cixous, and by extension, Chawaf, would be that the textual
confusion, or patchwork as I have called it in the case of Chawaf, is 'good',
but that its combination with calls for a female specificity which uses myth
to create utopias where all political and social problems vanish, is somehow 'bad'. It is this criticism which I earlier shorthanded as 'utopian
ghettoisation'.

Chawaf's writing does not attempt to elaborate an escape from the
Symbolic into the Imaginary, however, since it is explicitly operating on
patriarchal language and subverting it from within. We have just seen how
it does so by its explosion of clichés associated with women, but it is worth
summarising the other, more specifically narrative strategies already
mentioned before concentrating on the one which interests me most here.
There is, firstly, the dismantling of over-arching narrative, mentioned
earlier: a loose narrative base overlaid by a patchwork of discourses, where
the narrative line is occasionally gestured at by snippets of dialogue. There
is, secondly, the dismantling of syntax in favour of the materiality of the
word, examples of which we have seen in many of the extracts already
quoted:

> Syntax is taught to me, for example, by my organ of touch . . . Writing, for me, is,
> I think, trying to allow words and sentences to escape from their linguistic and
> arbitrary abstraction to connect with paste [la pâte], with mud, with what you
> knead. ('E', p. 71)

The third narrative strategy lies embedded in the text and is perhaps less
obvious at first sight, hence my wish to tease it out and discuss its implications. I mentioned above that in my view two of the most important
discourses in this text are the mythopoeic and the allegorical. There was an
example of the allegorical in the description of the male protagonist, and
an example of the mythopoeic in the description of the daughter's hair
which transfigures her in a halo of myth so that she joins the legions of earth
goddesses. I would contend that the arrogation of power by men which is
clearly referred to throughout the text symbolically by images of male
violence is paralleled at a formal level by a veritable struggle between
allegory, linked with male authority and hierarchy, as was clear in the

passage quoted above, and myth, linked with the closeness to matter and generosity, as well as generation, as was clear in the synesthesic world of earth goddesses. This struggle occurs most prominently in the second chapter.

The second chapter of the novel concerns the relationship between the male and female protagonists. In narrative terms, this chapter recounts, in a series of flashbacks, the woman's seduction, as she becomes caught in a web of sexual stimulation which she finds difficult to resist. At the beginning of the chapter the man is represented symbolically as a kind of Pan figure, associated with the night, the moon, the earth, and water, as the following notations suggest:

> He was the Master of the Night. . . The man made the moon come down to the earth . . . He would hurl himself on me, clasping me in all his roots, all his tufts and his mossy leafy beards, and his springs . . . He would stare at me with his brown, moonlike eyes . . . He would leave me, like a stream going underground. (*ST*, pp. 30–4)

The female on the other hand is linked with the sun:

> I am holding a sheaf of light in my hands . . . I am the Blonde Beauty . . . Woman embellished by love clothes me like jewellery, like the return of spring, like the rejuvenation of the sun . . . The sun surrounds my head with a diadem woven from my hair, and the nature of my blondness is transparent. (*ST*, p. 36)

The male is associated with the moon and with water, malevolent forces in general then, whereas the female is associated with regeneration and with the sun. At the end of the chapter, however, as we saw in the extract dealing with the allegorisation of the male, it is he who is associated with the sun, whose colour is no longer the colour of wheat, but the colour of military and religious gold. The myth of Ceres, the earth goddess has given way to the allegory of the master: 'I admired him enough to idealize him in an allegory' says the narrator (*ST*, p. 41). Effectively, the male has stolen and traduced the female principle of regeneration, erecting the rigid structures of patriarchal generation and logical thought. He has done so in the troubled confusion of the sexual act, which the female experiences as rape at the same time as she, apparently, longs for it (she speaks of the 'moment of rape when my blood flowed as I tried in tears to struggle out of his grasp but I was physically attached to what he had convulsed in my womb' (*ST*, p. 32)). The originary female myth of the earth goddess has been overcome by the hierarchy and authority of allegory.

This is consonant with what literary theorists have said about allegory, which can be summarised as the imposition of order and authority. We can make three points about allegory as order. First, allegory is often (or often refers to) religious ritual (A *Pilgrim's Progress*, for example), which orders the intuition/revelation of myth. Second, allegory is akin to scientific order, opposed to the dreamtime of myth; as R. Fletcher puts it, 'allegory makes an appeal to an almost scientific curiosity about the order of things'.[10]

Third, allegory orders chaos, whereas myth interprets it. Honig, for example, points out that 'the concept of allegory . . . hovers on the indistinct border between primitive mythological figurations and the more sophisticated structures of philosophical thought'.[11]

We can make two points about the authority of allegory. First, in allegory the writer imposes his/her control over the text. Northrop Frye points out that 'we have actual allegory when a poet explicitly indicates the relationship of his images to examples and precepts, and so tries to indicate how a commentary on him should proceed'.[12]

Second, allegory is an attempt to recreate (usually religious) authority, as is intimated by Honig in the following passage where he distinguishes two different types of allegory, the prophetic and the apocalyptic:

> Prophecy, taking its authority from the Word of God, calls attention to the covenant, the social contract, the moral obligations of men under divine law. It rehearses the law and stresses punishable infringements of the law . . . Apocalyptic, on the other hand, derives from the dedicated experience, isolated vision, and judgement of the solitary man, the seer, the unlicensed and obscure sage. In denying the possibility of mankind's improvement, apocalyptic casts a cold eye on man's social and moral nature, and criticizes the failures and imperfections of man and his laws. Apocalyptic frequently becomes the refuge of heretical imagination defying the contingencies of legalism and the status quo . . . In allegory, prophetic and apocalyptic elements often go together.[13]

Le Soleil et la terre thus enacts narratively and formally in its arrangement of symbols in mythical or allegorical frameworks the arrogation of power, and, by implication, of language, by men.

But does this not make Chawaf's text, precisely, an allegory, with all the implications of order and authority mentioned earlier? After all, the struggle between myth, or the female principle, and allegory, as the male principle, forms part of the wider allegory of male/female relationships which structures everything in the text, from the basic image networks (sun versus earth), to socio-political commentary (males are violent, females are not), even to its relationship to that other master-text which combines the sun, the desert, and disease, as an allegory for war – Camus' *La Peste*. Is Chawaf's text itself then not guilty of the imposition of utopian order, of a sort of female authority?

The simple answer is no, for several reasons. The first occurs at the narrative level. The narrator cannot prevent the war from encroaching upon her territory: 'I know that no war is ever ended, that war reigns supreme, that men the world over are mobilized . . . And the refuge is shrinking. And all that is left is a narrow strip of substance where the hand and the fingers can still project themselves' (*ST*, pp. 134, 163). As this passage might suggest, the allegorical thrust is clearly towards the idea that the narrator no longer has anything but language with which to change the world. But language itself is almost worthless: 'I must isolate myself from language, which cannot do anything anymore, which is useless' (*ST*, p. 137). Thus the allegorical level makes it clear that the desire to introduce female values has failed.

We can further claim that the text does not impose the order of allegory by returning to the formal level, but a patchwork of discourses, different, heterogeneous voices.

And, finally, at a theoretical level, we can claim that the text cannot impose the authority of female allegory in opposition to some assumed male language, since, by definition, the Symbolic Order which corresponds to the acquisition of language, is irremediably bound to the Law of the Father in Lacanian theory. Thus this basic theoretical point is paralleled in Chawaf's narrative by an apparently dystopic vision: the war reigns supreme, and will always do so. We can deduce from this that *écriture féminine* can only represent an irruption within language, a question needling through patriarchal language like lacework, to use one of Chawaf's favourite metaphors in *Le Soleil et la terre*, a metaphor which is systematically opposed to the *Brodeur*. The difference being that the latter covers space over with a layer of braid: 'the Braid-maker links his knot-worked embroideries together to make a solid body and he turns the earthly sky into an eternal sky whose golden silks project rays for the golden symbol to sit in glory, Thought', *ST*, pp. 41–2). Whereas lacework allows the body to breathe:

> Caressing needs the nimble fingers of a lacemaker, of a woman who makes lace by hand, so as to work the body, to work female matter, to make a network of breath and finest thread, the penetration of air in the lungs. (*ST*, p. 168)

Chawaf's text is like lacework, an intricate pattern woven from, but also through, patriarchal language. It relies on an essentialist perspective, but uses it as a deconstructive strategy amongst others. It is precisely the plurality of strategies in perpetual explicit conflict with patriarchal language which makes of her texts not a refuge in the undifferentiated bliss and plentitude of the Imaginary, but a political textual work within the Symbolic Order. Her texts are slow-motion bombs of lacework exploding through concrete.

NOTES

I would like to thank the University of Newcastle upon Tyne for a grant which helped me research this essay.

1. Annie Leclerc, *Parole de femme* (Paris: Grasset, 1974).
2. Toril Moi, *Sexual/Textual Politics: Feminist Literary Theory* (London and New York: Methuen, New Accents Series, 1985), p. 126.
3. *ibid.*, p. 120.
4. Chantal Chawaf, *Retable, la rêverie*, 1974; *L'Intérieur des heures*, 1987. (Both Paris: Editions des femmes).
5. Most particularly, 'La chair linguistique', *Les Nouvelles littéraires*, 2534 (26 May 1976), no. 18. Translated in E. Marks and I. de Courtivron, *New French Feminisms* (Amherst, Mass.: University of Massachusetts Press, 1980), pp. 177–8.
6. Chantal Chawaf, *Le Soleil et la terre* (Paris: Pauvert, 1977; Livre de Poche, No. 5219). Henceforth abbreviated in the text as *ST*. All translations of texts by Chawaf are my own.
7. Chantal Chawaf, 'L'Ecriture', in *Chair chaude* (Paris: Mercure de France, 1976), pp. 80–1. Henceforth abbreviated in the text as 'E'.
8. See for example Toril Moi, *Sexual/Textual*, pp. 104ff.
9. '*Etudes Féminines*: Women's writing and literary studies in theory and practice'. Colloquium at Liverpool University 21–2 April 1989. Hélène Cixous, in discussion.
10. R. Fletcher, *Allegory: The theory of a Symbolic mode* (New York: Cornell University Press, 1964), p. 69.
11. E. Honig, *Dark Conceit: The making of Allegory* (London: Faber & Faber, 1960), p. 25.
12. Northrop Frye, *Anatomy of Criticism: Four essays* (Princeton, N.J.: Princeton University Press, 1957), p. 90.
13. E. Honig, *Dark Conceit*, p. 107.

Chapter 7

Ambiguous Anonymity

The case of Madame de Lafayette

Anne Green

Madame de Lafayette is an illustrious name in the history of French literature. But this has not always been the case. During her lifetime only one of her writings – a brief portrait of her friend Madame de Sévigné – was published under her name. The rest of her work appeared either anonymously or pseudonymously, or else was not published at all until after her death.[1]

The explanation most frequently offered for Madame de Lafayette's decision to conceal her gender and identity as a writer is one of propriety: we are told that it was not considered seemly for ladies of a certain social class to display themselves in print. In the famous phrase of Mademoiselle de Scudéry, who published her own early novels under her brother's name, 'Ecrire, c'est perdre la moitié de sa noblesse' ('To write is to lose half one's nobility'). Moreover, if it was considered demeaning to publish one's writings, it was even worse to publish one's *novels*, which ranked very low in the hierarchy of seventeenth-century literary genres.[2] Feminist critics in particular have seen the opprobrium attached to women writers as an instance of the suppression of the female voice, and as an extension of codes of behaviour which inhibited women from public expression.

The view of Madame de Lafayette's anonymity as symptomatic of a social silencing of women needs, however, to be set in the context of the pubishing practice of the period. Far from being a female anomaly in a world of male discourse, anonymous publication was extremely common in seventeenth-century France. Indeed it had been so widespread in the previous century that civil and ecclesiastical authorities repeatedly insisted that publications must bear their author's name. By Madame de Lafayette's time these edicts applied only to political and religious works, but in other areas the tradition of anonymous publication continued: the majority of novels published between 1600 and 1700 were unsigned.[3]

Moreover, it has been suggested that Madame de Lafayette's name was withheld from the title page of *La Princesse de Clèves* not for reasons of propriety but as part of a carefully-orchestrated publicity campaign conducted by her publisher.[4] The suggestion is a persuasive one: the enigma of the unknown author would clearly appeal to the same public who enjoyed trying to solve the *énigmes* published regularly in *Le Mercure galant*, and who sent in their solutions under such elaborate pseudonyms that the editor was obliged to print a notice asking them kindly to restrain themselves.[5] But since Madame de Lafayette's other works were not published with the same fanfares as *La Princesse de Clèves* and since some were not published at all during her lifetime, we need to look for other explanations.

Joan DeJean has put forward a different hypothesis which also contradicts the notion that Madame de Lafayette's anonymity is a sign of self-effacement. In an astute analysis of *La Princesse de Clèves*, she sees the lack of signature, instead, as a 'carefully calculated strategy' which focuses the reader's attention on the text rather than on the author. She contends that in *La Princesse de Clèves* this strategy is an attempt 'to avoid the loss of authority that accompanies every public appropriation of fictionalized feminine desire and to create enigma from the protection of privacy, thus generating new privileges of anonymity.' Both Madame de Lafayette's choice of anonymity and the fictional princess's renunciation of marriage and public life are seen as affirmations of the woman writer's authority.[6]

But not all Madame de Lafayette's writing can be interpreted as having such an assertive message. Her motives were neither constant nor unambiguous. By exploring some of the ways in which she problematises not only her own name but also the names of female characters in the rest of her work, I shall suggest that she should be seen neither as a passive victim of silencing pressures, nor as a heroic pioneer struggling to change the reception of women's writing. Rather, she was a writer working out conflicting attitudes to her status both as woman and as author.

Some of the clearest insights into her choice of anonymity occur, paradoxically, in the one work that she did not sign – the portrait of Madame de Sévigné. This was her first publication and appeared in *La Galerie des peintures*, a collection of short word-portraits of members of the court which was presented to Mademoiselle de Montpensier in 1659. Contributors to the volume indicate their identities in a wide variety of ways: some give their real names, some give classical pseudonyms or initials, some give only an indication of their sex, some leave their piece totally unsigned. But Madame de Lafayette's contribution falls into none of these categories. It is *both* signed *and* anonymous: 'fait par Madame la comtesse de la Fayette, sous le Nom d'un Inconnu' ('written by Madame la comtesse de la Fayette, under the name of an unknown person').[7]

Clearly, Madame de Lafayette's pose of anonymity here is a deliberate literary conceit, a device whose advantages are explained in the portrait itself. First, it frees the writer from external constraints. If the author's identity is unknown, he or she cannot be blamed for what is written. Madame de Lafayette points out that conventional portraits are uniformly complimentary – authors dare not mention their subjects' shortcomings for fear of displeasing them. As an *inconnu*, however, Madame de Lafayette can tell the unpalatable truth without risk of repercussions. But then, with a clever twist, the pose of anonymity becomes an ingenious conceit: free to paint Madame de Sévigné's flaws, the writer can find none. Anonymity heightens the compliment.

The anonymous pose also appropriates additional power for the author. 'si je vous suis inconnu, vous ne m'êtes pas inconnue' ('although I am unknown to you, you are not unknown to me'), Madame de Sévigné is told.[8] The subject of the portrait remains in the dark, while the hidden author assumes greater authority through his superior knowledge.

I say 'his' advisedly, because the anonymous persona adopted by Madame de Lafayette for this piece is a male one. 'He' poses as an unrequited lover who bemoans the fact that Madame de Sévigné's affections are directed elsewhere – at none other than Madame de Lafayette herself.[9] By this curious, teasing sleight of hand, Madame de Lafayette purports to guarantee that she is *not* the author, but at the same time she draws added attention to herself *as* author by inscribing her own name within the text and repeating the signature printed at its head. Her portrait of Madame de Sévigné stands out from the rest of the collection not only because of the inventiveness and assurance of its argument but also because its ludic qualities tease the reader and focus attention on the author's identity. It is a more revealing portrait of Madame de Lafayette than of Madame de Sévigné.

Teasing and witty, anonymous yet signed, Madame de Lafayette's first venture into print shows a confident awareness of the positive benefits of writing without a name. This 'privilège d'Inconnu' ('privilege of anonymity'), as she calls it, was one which she would adopt for the rest of her fiction.[10]

But if her simultaneous absence and presence in this text is a deliberate literary contrivance, elsewhere it seems to reflect a barely expressible unease, a deep-seated preoccupation with alternative modes of being that echoes through the plots of her fiction. It is surely not fortuitous that words like *cacher*, *dissimuler*, *feindre*, and *secret* (hide, dissimulate, feign, secret) occur so frequently, or that much of her fiction turns on the delicate interplay between what is known, felt or said in private, and what is publicly displayed. The bold assertiveness of the *Portrait* is missing from her subsequent novels and short stories. In them, Madame de Lafayette's ambivalence about exposing and withholding her own name finds an echo in the titles themselves. Each of her four works of fiction is named after a female protagonist. But that apparently conventional naming is more problematic than it might at first seem.[11]

La Comtesse de Tende's title is that of a married woman. It conveys her public status, her identity-through-her-husband. The name's privileged position as title automatically prompts one to wonder who the comtesse de Tende can be. The answer that comes in the first sentence sets the tone for the rest of the story – it is both direct and evasive:

> Mademoiselle de Strozzi, fille du maréchal et proche parente de Cathérine de Médicis, épousa, la première année de la Régence de cette reine, le comte de Tende, de la maison de Savoie, riche, bien fait, le seigneur de la cour qui vivait avec le plus d'éclat et plus propre à se faire estimer qu'à plaire. (p. 339)[12]
> (Mademoiselle de Strozzi, the daughter of the *maréchal*, and a close relative of Catherine de Medici, married, in the first year of the queen's regency, the comte de Tende of the house of Savoie, a wealthy and handsome gentleman who displayed the greatest splendour at court and who was more likely to inspire esteem than love.)

We know her father's name and status, we know the family she belonged to, we know to whom and when she was married – but we still know nothing about *her*. Instead, the sentence slides on to describe her husband. Defined initially by her family and subsequently by her husband, by his family and by his status at court, the countess is presented, in that first sentence, as hemmed around by constraints.

But three details in this opening alert us to alternative possibilities. First, her Italian ancestry, strongly suggestive of passion and spontaneity, and so associated with the overthrow of approved 'womanly virtues'. Second, the close relationship to Catherine de Medici, archetype of the strong, active and astute woman, whose influence over French politics lasted for almost thirty years, and whose reign was associated with conflict and disorder. And third, the ironic deflation as the sentence comes to its close: the list of qualities which make the count outstandingly eligible as a husband ends with 'et plus propre à se faire estimer qu'à plaire', casting doubt on the value of preceding conventional attributes of wealth, beauty and prestige.

Critics have generally seen *La Comtesse de Tende* as a moral treatise whose portrayal of the suffering of an adulterous woman offers an unambiguous warning to the reader.[13] But this first sentence already shows hints of tensions and contradictions. They will be developed in the course of the story, although they always remain beneath the surface, quietly, almost sublimely, suggested.[14] The name 'La Comtesse de Tende' is thus fraught with double messages. On the one hand it evokes a cluster of social assumptions about marriage, status, lineage and woman's role; on the other hand, the story will unfold to show the eponymous heroine deviating from all these norms. Indeed, she deviates so far that the comte de Tende fails to recognise his own wife in Navarre's description of his unnamed mistress.

At the end, the name of Tende is eliminated. The countess dies in childbirth, knowing that her premature son, too, will die. She will not leave behind even an illegitimate heir to the title which is doomed to extinction: the count never remarries, the name cannot be passed on. Indeed the story itself ends in a curious self-suppression since all witnesses to the secret events – the countess, her baby, her lover, and Lalande (their only confident) – have died, and none, we are told, divulged the secret. There is no one left to tell the tale: logically, it is a story that cannot be told. So *La Comtesse de Tende*, by simultaneously expressing and erasing a dangerously unconventional perception of woman, echoes the authors' own ambiguous signature.

The title of *La Princesse de Montpensier* is equally problematic. The story is prefaced by a short note to the reader which states that the tale is completely fictitious and bears no relation whatsoever to the real Montpensier family. But what purports to be a conventional disclaimer turns out, on closer inspection, to be rather less than innocent. If the story that follows is no more than '*des aventures inventées à plaisir*' ('adventures invented for their own sake') as the author claims, then why has she decided that it is more appropriate to give her characters real names? Why in particular has she chosen explicitly to evoke the reputation of the real Mademoiselle de Montpensier while at the same time denying that she and her family have any connection with the fictitious story? For a contemporary reader this note surely cannot have failed to bring to mind the most illustrious Montpensier – Louis XIV's cousin, la Grande Mademoiselle – whole political and military involvement in the Fronde marked the climax of a period of female independence and activity, of *femmes fortes*, which had come to an end with Louis XIV's majority.[15] By simultaneously evoking and denying the memory of Mademoiselle's courage and independence, Madame de Lafayette effectively sets the tone for her story which will chart the shifting tensions between two conflicting codes of behaviour. The real Mademoiselle's strong qualities are implicitly set against the conventional feminine attributes of docility and silence that are associated with the fictional Montpensier princess.

We are first introduced to the future Princesse de Montpensier as the young heiress Mademoiselle de Mézières, an only child whose wealth and family make her a much sought-after marriage partner. Mademoiselle de Mézières is defined solely by her financial and genealogical inheritance. Political and dynastic interests determine whom she will marry, and she herself is presented as passive, pliant and consenting, a model of womanly virtues praised by so many writers of the period.

By the end of the story, however, she is in total moral and physical collapse. The last few lines hint again at the double perspective evoked by the ambiguous title:

> Elle mourut en peu de jours, dans la fleur de son âge, une des plus belles princesses du monde, et qui aurait été sans doute la plus heureuse, si la vertu et la prudence eussent conduit toutes ses actions. (p. 33)
> (She died a few days later in the flower of her youth, one of the most beautiful princesses in the world who would doubtless also have been the happiest if virtue and prudence had guided all her actions.)

Ostensibly a moralising conclusion, it nevertheless runs counter to a comment that comes immediately before. What has caused the princess's final agony is her discovery that her lover, Guise, has transferred his affections to the marquise de Noirmoutier. Unlike his feelings for the princess, his love for the marquis is not only intense but enduring: 'il s'y attacha entièrement et l'aima avec une passion démesurée et qui lui dura jusqu'à sa mort' ('he was totally devoted to her and loved her with an extravagant passion which lasted until her death'). We are not told much about the marquise de Noirmoutier, but what little is revealed throws light on the story's final judgement on the princesse de Montpensier. Both women are witty and beautiful, but the marquise 'était une personne qui prenait autant de soin de faire éclater ses galanteries que les autres en prennent de les cacher' ('was someone who took as much care to publicise her love-affairs as others do to conceal them') (p. 33). In other words, she is someone whose behaviour is antithetical to that of the princess. She does not possess the 'virtues' of self-restraint, discretion and prudent silence; she delights in displaying her love-affairs; and consequently, it is suggested, she inspires in Guise a passion of a kind that he never felt for the princess. We are told that the princess would have been the happiest person in the world if only she had behaved in a more prudent and virtuous fashion; and yet the marquise de Noirmoutier, by being neither prudent nor virtuous, by adopting that confident, vigorous and ourspoken mode implicit in the ambiguous title, lives happily ever after.

The thread of ambiguity continues in *Zaïde*. Zaïde herself not only gives the novel its title but also provides the narrative focus, the goal that has to be attained before the novel can end. Yet she is a largely hidden, silent, enigmatic figure. Her first appearance in the novel is as a glittering object washed up on the seashore and found by the male protagonist, Consalve. Gradually the limp, inert form is brought to life, but is nameless. She remains anonymous ('cette inconnue' or 'cette étrangère') until her otherwise incomprehensible conversation with Félime in a foreign tongue reveals that she is called Zaïde. Absent for much of the novel, the Zaïde we hear of is a figment of Consalve's imagination. He pursues her but cannot understand her – either literally (for they speak different languages, and repeatedly encounter physical barriers to communication) – or in the broader sense. The passive, silent creature of Consalve's fantasy fits uneasily with the picture of Zaïde that emerges from Félime's account towards the end of the novel. Zaïde as described by Félime is instead an adventurous, seductive, even teasing woman who revels in the admiration of a handsome stranger (Alamir), and who delights in having her boat go through unexpected manoeuvres to discover whether Alamir's vessel will follow.

That side of Zaïde is only hinted at. The central figure, the name of the title, remains a silent enigma. But her silences and misunderstood speech can be read as the metaphorical expression of the unsayable: they not only represent the impossibility of real communication between the sexes, but dramatise Madame de Lafayette's own ambiguous voice that simultaneously speaks and suppresses, echoing her ambivalent sense of appropriate female behaviour.

The *Histoire de Madame Henriette d'Angleterre*, which was not intended for formal publication, offers a final set of clues to Madame Lafayette's ambivalence about her authorship. In the preface, written towards the end of her life, she recounts the beginning of her friendship with Princess Henriette and the genesis of the work.[16] She describes how, after Henriette's marriage to Louis XIV's brother, the princess asked Madame de Lafayette to write down her story. Henriette would confide details of her life and of court intrigue to her, and Madame de Lafayette would then set them on paper and show the princess her work the following morning. She describes the difficulty of trying to tell the truth and yet present it in a way that would not offend Madame. For a time the princess was very enthusiastic about her memoirs, even writing some herself when Madame de Lafayette was absent for two days. But when Henriette began to tire of the project, Madame de Lafayette put it aside and began again only in the year before Madame's death.

In this preface, then, Madame de Lafayette presents the *Histoire de Madame* as a simple piece of amusement written with the sole purpose of entertaining the princess. The author portrays herself as little more than a scribe, an almost passive secretary who writes at the express wish of Madame, relinquishes her pen to her at one point, and stops writing as soon as the princess tires of telling her story. She seems to deny that there is anything of *herself* in the work: she indicates that it was not her idea in the first place, and that much of what she writes is a virtual transcription of Madame's account. [17]

But like so many of Madame de Lafayette's statements about her writing, this picture of self-effacement cannot be taken at face value. If she wrote the *Histoire* only to please Madame, why did she include a detailed account of Madame's death? And why did she return to the work many years later to add an explanatory preface to what purports to be quite a private piece of documentation? The answer can only be that Madame de Lafayette held greater store by it than she allows. Her suggestion that it was written solely for Madame's amusement has to be discounted. [18]

In this final example the reticence is more than balanced by self-revelation. For once, she admits in the text that she is indeed the author, and she even provides a deceptively modest self-portrait (written in the third person). Living on the fringes of a court where the slightest mark of royal favour was noted and envied, Madame de Lafayette must have derived considerable prestige from Madame's friendship and confidences. [19] So it is not surprising that on this occasion she was willing not only to acknowledge her authorship but to draw particular attention to her name. She begins the work with the story of Louis XIII's love and esteem for her sister-in-law, Angélique de Lafayette, and refers to the close ties between her uncle, François Motier de Lafayette, and the queen. Thus from the outset she firmly establishes that the name of Lafayette has long been associated with royal confidences. The main thrust of the *Histoire* concerns the rivalry between courtiers to win confidences from members of the royal family. By acknowledging her authorship, therefore, Madame de Lafayette announces her own status as superior to the courtiers about whom she is writing. She proclaims her social success, while at the same time disclaiming all responsibility for the text.

More important by shaping the account, passing judgement, displaying and no doubt suppressing details, Madame de Lafayette is controlling our understanding of history. A process inherent in the writing of *any* history is here made quite explicit. Throughout the text she shows members of the court using the transforming power of narrative as a means of furthering their own ambitions: they take charge of the flux of events by shaping them into written or spoken versions – into accurate or mendacious confidences or letters – and then spread these accounts to serve their own ends. The practice, however, is also shown to be a hazardous one. Generating rumours and writing letters may be ways of exercising authority, but they can also expose their authors to danger. If discovered, the authors risk punishment or disgrace: the versions of events they have created for their own ends can be turned against them. We see repeated instances where a letter falling in the wrong hands brings public shame to its writer, or where the instigator of a rumour is found out and punished. Thus the *Histoire* becomes a metaphor for the power and risk inherent in the act of writing. In other words, the act of creation creates hostages to fortune.

In the portrait of Madame de Sévigné we saw Madame de Lafayette making the teasing proposition that a named author is subject to risk, and confidently exploiting the benefits of anonymity while signing her name to the piece. Her subsequent work displays a more genuine ambivalence. The tensions and ambiguities present in her fiction and centred on her heroines' problematic names suggest conflicting values at which she can only hint. In the *Histoire*, however, her hesitation between self-effacement and self-exposure, between denying and proclaiming her authorship, is even more evident. That hesitation, discernible in the preface, is dramatised in the main body of the text through her focus on both the positive and negative consequences of writing: she shows it to be at once a means to power and a potential danger. Torn between their desire for active engagement and their fear of disgrace, the men and women at the court of Louis XIV, like the heroines of her fiction, are projections of the dilemma facing Madame de Lafayette herself, as woman and author.

NOTES

1. *Zaïde* was published under the signature of her probable collaborator, Jean de Segrais, and *La Princesse de Montpensier* and *La Princesse de Clèves* both appeared anonymously during her lifetime. Within forty years of her death three new works had been published under her name: the *Histoire de Madame Henriette d'Angleterre* (1720), *La Comtesse de Tende* (1724), and the *Mémoires de la cour de France pour les années 1688 et 1689* (1731). *Zaïde* and *La Princesse de Clèves* first appeared under her name in 1780 and *La Princesse de Montpensier* in 1804. More dubious attributions have continued to be made to her. On the other hand, Geneviève Mouligneau has attempted to cast serious doubt on Madame de Lafayette's status, arguing in *Madame de Lafayette, romancière?* (Brussels, 1980) that the principal authors of the works now attributed to her were La Rochefoucauld, Huet and, in particular, Segrais.
2. A distinction must be drawn between *writing* and *publishing*. It is clear that during her lifetime Madame de Lafayette enjoyed a high reputation as an author of distinction. By 1685 Adrien Baillet was referring to her as one of the most accomplished people

in the realm ('une personne des plus accomplies du Royaume'), and Boileau called her the most intelligent woman in France, and the best woman writer ('la femme de France qui avoit le plus d'esprit . . . et qui écrivoit le mieux') (Mouligneau, *ibid.*, pp. 16–18). In the Preface to her *Histoire de Madame* Madame de Lafayette herself admits that it was because of her reputation as a writer that she was chosen by Princess Henriette to write down her confidences. So it was clearly no secret that she wrote, and wrote well. Her writings, circulated among an intimate group of friends of appropriate social rank brought her admiration and esteem. It is only when she might seem to seek a wider audience that the issue of impropriety arises. See her distress when Huet passes a copy of *La Princesse de Montpensier* to his sister, telling her that Madame de Lafayette is the author:

> Elle croira que je suis un vray auteur de profession, de donner comme cela de mes livres. Je vous prie, raccommodez un peu ce que cette imaginative pourrait avoir gasté à l'opinion que je souhaite qu'elle ait de moy.' (*Correspondance.* edited by A. Beaunier, Paris: Gallimard, 1942, vol. 1, p. 175)
> (She will think that I am a real professional author, giving my books away like that. Please, I beg you, repair some of the damage that the lady's fertile imagination may have done to the good opinion I should like her to have of me.)

3. See Maurice Lever, 'Romans en quête d'auteurs au XVIIe siècle', *Revue d'histoire littéraire de la France*, LXXIII, no. 1 (1973), pp. 8–9. Writing in 1685, Adrien Baillet noted with disapproval that the device of anonymity had been fashionable in France for half a century. In a later work, he lists fourteen different reasons why an author might choose anonymity – including shame at publishing something unworthy of one's social status, disdain for transitory glory, fraudulent intent, the wish to avoid criticism, embarrassment at having a name which the reader might find ludicrous, and simple fun – 'le mouvement d'une pure gayeté de coeur.' *Jugemens des scavans sur les principaux ouvrages des auteurs* (Paris: Dezallier, 1685–6), vol. 1, p. 471; and *Auteurs déguisez sous des noms étrangers: empruntez, supposez, feints à plaisir, chiffrez, renversez, retournez, ou changez d'une Langue en une autre* (Paris, 1690), Part II, Chapters i–iv.

4. For example in Maurice Laugaa, *Lectures de Madame de Lafayette* (Paris: Colin, 1971), p. 14, ff.

5. *Le Mercure galant*, May 1678, preface (n.p.).

6. Joan DeJean, 'Lafayette's ellipses: the privileges of anonymity', *PMLA*, vol. 99, no. 5 (October 1984), pp. 884–902.

7. 'Portrait de Madame la Marquise de Sévigné', in *La Galerie des peintures ou recueil des portraits et éloges en vers et en prose* (1659), second edition (Paris: de Seroy, 1663), vol. 1, p. 200.

8. *ibid.*, vol. 1, pp. 198–9.

9.   Vous êtes naturellement tendre et passionnée; mais à la honte de notre sexe, cette tendresse vous a été inutile, & vous l'avez renfermée dans le vôtre, en la donnant à Madame de Lafayette. (*ibid.*, vol. 1, p. 200)
   (You have a loving and passionate nature; but to the shame of our sex, this capacity to love has been of no avail to you. You have confined it to your own sex by bestowing it on Madame de la Fayette.)

10. *ibid.*, vol. 1, p. 196.

11. For a discussion of the conventions of naming characters in the novels of this period, see English Showalter, Jr., *The Evolution of the French Novel 1641–1782* (Princeton, N.J.; Princeton University Press, 1972), pp. 161–9.

12. All page references in the text are to Madame de Lafayette, *Romans et nouvelles*, edited by E. Magne (Paris: Garnier, 1970).

13. See J. W. Scott, 'Criticism and *La Comtesse de Tende*', *Modern Language Review*, 1955, pp. 15–24. In 'La Terreur sans la pitié: *La Comtesse de Tende*', *Revue d'histoire littéraire de la France*, 1977, nos. 3–4, pp. 478–99, Micheline Cuénin goes so far as to call Madame de Lafayette a 'médecin de l'âme' ('doctor of the soul') because of the unambiguous moral perspective of this story.

14. For further discussion of the contradictions within this text, see my forthcoming book, *The Writings of Madame de Lafayette* (Bloomington, IN: Indiana University Press; and Hemel Hempstead: Harvester Wheatsheaf).

15. *La Galerie des peintures* (see above) was dedicated to this Mademoiselle de Montpensier. For a discussion of the *femmes fortes*, see Ian MacLean, *Woman Triumphant: Feminism in French literature 1610–1652* (Oxford: Clarendon Press, 1977), pp. 64–87.

16. The work was begun in 1664 and cut short by Madame's death in 1670; the preface, however, refers to Madame's daughter as 'la Duchesse de Savoie, aujourd'hui régnante' ('the now-reigning Duchess of Savoy'), which indicates that that section was written no earlier than April 1684.

17. The title may be held to reinforce this effacement. Is the *Histoire de Madame* perhaps to be read not as the 'story (or history) *of* Madame' but as a 'story *by* Madame', with Madame de Lafayette's part in it reduced to that of transcriber?

18. A. Beaunier suggests that the *Histoire* may have been started as a report for Louis XIV, who was conducting an inquiry about Vardes and the Spanish letter (see A. Beaunier, 'Madame de Lafayette et Madame', *Revue de Paris*, 1926, vol. 33, no. 6, pp. 73–100). The sharply critical comments about the king's behaviour, however, make it most unlikely that the version that survives was ever intended to be seen by him.

19. 'L'on croyait avoir atteint la perfection, quand on avait su plaire à Madame' ('one felt one had reached perfection when one managed to please Madame'), said Bossuet in his funeral oration for Henriette. *Oraisons funèbres, panégyriques*, edited by Abbé Velat and Yvonne Champailler (Paris: Pléïade, 1961), p. 87.

Chapter 8

'Femininity' and the Intellectual in Sontag and Cixous

Susan Wiseman

Susan Sontag is the example here in the service of a question – what is the relationship between the problematic (and disputed) ideas of the 'feminine' and the category of the intellectual?[1] Sontag's writing is used here to explore the relationship between the two. In mapping this relationship a central issue in the writing of both Cixous and Sontag is that of where the category of the 'feminine' belongs, where it is situated, by whom, and who wants it or uses it.[2] Morag Shiach pinpoints the problematic slippages in Cixous' writing between, on the one hand, '"man" and "woman" as culturally constructed signs', and, on the other hand, 'discussion of masculinity and femininity (with no inverted commas) as actually existing alternative economies'.[3] The questions one might ask of the 'feminine' in Cixous is how far it is socially constructed, and what exactly the status is of the signifier 'economy' in the term 'feminine economy'. Maybe it is possible to approach the way Cixous' writing deploys the 'feminine' by examining the appearance (and disappearance) of another idea of the 'feminine' as a culturally constructed other in Sontag's writing. How can the relationship between the idea of the intellectual, a 'mind' ranging free across a range of social, political, literary issues, and the 'feminine' be mapped?

There are few writers on cultural topics who have laid claim to the notion that the testimony of an (elite) individual can deliver something close to the truth as consistently as Sontag. But is her masterly, 'intellectual', writing – which explains to the reader our irrational fears, the 'meanings' of cultural artefacts, the typology of world events, what photography means – able to absent itself from material conditions of its production, including gender?[4] As well as attempting to erase gender her writing eschews, or treats with suspicion, the large discourses which support such pronouncements and cultural commentary.

One way of looking at the role of the 'feminine' in Sontag's writing would have been to compare her texts with those of Cixous; both are sceptical about master discourses, both concentrate always on the role of writing, language, the writer. Both write 'fiction'. Both struggle, ambivalently, with the rewards of mastery (as Cixous and Clément put it in 1975, 'Mistress woman or woman master?')[5] Moreover, Cixous writes for the theatre and Sontag has produced plays.[6] However, rather than making a comparison, this essay aims to use Cixous' ideas about the possibility of transforming hierarchised opposites (man/woman) in discourse as a way (albeit a problematic one) to read Sontag's writing in relation to gender, and especially the relationship of the social category of femininity to intellectual discourse. Perhaps Sontag's texts also offer a way to read Cixous. The 'feminine' must, in the case of Cixous, be seen as emerging from psychoanalytic discourse, even as it aims to destabilise psychoanalytic formulations of gender. However, the 'feminine' has other implications and meanings alongside Cixous' use of it to define a generous 'economy' of writing, and some of these can be explored in relation to Sontag's writing.

In the light of such differences, this essay aims to ask three questions: how does Susan Sontag's writing and even her 'persona' constitute itself in relation to the idea of the intellectual? Is the rational status of her intellectual production disturbed or disordered by the social construction of femininity? Does femininity contaminate the purity of relatively ratiocinative intellectual discourse?

'WHEN WE USE A MASTER DISCOURSE?'[7]

Sontag's position as an intellectual, a woman, a confessor and a political prophet contains – or fails to contain – contradictions. While on the one hand she offers herself as a part of an (increasingly) elite cultural group of intellectuals, on the other hand she eschews involvement in discourses that she regards as betrayers – history, sociology (though unavoidably even the most 'confessional' of texts engages with such discourses). For example, although she is clearly situated *within* the academy she is best known for her essay against interpretation. Even so she has written on Barthes, Artaud, Reifenstahl, Bresson. Instead these texts posit the response of the 'individual' – herself – as an alternative. The 'her' in this 'I' is never foregrounded, as if it was a 'one'. In many ways this combination of high academic distance and the 'I' produces exciting writing. It is as if the arguments make themselves up; the trace of gender is almost erased. Yet she appears photographed on the *front* of her books. Indeed one collection bears on the front the legend 'The cleverest woman in America' – putting the gender right back into a collection of essays which collectively ignore the question. The essays could be said to use identity as a guarantee of authenticity – but any sensibility represented as operating in the text is degenerate.

Unlike some texts produced by Cixous, Sontag's writing does not enter into circulation under the sign of gender, or the imprint of a feminist press (which is not to say that it ought to).[8] The 'I' however, plays a central role in many of the texts. The 'I' in the texts posits an answer to that question, who speaks thus? and also a guarantee of meaning and of sincerity. Sontag writes an ungendered 'I' without the presence of a female body other than as a disruption to the text. And why not? But can one be unsexed here, in the realm of writing and the 'intellect'? An example: in an interview which took place when Sontag visited Poland in 1980, reprinted in *Polish Perspectives*, the interviewer addresses Sontag as an Author, but also calls attention to the fact that she is in the socially constructed category of women – a small item that Sontag nowhere introduces. 'Let us now turn from the world of politics to the world of women . . .' So says the interviewer, neatly demarcating the spheres: 'Was it easy for you to make your way in what was predominantly a man's world?' To which Sontag replied,

> It is always easy if you are willing to make the sacrifices . . . certain sacrifices of one's personal life . . . It is always easier for a man because a man can have a wife. A woman always has to do more . . . I had to take care of the apartment, raise a child, put the shoes on him in the morning . . . and so on. You have to be stronger than a man.[9]

This is one of the relatively rare occasions on which Sontag has allowed herself to be drawn to address the relationship between her female body, her writing and her status as an intellectual. In the reply we might find the highly codified excusal given by the successful woman for her less successful sisters, those who did not have the 'strength' to make the 'sacrifices' that would permit them, as it does Sontag – to *transcend* gender.

The terms 'sacrifice' and 'strength' signal without interrogating the categories of 'woman's labour'. Moreover, she seems to be quite happy to operate with an unquestioned notion of 'separate spheres' – the academic, rational 'world of men' and the domestic 'world of women' which a woman must transcend in order to assume status as, for instance, an intellectual. Access to the 'man's world' is attainable only through an access of masculinity in excess of a 'man's'. One must become more of a man. Sontag's text here reinforces the binary hierarchy in which 'male' is privileged. In some ways, of course, exactly this is undeniably true and the discourse is familiar, mobilised by sections of the women's movement. But can the spheres be kept apart by the 'strength' of intellectual women? It seems that the feminine (which here I am using to mean that which is relegated to 'the world of women' in such a construct) constantly threatens to invade, to contaminate any 'world of men'. On the other hand, this is obviously 'up front', an acknowledgement of the way things are, on the other hand the feminine becomes that which must be repressed, 'sacrificed'.

The category of 'the intellectual' is beloved of Sontag and recurs through-out her writing. Whether in the service of 'the state' or otherwise, accord-ing to Gramsci's explorations of the idea, an intellectual puts ideas (not children) into circulation.[10] As a populariser, an intellectual spreads ideas perhaps a shade promiscuously, making them available. Sontag's fiction, as Gore Vidal pointed out, lays claim to the European intellectual tradition – that of Thomas Mann and Kafka and aims to popularise ideas drawing on this tradition within anglophone culture.[11]

In this 1980 interview, and elsewhere, she represents herself as an intellectual in a time and a place which is increasingly hostile to a role it does not understand. She says, 'I want to be a writer who is also an intellectual . . . But people are not educated any more to play this role.'[12] The role of the intellectual, which she describes as almost lost, is perhaps the quintessence of a 'man's world' or the demarcated spheres. A world inhabited, not exclusively but to a large extent, by men who are privileged by a ratiocinative ability which is endorsed by hierarchical status – or vice versa – and which enables them to *talk passionately* about ideas. The passionate talking is the privilege of those marked out as super-ratiocinative. A woman in such a position, or claiming such a position, is endangered in her status as an intellectual, perhaps, at the moment of entry into *passionate* talking. This is because the role of an intellectual might be said to offer, through its privileged status, a toehold for passionate – and therefore not hermetically superrational – thought, speaking.

Let us turn to two examples of the relationship between the un- or de-gendered category of the identity of the intellectual in Sontag's writing, and examine forces of instability (in Cixous' terms 'disorder', 'contamina-tion') which threaten it. This can be analysed in two different areas of Sontag's writing: first from her writing on aesthetics and then from her cultural confessional, 'Trip to Hanoi'.

In her writings on aesthetics from the 1970s, Sontag addresses the issue of the density and impermeability of all language. Diagnosing in some writing the worn out and used up condition of late modernity, she invokes as culture-heroes those writers who are separate from the generality, and whose sensibilities as expressed in language (as she sees it) offer the liberal bourgeois world their 'anti-liberal and anti-bourgeois' qualities. In an essay on Simone Weil she writes that in a writer, 'sanity becomes a compromise, an evasion, a lie . . . The truths we respect are those born of affliction. We measure truth in terms of the cost to the writer in suffering rather than by a standard of objective truth to which a writer's words correspond. Each of our truths must have a martyr.'[13] Here Sontag is exploring the person of the writer, the cult and mystery around the tortuous evidence of personal creativity in a late modern (though not yet post-modern) world. The writer as 'martyr' is set at a distance from the society which produced him or her. Indeed, the existence of the writer in its 'anti-bourgeois' state bodies forth a polar opposite, a binary other to the 'liberal bourgeois' society.

Elsewhere Sontag's theories of aesthetics formulate more abstractly the detached, antithetical relationship of the writer howling in the late modern wilderness of bourgeois society. In the early *Styles of Radical Will* (1967) the essay 'The Aesthetics of Silence' explores the question of lateness and the failure of language – primarily to provide the 'ritual' function which Sontag sees as fundamental (or as she puts it, 'essential') to writing. It becomes evident that a normative theory of language is operating in which the power of words *ought* to transcend a given historical context and provide access to a 'higher' realm of experience. The discussion of aesthetics takes on the present over-fed state of western consciousness. 'Perhaps', she speculates, 'the quality of attention one brings to bear on something will be better (less contaminated, less impoverished) the less one is offered.'[14] Sontag's modernist aesthetic of less is more (itself imbricated in the gender-histories of modernism) is presented to us in moral terms. With words like 'contaminated' we enter the zone of purity and defilement.

She continues to describe language as, on the one hand 'a human activity with an apparently essential stake in the project of transcendence', but on the other hand 'the most impure, the most contaminated, the most exhausted of all the materials out of which art is made'. Once again Sontag sets up a bipolar paradox with transcendence on the one hand as the ultimate goal in the chain of possibility inaugurated by the existence of language, but on the other hand, contamination and exhaustion as the given status of the present. Silence is offered as 'one approach to this visionary a-historical condition . . . silence is a metaphor for a cleansed, non-interfering vision.' But even silence is contaminated in the chain reaction of uncleanness and exhaustion that led to it: it must be purged in the new regenerate speech:

> Silence is a strategy for the transvaluation of art, art itself being the herald of an anticipated radical transvaluation of human values. But the success of the strategy must mean its eventual abandonment, or at least its significant modification: Silence is a prophecy, one which the artist's actions can be understood as attempting both to fulfill and to reverse.
>
> As language points to its own transcendance in silence, silence points to its own transcendence – to a speech beyond silence.

Thus discourses give way one to another in a temporal spiritual movement of language always on its journey towards the transcendental signifier, but always contaminated by its earlier contact with late, dirty modernity. Silence, if it is a metaphor for anything here, is a metaphor for the arms race of the spiritual, transcendental claims of Sontag's de-materialised, a-historical, clean-living language.

It is not difficult to locate in this writing a recurrent concern with pollution, and with prophecy of a kind of linguistic apocalypse or apotheosis depending on whether or not language manages to transcend the polluting present. As Mary Douglas puts it, 'the ideal order of society is guarded by dangers which threaten transgressors.'[15]

Here the ideal order is in the future when the language will again be purified and its access to sincerity and authenticity renewed. The relationship of identity between sayer and said will be restored, Sontag prophesies, only by the ritual purification of language, its separation from the impure elements.

For Sontag, more recently, elite writers are the 'guardians of language' which is to be maintained again, by keeping categories distinct – 'public language', must be prevented from contaminating elite language; 'the language of television is language at its lowest denominator.'[16] It does not seem excessive to read this as making a pattern in which 'good' language needs to escape 'bad' language to have access to the truth. But, like the 'worlds' of men and women posited by the interviewer, the binaries are, in fact, both unstable and independent. The threat of contamination (the return of 'bits of the body'?) is implicit within the binary itself.[17] In this way Sontag's writing sets up unstable and certainly hierarchised opposites, in which the privileged binary ('the world of men', 'pure' language) relies on the holding back of the always implicit other part ('the world of women', 'impure' language).

Alongside this concern with contamination in relation to authenticity Sontag's writing returns to the notion of the first person confessional guaranteeing the authenticity of an utterance. But, as becomes increasingly clear in her writing from 'Trip to Hanoi' to Aids and its Metaphors it is not any 'I' which guarantees authenticity, but only an 'I' whose confessional or prophecy is already itself guaranteed by political/intellectual status. This can be traced in her writing on socio-cultural topics.[18]

Sontag's cultural critique endeavours to place the 'I' at a distance from the hegemonic discourses of the United States. In 'Trip to Hanoi' (1968) Sontag distances her identity or persona from both America and the Vietnam which she represents as a unitary other. Charting her responses in that ambiguous form, the diary, the promise of authenticity of reported response appears to be fulfilled when in the early pages of the diary we hear from Sontag that she does not warm to this cultural 'other' she is involved in investigating. Gradually this reserve collapses and Vietnam becomes constituted within the text as the superior member of a binary opposition America/Vietnam.

The book substitutes a strategy of reporting the responses of one individual, an intellectual, to the war in Vietnam eschewing the discourses which purport to be objective politics, history, sociology. As Alf Louvre notes in his discussion of 'Trip to Hanoi', a nuanced and apparently immediate exploration of an alien culture is offered instead.[19] 'Trip to Hanoi' is written within the binary United States/Vietnam but attempts to turn the 'given' racist cultural implications – for western readers – upside down; America becomes alien for the text, Vietnam valorised. If we follow Cixous' well-known formulation masculine/feminine, United States/Vietnam, this might appear to be Sontag valorising that which is, in Cixous' terms, implicitly the 'feminine', Sontag is at pains to establish a distance between her identity and that of an 'American' – a bid for the text to be distant from its contaminating base which is similar to that traced in 'The Aesthetics of Silence'. She writes:

> Their cordial interest in America is so evidently sincere that it would be boorish not to respond to it. Yet somehow it chills me, for it seems a little indecent. I'm aware how their unexpectedly complex yet ingenuous, relation to the United States overlays every situation between individual Vietnamese and Bob, Andy and me. (p. 253).

However, she writes of her return to the United States in terms of her status as an alienated intellectual, and as she does so a third, privileged, position appears – the undesired but inevitable 'alienation' of the intellectual; 'Remembering the intimations I'd had in North Vietnam of the possibility of loving my own country, I wanted very much not to react crudely, moralistically, not to slip back into the old posture of alienation' (p. 260).[20] Something which is of note here is that Sontag is exploring her claim to elite status whereas later in her career – for example in AIDS and Its Metaphors – she presents herself as self-evidently distant from every average person.[21]

'Trip to Hanoi' has a political programme for its readers: to liberate a political reading which does not depend on master discourses and to problematise the cultural and political hegemony of the United States. The use of binaries here serves a political project in the insistence on Vietnam as the superior term in the binary United States/Vietnam.[22] The pattern of separation and potential contamination is repeated with the United States as the 'contaminator' of both Sontag and Vietnam, but Sontag reserves for herself the isolated position of the elite.[23]

Therefore, in both her aesthetic writing and her cultural commentary Sontag is looking for ways to shift issues out of an historical materialist, political context into a moral, intellectual and even metaphysical context. Sontag strives to avoid the deceitful discourses of imperialist America – the background babble of the talk talk talk of the political think-tank. At the same time, her writing erases or attempts to forestall gender which appears as the 'weak' domestic sphere. The intellectual's identity and finely-tuned personal response offer in Sontag's writing a more 'authentic' response than, say, 'history.' This intellectual as Sontag represents his or her role is always alien to and alienated from American bourgeois society. Further weight is put on the question of a identity and personal response because her prose retains the idea of a metaphysic, the idea of a spiritual trans-cendence, but without a logos or ultimate signifier for all authority. The intellectual, or this intellectual 'I', relies on the confessional and prophecy of an elite and far-seeing 'I', and one which is attempting, at times, to escape the hegemony of academic or 'state' language. However, this 'I' is also figured as de-gendered, in order to speak as part of the elite. Eschewing gestures to context except 'cosmopolitanism' such as 'I' is vulnerable to gendered recontextualisation.

'IF THE POSITION OF MASTERY CULTURALLY COMES BACK TO MEN?'

If, as is argued above, Sontag's aesthetic and intellectual writing uses an 'I' which is de-gendered and which is suspicious of the United States and to some extent of discourses from sociology to literary criticism, is the rational status of intellectual production disturbed or disordered by 'femininity', or the return of the 'woman's world'? Does 'femininity', as the repressed of Sontag's text, return to disorder the supremacy of the binary?

Sontag's writing constitutes itself as important, elite, intellectual, political, symbolic by eschewing investigation of the links of the binaries it attempts to separate. However, in February 1982 Sontag attended a rally of the American left for Solidarity at the New York Town Hall. Those in attendance included people from a range of literary, intellectual and political positions: Kurt Vonnegut, Gore Vidal, Pete Seeger. Her speech was reported in The Nation of 27 February which ran her edited version of it, and both Partisan Review and Encounter weighed in with their respective commentaries. The journalist Christopher Hitchens managed to write the story for papers of both the right and the left.

At this point the American left were attempting to negotiate a position on Poland that both took some account of the political complexities of the situation and differentiated itself as clearly as possible from the position which the Reagan administration had adopted with the slogan – 'Let Poland Be Poland'. Indeed Sontag drew attention to this when she mentioned the message sent by the writer Carlos Fuentes which adapted the government's slogan – 'Let Poland Be Poland – Yes. But let El Salvador be El Salvador'. Sontag is aware here of the dangers of political fudging which directs attention to the investments of the United States at the expense of other political questions.

The role of the American government in relation to communist countries was one issue in 1982; perhaps an equally difficult issue for the left to negotiate was the use of the word 'communist' within the United States. This word became a focus of the debate on the left, and Daniel Singer wrote an article in *The Nation* of 3 July which went some way towards articulating the issue of the disputed meaning of the word 'communist'.[24] Sontag used it as follows.

> We meet here tonight to express our solidarity with the people of Poland, now languishing under the brutal oppression of what one can only call – if that word has any meaning – a fascist regime . . . The present government has not only adopted the standards of fascist rule; it has offered fascist rule as a whole arsenal of new techniques.
>
> All this is obvious, or almost, when one uses the word 'fascist' to describe the present Polish government. But I mean to use the word in a further sense. What the recent Polish events illustrate is something more than that fascist rule is possible within the framework of communist society, whereas democratic government and worker self-rule are clearly intolerable – and will not be tolerated. I would contend that what they illustrate is a truth that we should have understood a very long time ago: that Communism *is* fascism – successful fascism, if you will. What we have called fascism is, rather, the form of tyranny that can be overthrown – that has, largely, failed. I repeat: not only is fascism (and overt military rule) the probable destiny of all Communist societies – especially when their populations are moved to revolt but Communism is itself a variant, the most successful variant, of fascism. Fascism with a human face.
>
> This, I would argue, must be the starting point of all the lessons to be learned from the on going Polish events. And in our efforts to criticize and reform our own societies, we owe it to those in the front line of struggle against tyranny to tell the truth, without bending it to serve interests we believe are just. These hard truths mean abandoning many of the commonplaces of the left, mean challenging what we have meant for many years by 'radical' and 'progressive'. The stimulus to rethink our position, and to abandon old and corrupt rhetoric may not be the least of what we owe the heroic Poles, and may be our best way to express solidarity with them.[25]

The Nation reprinted this speech, including an attack on itself in which Susan Sontag had also claimed that between 1950 and 1970 a reader of *The*

Reader's Digest would have been better informed about the 'realities of communism' than a reader of The Nation or The New Statesman – 'the answer', Sontag said, 'should give us pause. Could it be that our enemies were right?'[26] Sontag here adopts the familiar role of the politician predicting the future as a moral terrorist. The language is prophetic rather than ratiocinative and full of possibilities of deceit, collapsing categories, tautology: 'When enormities go on mounting up . . . we say "It can't get much worse now". It seems that the day of judgement is at hand.'[27]

Fascism and (now articulated as the same) communism collapse and reverse places. Through the rather surprising organ of The Reader's Digest the right become the custodians of Truth. Communism becomes fascism 'with a human face'. The blindness of the seers of the American left (particularly Sontag) is dissolved as the veil drops from her eyes in a moment of visionary, prophetic truth – undefiled by propoganda – as she confesses, articulates guilt, prophesies the future. Her use of the term 'communism' confounds political ideas with a very specific manifestation of the nation state. Her language circles the world but leaves it overdetermined and de-historicised at the centre of her text: its signification collapsed within her discourse into that of fascism.

In terms of the argument traced above, we could read this as a moment at which the binaries which Sontag elsewhere constructs collapse, the privileged binary 'communism' in the already problematic dyad communism/fascism becoming equivalent to its opposite.

Sontag's response hit the left at a time when they were beginning to rethink European politics. Printed reaction to this speech was extensive. Moreover, commentators of right and left responded by bringing the gender of the author into play in relation to her status as an intellectual and her access to political discourse. For example, The Nation, in an introduction to Sontag's denunciation, calls attention to her narrative strategies. It writes that it is 'happy to enter the lists about this or any other periods of history (even periods of history that took place before Sontag was born, and thus are not covered by her own personal experience and confessional)'.[28] On the right, Encounter was delighted.[29] In the Partisan Review Leon Wieseltier referred to the speech as 'the political apology of an unpolitical person', figuring Sontag as an invader of the separate sphere – here the world of politics – which she had seen as separate from the 'world of women'.[30] Diana Trilling, the one woman The Nation invited to respond to Sontag, referred to Sontag as 'Miss Sontag' (apparently a term of abuse) throughout the article. Response from the left indicated that Sontag had made a fool of herself and had transgressed some peer decorum. The right made hay – and metaphors of fashion and femininity. Hilton Kramer wrote

in *The New Criterion* (in September 1986) that 'in . . . the Sontag circle
. . . it is no longer considered *démodé* to be anti-communist. Indeed it has
become positively smart', relegating Sontag to the position of an elderly
centre of a fashion salon.[31] Later he wrote, 'The truth is, Susan Sontag
doesn't have much of a mind for politics . . . [she is] hopelessly in thrall to
the winds of fashion, forever in search of the 'turn-on' that will serve [her]
narcissism.'[32]

Despite Susan Sontag's attempt to detoxify her texts and remove traces
of that dangerous agent femininity, the possibility of the contamination of
the ratiocinative by the other sphere, the unspoken gender of the 'I', exists
with every sentence. The questions that Sontag raised (and obscured) at
the Town Hall were lost in the shock of her rhetoric of reversal (and that
rhetoric was relentlessly gendered by the press).

DESIRE, THE IMAGINARY, CLASS-STRUGGLE – HOW DO THEY RELATE?

What are the meanings of this story for the question of writing under the
sign of gender, or attempting to subvert or eschew that sign? How can we
think of the social category of woman, and the role of the intellectual?
Cixous' writing suggests that categories such as man and women (as used by
Sontag) need to be destabilised. Instead, she offers the terms 'masculine'
and 'feminine', with reference to writing, or libidinal economies within
writing (in itself perhaps a rather obscure notion) as terms which can be
used to locate and in the future produce a generous kind of writing. Cixous
writes, 'what I call "feminine" and "masculine" is the relationship to
pleasure, the relationship to spending.'[33] She insists also on the role of the
question as the motor of investigation.[34] The ways in which these insights
help us to trace (or invent) the problematic operations of binaries and
disruptions in Sontag's texts help us to offer an analysis of femininity, in
terms of the social category of women, as the repressed of Sontag's text. But
does changing the ground to that of the written eliminate the man/woman
opposition from masculine/feminine? This is made especially difficult when
we find that alongside masculine and feminine in writing Cixous also uses
woman as something (someone) which her texts write 'towards', and as
something (someone) which can speak itself. Obviously, these are quixotic
accusations to make of terms which themselves are disordering the Lacanian ideas of female desire. But there does seem to be a problem with the way
in which the feminine economy escapes woman, only for her to reappear,

not as a social category, but as something written towards or, equally, writing herself. Here, perhaps, we might want to recall something of Sontag's insistence on up-frontness, on stating the status quo.

If the feminine can be read as the repressed of Sontag's texts, themselves positioned in relation to political events, the role of the intellectual, Cixous' texts investigate, question, explore the possibilities of the feminine. She finds in the writing of Clarice Lispector 'all the possible positions of a subject in relation to what would be "appropriation", use and abuse of owning', and this is where she investigates the categories which Sontag takes for granted, and I have tried to suggest the ways in which such investigations offer a critique of Sontag's unproblematised acceptance of the problematic of the binary man/woman.[35]

But the relationship between Cixous' neo- and anti-Lacanian uses of 'femininity' and the social category of women remain fraught for any reader. The feminine is valorised in Cixous' text but it is located wholly in writing. For example:

> The problem is with women who have produced, who have written, because culturally, they have been subjected to the obligations of masculinization in order to hoist themselves on to the scene of sociopolitical legitimation. With the result that most of the texts by women up to our own time have been terribly marked by the 'masculine' economy.[36]

On the one hand this formulation offers us a way to think of 'femininity' and 'masculinity' as mutable, and perhaps also offers a way to think about de-gendered 'I's as part of a process of 'sociopolitical masculinization'. But the scene of the masculine or feminine 'economy' is the text, and this leaves the question of where we might locate the 'economy' of a text. The sociopolitical signifier is there, but its connotations seem to be limited to either a psychoanalytic, libidinal economy, or one located somewhere within language. Cixous' investigation of the category of feminine is, obviously, 'political' in its radical questioning of categories, but we might also want to ask what work the political, even Marxian, language does. How does the step from masculine and feminine 'economies' take place?

At moments, differences and the possibility of multiplicities seem possible *loci* for change. More than ten years ago, Kristeva, writing about femininity and the idea of the intellectual, brought the questions of sexual difference, politics and 'thought' into focus, just for a moment, around Hegelian history. She analysed the intellectual/dissident as a configuration of linguistic and political potential:

> A spectre haunts Europe: the dissident.
> Give voice to each individual form of the unconscious, to every desire and need.
> Call into play the identity and/or the language of the individual and the group.

Become the analyst of every type of speech and institution considered socially impossible. Proclaim that we reveal the Impossible.

But an eruption of languages, like that in our own age, has rarely produced such a clear awareness of the closed nature of society and its safety mechanisms, which range from the group (the Family, the Nation, the State, the Party) to its rational technological forms of discourse. The intellectual, who is the instrument of this discursive rationality, is the first to feel the effects of its break-up: his own identity is called into question, his dissidence becomes more radical.[37]

By virtue of this assumed perception of ideology Kristeva (perhaps rather briskly) co-opts women as dissidents: 'And sexual difference, women: isn't that another form of dissidence?'[38] Although there are obviously problems with the way women appear in the argument as a revolutionary force like a rabbit out of a hat, Kristeva brings together an elaboration of a quasi-Gramscian model of the revolutionary potential of the intellectual with the linguistic and psychic structures which both support and endanger both identity and the status quo. At this moment she situates the potential for change in the dissolution of stable categories and that in the perception of such dissolution. She writes, 'now that reason has become absorbed by technology, thought is tenable only as an "analytic position" that affirms dissolution and works through differences.'[39] Kristeva suggests that women can be mobilised as this new type of intellectual and dissident.

But where multiple difference, though particularly sexual difference, is important to Kristeva's analysis, the distinctions that Sontag's writing strives to keep in place are between high and low, between the pure and the contaminated, between the elite intellectual and the rest acknowledge the power of the *social* category of the feminine. Just as Kristeva's analyses leave the female subject, reader, balanced (or speared) on the horns of the dilemma of difference as a motor for change, Sontag's embracing of the unchanged categories leaves the rational and the invasively irrational, the sacred and the profane, in a dyadic and mutually threatening relation.

For Sontag the intellectual and the social category of the feminine can coexist only at the exclusion of the second category, in Kristeva's essay the two are mutual in their imbalance as part of potential force for cultural transformation. A question we might ask of Cixous' 'feminine' is why the signifier 'feminine' is any less trapped by social construction than the binary man/woman. It seems that the binary man/woman (social categories) is, for Cixous, firmly and inescapably grounded in the problematic of binary, logocentric signification – a product and generator of the traps of gender – where the binary masculine/feminine, at least in writing, is represented as floating free of logocentric categorisation. But even so, woman, in some way, exists in her writing. In reading Cixous perhaps the double slippage between writing and action, feminine as a social and then as an absolute and free-standing category, destabilises the binary categories, perhaps it allows the feminine to be valorised in writing. But such a slippage leaves a puzzle about where and how change might happen – how can we map more fully the relationship between a 'feminine economy' in writing and potential for the transformation of socio-political categories?

NOTES

1. Sontag's fictional writing and cultural commentary is characterised by a continuing concern about the role of the intellectual. See for example *The Benefactor* (New York: Farrar, Strauss and Giroux, 1967), pp. 7–8. For an incisive but critical analysis of Sontag's part as an intellectual in the United States see Walter Kendrick, 'A gulf of her own', *The Nation*, 23 October 1982, pp. 404–6.

2. See Rachel Bowlby on psychoanalysis, feminism and the repudiation of the feminine in 'Still crazy after all these years', in Teresa Brennan (ed.), *Between Feminism and Psychoanalysis* (London and New York: Routledge, 1989), pp. 40–59, especially pp. 50–5. As she puts it, 'Feminity is thus the place where no man – male or female – wants to be, and its repudiation is the attitude that characterises both the "normal" man and woman who has remained masculine, refusing or failing to change her first, masculine, nature for femininity' (p. 48).

3. Morag Shiach, 'Their "symbolic" exists, it holds power – we, the sowers of disorder, know it only too well', in Teresa Brennan, *op. cit.*, p. 156.

4. On the topic of Sontag and the elite ethos of the intellectual see Andrew Ross, *No Respect: Intellectuals and popular culture* (London and New York: Routledge, 1989). He makes the point succinctly with regard to Sontag's treatment of general versus art photography (see pp. 111–13).

5. Hélène Cixous and Catherine Clément, in their 'Exchange', in *The Newly Born Woman* translated by Betsy Wing (Manchester: Manchester University Press, 1986) (first published Paris: Union Générale d'Editions, 1975), p. 140.

6. Hélène Cixous, 'Le dernier tableau ou le portrait de Dieu' in her *Entre l'Ecriture* (Paris: Des femmes, 1986). On Cixous and theatre see for example *Portrait of Dora* translated by Anita Barrows in *Benmussa Directs* (London: John Calder, 1979) and *L'Histoire terrible mais inachevée de Norodom Sihanouk, roi du Cambodge* (Paris: Théâtre du Soleil, 1985). For Sontag's production of Pirandello's (1930) *Come tu mi vuoi* see Jennifer Stone, 'Beyond Desire: A critique of Susan Sontag's production of Pirandello's *Come tu mi vuoi*', *The Yearbook of the British Pirandello Society*, 1981, no. 1, pp. 35–48.

7. Hélène Cixous and Catherine Clément, 'A Woman Mistress', *The Newly Born Woman*, p. 136. Other headings also taken from *The Newly Born Woman*.

8. Thanks to Jill LiBehan for a discussion of this.

9. 'A Life Style is Not a Life: An interview with Susan Sontag', Monika Beyer in *Polish Perspectives*, September 1980, vol. 23, no. 9, pp. 42–6 (abridged from *Polityka*, p. 45).

10. Antonio Gramsci, *Selections From the Cultural Writings* edited by David Forgacs and Geoffry Nowell-Smith, (London: Lawrence and Wishart, 1985), section on 'People, Nation and Culture', see for instance the note, 'The Study of the Historical

Formation of the Italian Intellectuals', pp. 216–7. See also, *Letters From Prison*, selected and translated by Lynne Larner (London: Jonathan Cape, 1975), p. 227. For an analysis of the feminine as inscribed in philosophical discourse see Jacques Derrida, *Spurs* (Chicago: University of Chicago Press, 1979) pp. 41–67.

11. Gore Vidal, 'Miss Sontag's second new novel', in his *Reflections Upon a Sinking Ship* (London: Heinemann, 1969), pp. 41–7.
12. *Polish Perspectives*, p. 43.
13. Susan Sontag, *Against Interpretation*.
14. Susan Sontag, 'The aesthetics of silence', in *Styles of Radical Will* (London: Secker & Warburg, 1967), p. 13. Subsequent references in text.
15. Mary Douglas, *Purity and Danger* (first published 1966) (London and Boston: Ark, 1985), p. 3. See also Cixous, 'The guilty one', *The Newly Born Woman*, pp. 32–9.
16. 'Under the sign of Sontag', interview with Michael Cronin in *Graph*, no. 5, Dublin, Autumn 1988, pp. 16–8.
17. Hélène Cixous, 'The guilty one', in *The Newly Born Woman*, p. 33.
18. Susan Sontag, 'Trip to Hanoi', in *Styles of Radical Will*, pp. 205–74. Subsequent references in text.
19. Alf Louvre, 'The reluctant historians: Sontag, Mailer and the American culture critics of the 1960s', *Prose Studies*, May 1986, vol. 9, no. 1, pp. 47–62, especially p. 47.
20. Thanks to Linda R. Williams for her comments on this and other sections of the essay.
21. A recent example of Sontag putting herself at a distance is to be found in *AIDS and Its Metaphors* (New York: Farrar, Strauss and Giroux, and Harmondsworth: Penguin, 1988). Sontag writes of other people with cancer, 'They seemed to be in the grip of fantasies about their illness by which I was quite unseduced', p. 12.
22. See also Cary Nelson, 'Soliciting self-knowledge: The rhetoric of Susan Sontag's criticism', *Critical Inquiry*, vol. 6, no. 4, 1980.
23. This pattern is repeated with Poland and more recently, Ireland, but the valorisation of European cultures in Sontag's writing takes very different forms. In the interview in *Polish Perspectives*, Sontag appears to think of Poland, too, as an 'other' superior in many ways to America. Again the absence of a role for her conception of an intellectual is voiced. Here it is linked explicitly as in 'Trip to Hanoi' to the idea of America. She talks of the hegemonic discourses of nation in which 'free speech' is present but colonised by imperialist ideas about reality: 'We have an extraordinary tradition of freedom . . . but America is still a very stable conservative society. This constant talk is like music that is going on all the time . . . our society does not prevent dissidence. Or rather, it does not allow it. If we say everybody can be a dissident, then are are no dissidents. You could say, and people have said it, that it is a more sophisticated form of censorship. So in America you cannot be a dissident because you would get your picture on the cover of *Time* magazine . . . I do not say that I do not like the system, but I also see that in a way it is very diabolical.' (*Polish Perspectives*, p. 43). See also *Graph* no. 5 p. 18.
24. Daniel Singer, 'Solidarity – lest we forget', *The Nation*, 3 July 1982.
25. 'Communism and the Left', *The Nation*, 27 February 1982, pp. 229–38. See also Daniel Singer, 'Solidarity – lest we forget', *The Nation*, 3 July 1982.
26. *The Nation* 27 February 1982, p. 229.
27. Immanuel Kant, 'The contest of the faculties', in *Political Writings*, edited by Hans Reiss translated by H. B. Misbet (Cambridge: Cambridge University Press, 1970), p. 179. See also pp. 177–80. Thanks to John Philips.

28. *The Nation*, 27 February 1982, p. 229.
29. *Encounter*, May–July 1982, vol. 58, nos. 5 and 6, vol. 59, no. 1.
30. Leon Wieseltier, *Partisan Review* 1982, vol. XLIX, no. 3. See also Noam Chomsky in *Partisan Review* 1983, vol. L, no. 2., and 'Intellectuals and Politics', *Partisan Review*, vol. L, no. 4, pp. 590–617.
31. Hilton Kramer, 'Anti-communism and the Sontag circle', *The New Criterion*, vol. 5, no. 1, pp. 1–7.
32. *ibid.*, p. 6.
33. Hélène Cixous, 'Extreme Fidelity', translated by Susan Sellers in Susan Sellers (ed.), *Writing Differences: Readings from the seminar of Hélène Cixous* (Milton Keynes: Open University Press, 1988), p. 15.
34. Hélène Cixous, 'Le dernier tableau ou le portrait de Dieu', (1983) in *Entre l'Ecriture* (Paris: Des femmes, 1986), pp. 191–2.
35. 'Extreme Fidelity', p. 17.
36. 'Extreme Fidelity', p. 25.
37. Julia Kristeva, 'A new type of intellectual: the dissident', in Toril Moi (ed.) *The Kristeva Reader*, p. 295.
38. *ibid.*, p. 296.
39. *ibid.*, p. 299.

Chapter 9

Metaphorical Thinking and Poetic Writing in Virginia Woolf and Hélène Cixous

Françoise Defromont

Focusing on women's studies also implies analysing women writers' own approach to theory and thought, for even though they are now increasingly being studied as outstanding artists, they are still overlooked as remarkable thinkers. At the least, their original approach to theory is overlooked, which undermines the very logic of some theoretical discourses.

Reading over some great women writers whom I love because of their unique connection to the feminine – Hélène Cixous, Virginia Woolf, Katherine Mansfield – I realised that whether I plunged into their fictions or their essays, something very strong unites them, which has to do with the poetic fabric of the text.

Many questions then come up: what is the connection between theory and practice in such texts? Should we examine the connection between theory and thought, or theory and poetry? or theoretical thought and the practice of thinking? . . .

The first feature that struck me about this kind of writing was that the metaphorical network was, as in poetical works, very dense, unlike most theoretical essays. 'Theory' did not seem the appropriate word any more, so I shall rather call it metaphorical thinking.

Then I realised there was no gap between so-called theory and the practice of writing fiction – just a flowing continuous prose – which raises the question of the status of theory in women's thinking.

The last point I would like to tackle is how practice and theory interweave in Hélène Cixous' texts; the poetic embracing the political through the tongues of ecstasy.

METAPHORICAL THINKING

The essays of Virginia Woolf and Hélène Cixous swarm with metaphors, and it may appear surprising that they should express deep intellectual thought. The most obvious example is *A Room of One's Own*. This well-known title is a metaphor of the feminine writing identity, and is thus anchored simultaneously in the necessity of a material as well as symbolical place from which one can stem as a writer.

But behind the title which now almost seems too obvious, the very essay as a whole is metaphorical even in the settings Virginia Woolf has chosen: the walk through Oxbridge is a metaphor for women's position in the world of knowledge – just outsiders accidentally strolling there, as if astray in a country inhabited by men only. The metaphor continues with the British Museum. It deals with the symbolical position of women in the world of literature and culture, as objects to be studied rather than subjects. The perusing of books in the British Museum thus appears as a metaphor for reading, revealing that there is no space for women in the history of literature.

However brilliant this approach may be, it is not the most innovative part of the essay, whose originality and strength lie mostly in the way Woolf deconstructs the concept of thought itself and reveals its very working through metaphorical thinking.

She expresses her doubts on making theories about women and writing from the very first page, and goes on undermining the concept of thought in the following way:

> Thought – to call it by a prouder name than it deserved – had let its line down into the stream. It swayed, minute after minute, hither and thither, among the reflections and the weeds, letting the water lift it and sink until – you know the little tug – the sudden conglomeration of an idea at the end of one's line: and then the cautious hauling of it in, and the careful laying of it out. [1]

This passage illustrates a metaphorical approach to the very concept of thought, which deconstructs it into flowing thinking thus recapturing the process of thinking itself as something free and mobile, as something which is part of a whole, a landscape with trees and a river.

But Woolf goes even further, for she debunks 'proud' thought from its position of phallic object, turning it – to use her own metaphor – into a small fish, which she expresses in the following way: 'Laid on the grass how small, how insignificant this thought of mine looked'. This small fish is flowing thinking to be opposed to thought:

I should never be able to fulfil what is, I understand, the first duty of a lecturer – to hand you after an hour's discourse a nugget of pure truth to wrap up between the pages of your notebook and keep on the mantlepiece for ever.[2]

It then becomes a nugget, not something alive like a fish, but hard gold, to be displayed, in fact something of a phallic object, cut off from its context and in a position to be looked at. The difference between these two approaches almost amounts to the difference between two concepts.

However, the question is: how should such an approach be assessed insofar as depth, accuracy and power are concerned? It is time to go back to linguists' definition of metaphors.[3] First, metaphor implies the substitution of one word for another (or of one context, or even one semantic field for another); it produces a shift of meaning, as the metaphor of the stream and the fish shows, for instead of shutting us out in the arid world of abstraction Woolf carries us away into nature and one of its beautiful landscapes, as if at the moment of coming to grips with a deep intellectual question she felt like drifting into a kind of reverie – metaphorical thinking. Is metaphorical thinking, then, to be considered as serious and efficient?

One answer has been suggested by philosophers, for metaphors have always been at the very centre of metaphysics; philosophers such as Paul Ricoeur and Jacques Derrida have debated them extensively. As Julia Kristeva points out, something very significant happened in the philosophical field in the seventeenth century with Descartes.[4] As she emphasises, rationalism banned anything connected with metaphors in order to focus on the actual basis of reason rather than on its working, thus eradicating analogies, because of their likeness to reality – as if they dimmed the pure vision of abstractions. So even in the philosophical field, if metaphors have been acknowledged as useful they have also been rejected. Metaphors are seen as the opposite of a rational and scientific approach, something to illustrate or adorn thought, or something producing idealisation . . .

It is very interesting to note that at about the same historical period, the seventeenth century, new scientific theories on cosmology and physics were spreading in France and were publicised by such authors as Fontenelle.[5] Some essays popularising science were written for women; they staged beautiful marchionesses courted by philosophers, science being tackled through a whole set of metaphors, as if this were the best way of giving their inferior minds access to abstract ideas.

So if women have long been considered as not much above the level of metaphors, that is capable only of poor thought, I would say that it is now time to consider metaphorical thinking not only as an illustrative or ornamental way of thinking but also as a very fertile one. Derrida's own approach has made this explicit, for his deconstruction of philosophy partly relies on the deconstruction of concepts through metaphors, as he develops it in 'La Mythologie blanche'.[6] If some political, literary and feminist essays written by women swarm with metaphors, should this be seen as a connection with deeper essences or ontological questions – the kind philosophy puts forth? Anyway, metaphors appear as linked with the most primitive expression of language, as images coming forth before proper words or ideas, as Derrida states it, quoting Rousseau.[7] How can we connect all these elements with women and metaphorical thinking?

Cixous herself seems to express some kind of distrust towards metaphors in *La Venue à l'écriture* when she comments upon her feeding on books, adding that it is not a metaphor; what does this mean exactly? The very texture of her own writing is so deeply metaphorical that I can only interpret this as a distrust of tropes, or rather of ornamental writing. She explicitly aims at releasing the literal meaning of the word, not its figurative one, so that, under the congealed expression, the real living word breathes again and can be felt full of flesh.

And this is exactly what metaphors give to thought: flesh. For if they are connected with a primitive form of language it is because they anchor thought into matter, embodying ideas, giving them something of a body – instead of being just ideas, they become thinkable – hence their necessity in the philosophical field, as well as their subsequent rejection. The assumption I then make is that women thinkers such as Cixous and Woolf do not *need*, in order to think, to withdraw from, as the etymology of the word abstraction suggests it. The thinking movement, on the contrary, takes place in the full stream of life and does not stem from the eradication of their own bodies – it is not a nugget on the mantlepiece – it belongs to the body of life, and as such it belongs to a whole, a river, willows and a fisherman. The thinking body is completely immersed in its present context at the moment when the thinking is taking place, even if the necessary step backwards is there, metaphorised through hauling the fish out of the stream.

The shift of meaning occurs together with an excess, and an overlapping, and an overflowing between genres – for is metaphorical thinking mostly poetic, philosophical, or political? It appears as multidisciplinary with none of the usual categories between theory and practice or even between theory and fiction.

THE EBB AND FLOW BETWEEN THEORY AND PRACTICE

The approach of Virginia Woolf, the thinking movement embracing the very context where it takes place through the use of metaphors, not only catches the thinking process itself and gives it a poetic scope, it also implies a different handling of theory. No disruptions, no gaps, no tearing apart between theory and the writing of fiction: writing is a rhythmic whole whether it includes thinking or not. This is what Woolf explicitly says in *A Room of One's Own*, to explain how she is to tackle the subject of women and writing:

> Fiction here is likely to contain more truth than fact. Therefore I propose, making use of all the liberties and licences of a novelist, to tell you the story of the two days that preceded my coming here – how, bowed down by the weight of the subject which you have laid upon my shoulders, I pondered it, and made it work in and out of my daily life.[8]

This is a key passage which may very well serve to analyse what metaphorical thinking means, that is, a deconstruction of phallic thought – a burden she manages to get rid of through 'fiction' and what she calls the working in and out of her daily life. Thinking interweaves with everyday life; thinking as part of the trivia generally associated with women; feminine thinking – if I may use such an expression. The 'in and out' recaptures the process itself, but it is not a mere metaphor, for it describes how she writes so called theory.

Woolf's writing of theory is remarkable for it breathes in and out, it is pure movement. It ebbs and flows with the same rhythm as her fictions, as we can see in the following passage where she muses over poets:

> The illusion which inspired Tennyson and Christina Rossetti to sing so passionately about the coming of their loves is far rarer now than then . . . For truth . . . those dots mark the spot where, in search of truth, I missed the turning up to Fernham. Yes indeed, which was truth and which was illusion?[9]

Walking to Fernham is part of her thinking, and as the sentence shows nothing separates one from the other: they are one, and this is the most striking characteristic of this essay.[10] Her thinking keeps flowing – style and meaning, University as a sanctuary, novelists' conventions etc., whereas she constantly keeps in touch with 'the willows and the river and the gardens'[11] and 'the spring twilight'.[12] She is herself 'aware of a current setting in of its own accord and carrying everything forward of its own';[13] this current is what ebbs and flows in the lives of her protagonists, a stream of consciousness, or what I would call her 'stream of consciousness thinking', as if writing, thinking and living were just one continuous whole.

This continuity, which may be one of the striking features of women's writing, whether it is fiction or theory, can also be found in Cixous' works, as for example in *La*, supposedly a fiction, and in *La Venue à l'écriture*, supposedly an essay. Language is beautifully celebrated in the two passages; here she speaks of the woman's 'art for . . . giving way to alterations, mutations, adoptions, for boldly pushing connections to the point of breaking free and embraces tongue to tongue beyond the country of sense'.[14] In this extract she describes how words mix, meet and intertwine tongue to tongue, creating a newborn language of a new kind.

The second extract is also about the flow of words in this new linguistic space: 'Languages pass into my tongue, understand one another, call to each other, touch and alter one another, blend their personal pronouns together in the effervescence of differences.'[15] In this passage the emphasis lies on the exchanges and the very movement of language itself as a mobile and streaming continuity. The main metaphors in the two extracts connect the language with the body (*langue/sens/se touchent/sein*). The body which is the key metaphor in Hélène Cixous' works. The body which is here to inscribe new linguistic practices related to newborn women: metaphorical thinking again. (Although it is not quite a metaphor, for Cixous deconstructs it, as I will show later.)

Besides, there is so much fluid continuity between these two passages that they seem to belong to the same text, although one is from *La* and the other one from *La Venue à l'écriture*. They have the same texture, the same density and the same rhythm as if such an essay or such a fiction or such a poem were just one piece of writing, one piece of weaving, with the ebb and flow between theory and practice, or between the poetic and the political.

The political is woven into the poetic fabric with its own inner modulation beating the tempo in *La Venue à l'écriture*. It is a voyage through different spaces including the loose autobiographical pattern of the newborn woman as well as key issues; writing faced with the metaphysical and dialectic process of going through death towards life; the ontological question of thinking 'I'm a woman'; the pressure of patriarchal culture meant to ban women from writing; or just the urge inside the body to write. Such moments come upon us as waves, one after the other, and raise over and over again the question of what it is to be growing into a woman writer.

Becoming a woman writer is approached through the metaphor of a rending but thrilling birth delivery, as if writing were born from two powerful tides; the embrace between living a body of one's own and thinking it out. For political thinking on women's writing, identity is inescapably connected with what may be called body language:

> History, love, violence, time, work, desire inscribe it in my body . . . the whole of reality worked upon in my flesh, intercepted by my nerves, by my senses, by the labour of all my cells, projected, analysed, recomposed into a book. Vision: . . . scrolls are imprinted and unfurled throughout time and on the same History, all the stories, ephemeral changes and transformations are written, I enter into myself with my eyes closed, and you can read it.[16]

Change and continuity – the inside of the body, every single nerve and cell, contains the whole of History, whether this is in the personal or the collective dimension, as if the body had become political. The body has become a room of one's own, the very place of inscription of writing, a political space in itself which abolishes centuries of colonisation of the feminine body, including by literature.

Closely knitting together the body with the book – that is, nature with culture – means abolishing the old antagonistic dualism separating nature from culture, whether it associates women with nature and men with culture or whether, as sometimes happened with feminism, women are turned into cultural beings at the expense of their bodies. The continuity Cixous establishes between nature and culture dismantles the idea of hierarchy between the two.

The body is then given a full cultural dimension; the writing self no longer appears as just the intellectual self, or even as the androgynous mind, to quote Virginia Woolf's expression; the writing gesture is revealed at last as a physical act.

Nature and culture, equally and powerfully balanced. A tremendously powerful world of words. This world is strongly constructed and built into a universe, and as such, it is as elaborate, as abundant and as rich as James Joyce's writing, for example. This extraordinary flow of words suggests here again an excess, an overlapping, the body being a full cultural and symbolic space that is explicitly connected with the feminine. The body is then simultaneously the beloved object to be written about, and the writing subject which supports the rising of the feminine identity. Access to the symbolic order of language – that is, to culture – occurs through the body – that is, nature – thus bringing about a continuity of a new kind, raising both the book and the flesh to their highest pitch.

THE TONGUES OF ECSTASY

Through the use of metaphors and a continuity between theory and fiction, and through other practices, Hélène Cixous generates a linguistic revolution I would like to analyse more closely. This linguistic revolution may be seen as a movement towards a literal language, which, as I have already mentioned, has to do with metaphors. Derrida has used metaphors to deconstruct concepts (but not metaphors themselves) in the field of philosophical theory; as for Cixous, we may say that she deconstructs metaphors, pushing them towards their literal meaning because of her approach to the body. For example, the word blood (*sang*) in the next extract is to be heard as such because of its strangeness in the sentence which prevents us from reading it as any other word, and so enables us to perceive its meaning literally and inscribe the body.

Words and sounds interplay so that the barrier between the signified and the signifier dissolves as the musical sound is heard, or as Cixous plays with the fictive or real etymological root. The following extract is like a pure modulation of sounds, as if nothing were to be understood by these words except through their spelling:

> In me the song which, the moment it's uttered, gains instant access to language: a flux immediately text. No break, soundsense, songsound, bloodsong, everything's always already written, all the meanings are cast. (En moi le chant mais qui, dés l'émission, accède au langage: un flux immédiatement texte. Pas de coupure, sonsens, chantson, sangson, tout est toujours déjà écrit, tous les sens sont jetés.)[17]

Theoretically, from a semiotic point of view, the barrier between the signified and the signifier cannot be trespassed; however, something of a vacillation occurs in this passage in which flickering exchanges between sound (*son*) and meaning (*sens*) take place. 'Son' moves throughout the sentence as a signifier (*sonsens/chantson/sangson*) just as the signified, '*sens*', does – but is it a signified or a signifier? The interplay between the two words '*sonsens*' and '*sangson*' is worth questioning; the spelling inscribes a difference which disappears when they are pronounced – except that one is the reverse of the other . . . The same or the opposite? The word or the sound? The possible answers are all the more baffling since the connection between '*chantson*' and '*sangson*' is of the same kinds. In fact, is it the same word said (or written) twice, but in a different way – once as a signified and once as a signifier? First, it calls forth the very sound of the song in the word itself (*chantson*) and then it is said again, as a child would, lisping the '*ch*' and also giving it its fleshly dimension with '*sang*' (blood). Therefore, does this working of language focus on the song of the word woven into its meaning, or on its organic substance? Whatever the answer is, the approach can only be seen as revolutionary, for the barrier separating the signified and the signifier is actually deconstructed, liberating the musical self of the word beyond its meaning.

Language is thus made to stretch, to shift or even to swell as though it were matter and as though we could hear its working – a musical modulation, the singing of the signifier, of the musical flesh of the word. And this is what gives a different status to Hélène Cixous' use of language. It could very well be said to have common characteristics with Joyce's handling of words. But it is not a pure intellectual and linguistic game, for it springs from the body; the writing self has changed. Just as the very direction in which it is going has changed too; it proceeds towards a primitive expression, towards the literal meaning (even if it is an elaborate language) through Cixous' toying with the music of words and through her use of metaphors – images prior to language – both revealing the body of language and producing a body language.

Here is another example of the musical modulation to be heard in Cixous' writing: the word 'animots' (animals spelt 'mot' like 'word'), [18] or 'chamot' ('camel' spelt like 'word' as well), or even 'chatmeaux' (this time spelt like 'cat'). [19] This is a wide scope: all the colours of the spectrum seem to combine and shift before our eyes. It enables us to get in touch with something else in words, what I would call their animal-like and physical self (animot), or at the other end of the spectrum, their anima, their spiritual self.

This writing practice has a strong poetic impact for it produces a new creative tongue, as dense as a pure poem. It reaches a climax in the very process of dissolving the barrier between the signified and the signifier – and it is an erotic one: 'To write: making love to writing. To write through loving, to love through writing. Through writing, love opens the body without which writing shrinks.' [20]

Erotic ravishment produces an endless syntaxic and lexical turmoil at the very moment of the ecstatic embrace between words and the body. This is what Cixous labels 'étymolorgiaque', another of the numerous words she invents, from etymology and orgy, which illustrates the combination of two different kinds of words, one connected with language and the other one with delight. [21] Their union gives birth to a new word in this prolific chain woven into a polysemic language. But is it a union or a fusion? For this neologism, this newborn word melted into a new mould, could very well live on; it comes out of a musical mould shaping words to be heard as sounds – as though the process taking place were something of a fusion. I shall call it the embrace of the tongues of ecstasy. The fleshly tongue becomes one with the linguistic tongue, for in French there is a word, 'langue', which inscribes such a union, and the double scope of the word, flesh and language, sound and meaning.

But Hélène Cixous' practice, a poetic one, has even more to it, for political thinking is in its very heart.

Her political thinking does not dissolve in her practice for there is a dialectic interplay between the poetic and the political insofar as the poetic fusion experienced in words does not erode her political thinking. The linguistic breakthrough based on fusions inside words interplays dialectically with some of her concepts, for example her concept of 'difference', which challenges the feminist concept of 'equality'.

The concept of 'difference', originally stemming from Freudian theory, was much debated and even criticised, especially by American feminists, for it was seen as an 'essentialist' point of view which divided the sexes through a binary system. I think the concept of difference points to a very important step because it means breaking free from the trap of 'sameness' – which is likely to entail identification to the masculine model – implied by the feminist claim of equality. In my opinion it also deconstructs the long-lived stereotype of 'women's difference', for it is strongly connected with power associated to date with the masculine, or rather the phallic – which overthrows the very idea of an essentialist binary system. I would then stress the fact that this concept was a breakthrough because it meant a shift of perspective; the issue was at last not only seen from a social point of view, but also from a symbolic one, opening the way for a reassessment of the feminine (writing) identity . . . Fusion and difference, the two poles between which theory and practice move and interplay in Hélène Cixous' writing and thinking, involving both the poetic and the political . . .

All the characteristics of Cixous' practice point to freedom; indeed the laws of literary genres, of grammar and correct spelling, are being transgressed through her texts that teem with all kinds of neologisms, as I have shown; for as she expresses it herself, spelling has to do only with the needs of one's unconscious. It is true her writing is as free as if she were writing under the spell of her unconscious. Through the vacillation between meaning and sound in words, her language can be seen as refusing to submit to the phallic as well as symbolic order which tear away words from the body, according to Lacanian theory. Her tongues of ecstasy are then set free and they flow, spill, and stream in every direction, producing the very ebullience of ecstatic creation.

Besides, her outlook on the creative act itself represents another breakthrough, because of the emphasis it lays on delight (let us not forget she was the first one to do so, even if she does take into account the suffering) and as such it has a strong political impact, for it breaks free from the long-lived clichés about creation. The nineteenth century, among others, staged the scene of creation, strongly stressing pain, torment and guilt. Is this not an expression of the Judaeo-Christian guilt which surrounds the body, and hence the creative act as a physical act, which is therefore to be obliterated as carnal?

On the contrary, Cixous' texts endlessly celebrate the pleasure of writing, as she beautifully does here even if she speaks elsewhere of the tearing apart of one's bowels which writing implies:

> Her art of roaming through languages night and day, of roving, pirating, patting, piloting, intoxicating them . . . of enjoying the fleshly joy of her full tongue.[22]

In this passage she describes the process of writing just as she is enjoying it – so that we have a reflexive approach, that is, simultaneously, her practice and the thinking she produces. Such a language is the embodiment of a revolutionary practice creating poetic and political thinking about the very delight of language and of writing.

Virginia Woolf and Hélène Cixous have not only produced major thinking on the question of the feminine writing identity, they have also produced innovative metaphorical language which should be taken into account to redefine the question of theoretical discourses. Furthermore, their thinking leads the way to delving deeper into women's access to language and to their approach to the symbolic order of language, which may well be reconsidered with regard to Lacanian theory – for are not such hard gold concepts – nuggets – still under masculine control?

NOTES

1. Virginia Woolf, *A Room of One's Own* (London: Granada, 1977), p. 7.
2. *ibid.*, p. 5.
3. Julia Kristeva, 'Histoires d'amour', *Folio*, September 1985, p. 337. I would like to add a remark to stress the fact that this very essay, although it specifically deals with the question of metaphors, does not itself use metaphorical language and does not question it through the feminine. It uses what I would call strict theoretical discourse, contrary to the essay called 'Stabat Mater' which deals with the mother image and where even typography appears as metaphorical, although it gives a cleft image of the feminine for the typography inscribes: 'mother/discourse', with a bar in the middle. I see this as doing away with the woman through the mother, who is herself banned from discourse – a very significant process which sets up a gap between the mother and the woman as metaphors, or, here again, nature and culture. Is this because when producing discourse on some topics – metaphysics, in this case (none of women's business!) – one should stick to close (masculine?) reasoning, whereas when dealing with the feminine no such compulsion appears . . .?
4. *ibid.*, p. 341.
5. See the paper read by J. Pfeiffer at the colloquium 'Sexe et Genre' at the CNRS in Paris in March 1989.
6. *Marges de la philosophie* (Paris: Minuit, 1972).
7. *ibid.*, p. 322.

8. *A Room of One's Own*, p. 6.
9. *ibid.*, p. 16.
10. See Rachel Bowlby's paper given at Paris X in April 1989 on 'Walking, women and writing: Virginia Woolf as *flaneuse*', to be published in *Tropismes*, No 5. 1990.
11. *ibid.*, p. 16.
12. *ibid.*, p. 17.
13. *ibid.*, p. 20.
14. *La* (Paris: Editions des femmes, 1976), p. 84. All the translations from the text are mine.
15. *Her Arrival in Writing*, translated by Ann Liddle and Deborah Carpenter-Jensen, (Boston, Mass: Harvard University Press, 1990), p. 31.
16. *ibid.*, p. 63.
17. *ibid.*, p. 69.
18. *La*, p. 94.
19. *ibid.*, p. 95.
20. *La Venue à l'écriture* (Paris: Editions des femmes, 1988), p. 52 (my own translation).
21. *La*, p. 84.
22. *ibid.*, p. 89.

Part III

Gender and Texts

Introduction

It is inevitable that in a collection such as this, one should encounter Simone de Beauvoir. Not only does she seek to provide a compendious description of the female estate from childhood to motherhood and beyond to *la vieillesse*, and from female narcissism to female mysticism, she also seeks to provide an image of woman in male writing; in Montherlant, in Claudel, in Breton, in D.H. Lawrence, in Stendhal, exhausting, one is tempted to say, the different varieties of male. Her study of Stendhal has a currency beyond feminist readings of a male author, having been reproduced both in French and in English in volumes of critical essays aimed at undergraduate readers of French literature. Her presence here, then, is welcome, even if in the 1970s she was denounced as being too much of a Hegelian to be an adequate guide or standard bearer.

But forty years on, *Le Deuxième Sexe* is still seen in France as a missionary text, that is, as a life-transforming text and potentially a world-transforming one: witness the recent meeting (December 1989) of the *Association Les Femmes sont pour* held at the Sorbonne in Paris with the title: *Simone de Beauvoir: de la mémoire aux projets*.

It would nonetheless be unwise to use Simone de Beauvoir to raise a divide between writing and the theorisation of problems, on the one hand, and practical action on the other. As Naomi Segal notes in the following pages: 'The difficulty of perceiving or theorising the mother as a subject is very general'. This notion is at the heart of the section Simone de Beauvoir devotes in *The Second Sex* to 'Woman as Mother', even if the first focus is upon contraception and abortion. There is, however, and this point is crucial, a difference of tone, if one compares what Beauvoir has to say about mothers and daughters, with the triumphalist conclusion to Segal's essay, 'Patrilinear and Matrilinear'. The difference is due, one suspects, at least partly to the fact that since 1949 women have effectively measured themselves against psychoanalysis and have not found themselves wanting. But this triumph itself suggests the need to read, re-read and re-discover the texts of those women who, how knowingly is uncertain, have in an earlier age subverted established hierarchies. One thinks of George Sand and her *Mauprat*, where conventions of naming break down, potentially – since no child is born – confusing lines of descent, and where the transmission of wealth ceases to follow established patterns. One thinks, too, of Emily Brontë and *Wuthering Heights*, which beyond its own explosive force owes much, as Patricia Thompson in her *George Sand and the Victorians* has shown, to Sand and precisely to *Mauprat* in these crucial respects.

A further step may be taken whereby male and female voices are ultimately in consort, which is of course Sand's wish. But I am following the logic offered by this collection of essays, and what I have in mind is the unexpected collocation of an aristocratic English libertine poet, Rochester, and a free and unsupported woman writer, Aphra Behn. The theme which brings their two voices and other female voices, together, though in no obvious harmony, is both aptly and mysteriously chosen – *Absent from Home* – a theme depending ultimately upon a biblical text; 'in my father's house there are many mansions'. The reader of modern English novels is thereby driven to a further series of juxtapositions or collocations. Firstly, to Susan Hill's *Strange Meeting*, where in the entirely masculine world of World War I the notion of 'home' and 'homecoming' is powerfully mediated by a woman absent qua woman from the world she represents in writing; then to Philip Larkin's novel *A Girl in Winter*, where a homeless Jewess copes with a wintry wartime unhomely England she had known as homely, and provocatively so, in peacetime.

Such juxtapositions, Rochester, Behn, Hill, Larkin, suggest a canon where comparison is all and where syncretic values may predominate. Such comparisons indeed serve better than attempts to characterise women's writing by its own alleged thematics.

The question of a canon may arise in other contexts, and it does here, apropos of Rabelais. In one of the essays that follow it is suggested that Rabelais may well be under a feminist interdict, to the detriment of women. The charge is a real one, at least historically, and is derived from the *ukases* coming out of America in the 1970s. Rabelais, of course, can be interpreted in terms of tenets common to the Russian formalists and to German theorists of the reception of literary works. Literary texts, it is held, destabilise value systems, and this Rabelais does. And women should profit thereby. Rabelais destabilises, Clarice Lispector, to take another symbolic name, destabilises. Is there a common measure between the two? Is destabilisation an *impossible* notion, which makes it appear desirable; or a cosy concept to frustrate male and female writers, once again, of their specificity?

K.M.

Chapter 10

Patrilinear and Matrilinear

Naomi Segal

Here is a puzzle. I have twelve socks loose in a drawer; six of them are red and six are blue. How many do I need to take, in the dark, in order to have a pair?

The answer is three, because I need the number of possible colours plus one, which is certain to give me two of the same colour: a pair. But a curiously large proportion of people asked this puzzle, after reaching the first stage of the logic – that I need the whole group plus one – give the answer seven. Their reason is that I need one red and one blue one to make up a pair. When pressed, they laugh and realise the error but not perhaps the pervasiveness of the assumption on which it is based.

We all know that a pair of socks is two socks identical in form and colour. But most people think of a pair rather in terms of a couple, in which complementarity is supposed to be the basis of juxtaposition: two things not of a kind but of two mutually adjusted kinds, a complete set, a pigeon pair, male and female plugs.

Until recently at least, childcare advice in books and magazines universally referred to the child as 'he'. A reason commonly cited (in the years when this began to be an issue) was that it would be most confusing, since the mother must be a 'she', to deal in two alike pronouns all the time. A similar point is made in a study of 1977 by the critic Roy Pascal, discussing the narrator of Jane Austen's novels: 'so truly is this impersonal narrator the "spirit of the story", that one cannot ascribe him/her a sex, and it is misleading to use either "him" or "her" for this function; I use "him" throughout this study in the same way one uses "man" for "mankind" (in Jane Austen's case it usefully makes a clearer distinction between the author and the narrator).'[1] In both these cases the anxiety to make a complementary pair of mother and infant, author and narrator is something very special – it never takes possession of people writing about doctors and patients or about Balzac and *his* spirit-of-the-story narrator. Here (unlike the case of the socks, in which something rather different is at stake) the commentator is dealing with a woman in the position of subject in a pair in

131

which the second figure functions as her other; she is, in both cases, in the place of the mother. What each commentator does is preempt the possibility of a different complementarity of two females. They make the other a male because in this way, I suggest, the mother is subtly stripped of her status as subject.

We all know women are the second sex. There is one couple in which the first, the author, is always a woman, and this is the mother–child couple. But if many, most, of us are not mothers, all of us are or have been children and if transference is the key trope which shapes our reasoning, we continue to be and think as children as long as we live. Thus when we speak of the mother–child pair we more readily put ourselves in the shoes of Oedipus, not Jocasta, the infant marked by the phallus and not the legislative mother. For the mother is never perceived as legislative. Law, reason, power, language are real insofar as they are perceived as coming late, coming from the father, 'being inserted' disruptively into a pair that drops apart to let the father 'insert' the child into the symbolic. Dorothy Dinnerstein has argued that the childcare system wherein infants are nearly always mothered by women causes the child (and the remembering adult) to find all initiatives of power from women uncanny and overwhelming, and to prefer to attribute the canny, motivation, reason to males. A sentence in which the mother is subject is almost impossible to form. If she appears in that position, we tend to mark the limit of her function with an other who is masculine – son or son *manqué*.

The difficulty of perceiving or theorising the mother as a subject is very, general. Observe the switch in the second sentence of the following remark by Julia Kristeva: 'c'est vers la mère que convergent non seulement les besoins pour la survie mais surtout les premières aspirations mimétiques. Elle est l'autre sujet, un objet qui garantit mon être de sujet' (we direct towards the mother not only our needs for survival but above all our earliest mimetic aspirations. She is the other subject, an object that guarantees my being as a subject).[2] The rapid changeover here shows how the mother's subjectivity is strictly constrained by the child's desire for her as mirror. Her being as a subject is allowed to be no more than a mimetic function – effectively she is, by her very moves or initiatives, put back into the passive, the object position.

Psychoanalysis endorses this constraint on the possibility of the mother's knowledge. In Freud the authority of the analyst as father survives the concept of counter-transference. It has been well observed how in the 'Dora' narrative Freud fails to incorporate the desire of Dora for Frau K., so that their mutual communication – always over the question of teaching and speaking sexuality – is marginalised in favour of the more easily palatable possibility of Dora's desire of Herr K. and a consequential chain of transference from her father onto the analyst. Several commentators note how this squeezes out not just Dora's homosexual desire but also the repressed tie to her mother, in which Freud willingly colludes. John Forrester has suggested that the most deeply repressed countertransference is that in which Freud would have to recognise himself as taking up the role of mother to Dora: 'as likely as not, for both of them, the secret lay in the picture of the Madonna – but they preferred not to find the word to say it'.[3] What silences both the daughter and the analyst is the impossibility of the mother's subject position. The whole phenomenon of countertransference is a masculine move, based upon a knowledge that must be that of the father.

The analyst's knowledge is, as Lacan insists, a fiction in which the patient partakes by suspending disbelief. But this very observation implies that the analyst can (and should) know something the patient does not: the genuine limits of that supposed knowledge. Thus, here too the analyst has an advantage without which countertransference could not function in the cure. The unconscious feelings of the analyst differ from the transference of the patient in that it is the analyst's job to pre-empt them, make them conscious, make them work for him. Placed initially in the object-position, he overturns this by his pre-emptive knowledge, making himself master of the unconscious processes of both people, the patient's because these are the object of the work, and his own because they similarly serve the cure. Feeling is changed into knowledge, and precisely as he sites the origin of everything in the patient's psyche, he makes his own the organ of control. The patient ends up, like the mother, a subject that is more really an object: initiating only at the price of ignorance. The analyst develops in this sea-change nicely from infant to father.

If the fathers and the sons think thus about mothers, what about the daughters, and the mothers themselves? There is a curious fact about the many feminist studies of the mother–child relation published in the late 1970s and early 1980s. Those which spoke from the position of mother were almost all written by the mothers of sons; those which dealt with the mother–daughter relationship were spoken from the position of the daughter. Judith Arcana's pair of popular studies, *Our Mothers' Daughters* (1979) and *Every Mother's Son* (1983) show a typical morphology. The first, shorter in length by about a third, is a consciousness-raising act of reassessing the position of the feminist daughter: how are we to understand our mothers? It concludes on a note of optimism based in an upturning of the power-roles: daughter will re-educate mother, teaching her 'mother–daughter sisterhood [as] the consciousness we must seek'. In this it is similar to many other discussions of mother–daughter reconciliation, which begin by biting back expressions of anger and end with the offer of elder-sisterhood. What precisely happens to bring this about? 'Sixty-three per cent of women I studied', Arcana declares, 'said that they consciously tried not to model themselves as women after their mothers'.[4] Individual interviews in this book (and by implication the questions that provoked them) show that the daughter–mother pair is perceived as a metonymic phenomenon: behind the resented mother is a social structure of which she herself is a victim–daughter. The tendency to read back the dyad as a chain without origin is characteristic of all these analyses. To blame the mother is so tempting that the only way it can be avoided is to cast her as unknowing once again, herself a helpless daughter, dominant only as the channel of the others' control.

Arcana's second book could, no doubt, only be written after the first. Its title borrows a ready-made phrase, and has a subtitle which already delimits the woman's function: 'the role of mothers in the making of men'. Dedicated to the author's son, 'who is both the question and the answer' – so where is the place of her authorship? – it begins with a chapter called 'The Book of Daniel' and proceeds to others named 'Raising Sons', 'Making Men' and 'Fathers'. In the perplexity that is the woman's encounter with her beloved enemy, the boy elbows for his space and she debates how she is to give him it.

The other best-known studies from the mother's place similarly come from mothers of sons: Adrienne Rich, Jane Lazarre, Mary Kelly, Julia-Kristeva. What they have to say is indeed urgent. And I confess it, I decided on this topic for a book when I discovered my second child was going to be a son. The reason is not far to seek. There is something uncanny – for some an anticipated triumph, for others a new crisis – about our known body reproducing itself as a gendered other. How is a woman to hold power over the creature that will soon hold power over her? What is it for a feminist to be fulfilling Freud's promised second-best by giving birth to the penis through her 'not-all' genital? How is she then to nurture a good man in a world that requires her to produce soldiers and pornographers? Or how to follow Winnicott's injunction to know exactly when to stop holding and start letting go lest the child be castrated? Architects of our own rejection, we can perhaps only find some mode of control over this bizarre process of loss and self-loss if we make a study of it in writing. So the mothers of sons frame and date each nappy and tooth and the mothers of daughters seem not to record, not to puzzle over, their girls' moves or their own passion for them. Is this because, as the Lacanians would argue, the arrival of the phallus here as elsewhere precipitates the accession to language – we speak with, of and after the male input? Are the daughter–mother studies gestures of separation which must precede the real debate of how to contend with and speak fitly of our once-only and brief position of power over a male? Why does the mother of the daughter not write?[5]

Nancy Chodorow's non-Kleinian object-relations theory, in *The Reproduction of Mothering*, has been hugely influential over the last ten years.[6] She argues that mothers cannot cathect male and female children differently: their relation to their daughters is characteristically pre-oedipal and narcissistic, a relation of like to like; with their sons they encounter an other to whom they respond sexually, oedipally. Mothers thus collude in the process whereby, as is so frequently argued, men become men by separating from the woman who mothers them, recognising her as different in all the ways patriarchy sets, and aligning themselves with the father in a joke that excludes her. In this same argument, girls separate less radically, encounter the mother as another themselves, stay with her on the social margin, servicing those who more nearly have the phallus. Viewed positively, by Chodorow or Carol Gilligan for example, this means an aptitude for alliance, a warmth and readiness to feel; viewed negatively it means failure to take off, at worst a Freudian neurosis or Lacanian psychosis.[7]

The view that mothers cathect their sons and daughters differently is, I believe, based on the same knee-jerk reaction that makes us consider a pair has to consist of one red sock and one blue sock, as a mother requires a son to complete her sentence, and make passive sense of her position as subject. Three books give three different reasons for it. Dinnerstein in 1976:

> The mother . . . is likely to experience a more effortless identification, a smoother communication, with a girl baby than with a boy baby. With him, there is more difference and separateness, more of a barrier to be bridged.

Luise Eichenbaum and Susie Orbach in 1983:

> Built into a mother's experience with a son from the beginning of his life is the knowledge that he will become his own person in the world. She accepts the fact that he will become a man and move out into the world to create and commit himself to a family of his own. But although she expects her daughter to have a family too, she expects this to be an extension of her own family rather than a separate entity.

Rosalind Coward in 1984:

> Some women have described the experience of finding their sons utterly different from the outset, a difference based just on the strangeness of the body. Baby boys have bodies which do not invite identification but rather fascination for women.[8]

All these arguments represent something real but they feel particularly like excuses. The separateness Dinnerstein cites is precisely what follows, not what causes, the perception of a gendered other. Eichenbaum and Orbach get into a tangle in which the exchange of women which prescribes that, as Luce Irigaray puts it, women's genealogy is dissolved into men's, is whisked away to be replaced by the loss of the son into his own family and the daughter still under your roof.[9] The strangeness Coward cites is just the beginning of the enigma: what can we be sensing as masculine in the boy baby's body, which is just as soft (including his penis) as a girl's – as the protagonist of 'Verity Bargate's novel *No Mama No* discovers to her surprise, when her infant son, dressed in girl's clothing, turns out to be 'all softness, nothing male about that sweet pliable body'.[10] In each case, the fundamental reasons for our differing reaction (if indeed we have a different reaction) are left unexplored, as though once again it were not the mother's place to have knowledge of what she does.

If we women indeed find it difficult to take up knowledge of our experience of motherhood, that is surely because of something at once deeply unconscious and abstract in our encounter with the question. We are embedded in a system which perceives maternity as a function: the mother receives, carries and gives forth to the paternal family a child stamped with that family's name. In this she plays a role less in a pair than in a chain.

I want to argue that there are two genealogical chains in which the mother may function. Either she is positioned in a patrilinear structure, giving a son to her father or husband, or she functions in a matrilinear chain, offering a daughter to her mother. In the first case, the male child makes her a negative, a producer of what she is not; she is, as Freud prescribes, the temporary owner, the partial maker, of a penis which proves her sex a no-thing. In the second case she reproduces herself, finds herself confronted by an other that contradicts the premise of pairing by complementarity. To the woman she makes she has the crisis of seeing a self in the object position that makes her subject. It is not very surprising that this is rarely written. We have little language that can encompass this relation of otherness, for it prescribes that the grammar of pronouns must be surpassed into a naming free of the *nom du père*. Both the name of the mother and the no of the mother – that is, the mother as authority in the world or as internalised superego – have little place in the discourse of patriarchy. The power of motherhood, its dual function as knowledge and as desire, is as yet largely unwritten.

I have space to offer only two sets of examples of patrilinear and matrilinear mothers. The first comes from the male-authored novel of adultery.[11] In those novels (and they are among the most celebrated) where the woman is a mother, she tends to fall into one of two roles. In such fictions as *Le Rouge et le noir*, *L'Education sentimentale*, *Anna Karenina* and *Pierre et Jean*, she is the mother of one or more sons. Desired by the hero, she has a husband presented after the model of cuckolds as weak, laughable, no serious rival for desire. But her son is more precisely a threat. When the author chooses to oppose a real barrier to desire, he tends to make the son fall ill, the mother succumb to pangs of guilt, the paternal God appear as proscriber of illegitimate love. The woman is thus re-placed in the chain from which the young man's desire might have seemed to emancipate her, and she becomes once again the mother who cannot know her own desire. Even if the hero 'overcomes' her love of the son it is by reinstating her in the maternal position as central, non-functioning link in a patriarchal genealogy. By only a small adjustment, the homosocial bond is kept intact.

Women who have children in male-authored fiction are a small enough group, commonly becoming pregnant – frequently as the result of a super-potent wedding-night – in order that they can suffer obstetrical trauma. Women who give birth to daughters are an even smaller sub-group and a startlingly high number of them are adulteresses – Emma Bovary, Hester Prynne, Effi Briest, Anna Karenina, the mothers of Atala or Alissa (more scarlet letters) – not to mention other sinners such as Thérèse Des-queyroux, Germinie Lacerteux, Nadja. There is something in women who are perceived as desiring which, it seems, deserves the punishment of reproducing themselves; they have disqualified themselves from the uniquely gratifying form of motherhood that Freud identifies in the birth of a son. Emma Bovary discovers after a long labour that the baby is a girl; she groans and turns her face to the wall. Anna Karenina is condemned to adore her son by Karenin and neglect the daughter she has by Vronsky. But something else occasionally happens. Between Hester Prynne and Pearl or the matrilinear Effi Briest and her maid Roswitha (the daughter as the absent centre of their bond) an enclosed social unit is formed in which, for all the tensions of internalised guilt, there is something not just of narcissism and self-repetition but a potential other-world in which women speak or love.

These are men's readings of the mother–child couple. They show up as two possible structures: the woman transferred from one paternal chain to another, or the woman marginalised into a cellular space in which the paternal is in abeyance, a matrilinear chain held up as negative utopia, harem, gynaeceum, prison.

In the novel of adultery, the male author creating a mother of sons offers one wishful fantasy: her love is his one way or the other, directly or indirectly she welcomes him to her bosom. In the mother of daughters he incarnates a less readily avowed wish: to see in what occult manner she loves the child more exactly of her flesh, in whom no mark of the husband remains, the scarlet letter shows up and shares the unique 'wound' that makes her mother.

I have no space to go further than a brief suggestion, but it is only through the feminist critique of anthropology, I believe, that we can begin to understand this idea of the mother as wounded. The theory that women are not complete but castrated, on which psychoanalysis and some versions of feminism depend, is based on an implicit conviction that when a body bleeds it must be from a wound. But the bleeding of menstruation or birth signals no damage. The reason for the conviction is perhaps that, while not all of us have given birth, we have all been born, and transference dictates that it is tremendously difficult for us to imagine that once we have left it the mother's body can be whole. If we examine an extreme version of the masculine rite of passage, penile sub-incision as it is practised in some aboriginal tribes (and let us not ignore that all such rites, including the benign and perhaps hygienic practice of circumcision, separate the boy from the mother, surround him with men and mark him with a cut), we can see this particularly clearly.[12] In these tribes, where the men gather in groups to anoint each other with blood from their cuts, women who are menstruating or giving birth are kept rigidly apart from each other. The self-inflicted wound, vicarious imitation of a benign bleeding the men cannot reproduce, is the horrific representation of something tabooed because powerful, powerful because uncanny, uncanny because it is *not* castration. We know that women living together tend to have synchronised cycles. Is, then, the occulted space in which women are perceived to speak, act or bleed dangerously, both the original and the signified of those rituals that subtend any communication of man and man?

My other example of patrilinear and matrilinear mothers comes from that most male-authored of all texts, the Hebrew Bible. I want to offer a comparison of two mothers from either end of the text and the lineage, Sarah and Naomi.

In a study of mothers in the Bible, Esther Fuchs takes from Robert Alter the following topos: it 'consists of three major thematic components: the initial barrenness of the wife, a divine promise of future conception, and the birth of a son'.[13] Fuchs goes on to discuss the developing variants in the stories of Sarah, Rebecca, Rachel, Hannah and the Shunamite woman. In each narrative, the autonomy of the woman is increasingly recognised and portrayed, although all the women continue to be presented as wives whose desire is consonant with the continuance of the male lineage and whose satisfaction is at one with their role as essential link. The only hint, perhaps, of the quirkiness of biblical genealogy is in God's repeated preference of young sons over older, a preference both Rebecca and Rachel anticipate. For these two women, as for Hannah and the Shunamite, the husbands (and other men) play the role almost of cuckold, well-fooled by a more perspicacious woman and a God she comes to address directly. But I am not aware that the figure of Naomi has been discussed as a late and matrilinear version of this topos. In the comparison I wish to make, the story of Naomi's progress from aged barrenness to the nurturing of a baby not even related to her is a matrilinear process that depends on the voluntary alliance of women.[14]

First, Sarah. The death of Sarah appears in the text immediately after the narrative of the binding of Isaac. Rabbis have interpreted this juxtaposition as an indication of how deeply wounded she is by the willingness of her husband to sacrifice the son of their old age. In their eyes, typically of the mother of the patrilinear bond, she holds the maternal role to be her whole existence, its near-transgression must cause her death. But we could look somewhat differently at the timing and significance of Sarah's death.

Abram, the founder of Judaism, is promised that his seed will become a great nation as numberless as the stars, but he is eighty-five and his wife Sarai ten years younger and they have no children. Sarai then decides to offer her handmaid Hagar to Abram as a surrogate mother: 'go to my maid; perhaps I will get children through her' (Genesis 16: 2). When Hagar conceives, she despises her mistress and Abram allows Sarai to send her away into the desert. Found wandering by a fountain, Hagar is consoled by an angel who tells her her son will be a misanthrope but father to another great nation; she returns and gives birth to Ishmael.

In this first phase we see Sarai's attempt to fulfil her wifely role indirectly founder on the perennial risk of surrogacy: the barren woman displaced by another in the significant chain. But thirteen years later God changes their names to Abraham and Sarah and promises that she will indeed bear a son. At the first announcement, Abraham laughs to himself; at the second (by divine messengers) Sarah, overhearing, laughs to herself. She is well past the menopause, her husband is almost a hundred: 'now that I have passed the age of child-bearing, could I have such pleasure, with my husband an old man too?' (Genesis 18: 12). God's response to Abraham's laughter is to prescribe the name Isaac ('Yitzhak: he shall laugh') for the child; his response to Sarah's is to chide her for thinking anything – from hearing laughter in the heart to inducing conception in a woman of ninety – is beyond his powers.

Thus the woman's moment of irreverence is stifled in the gratifying production of the son who will breed multitudes. The first of the matriarchs, she earns her place as the mother of the nation, as it were replacing Eve the sinner. Her name means princess, sovereign. Almost an equal to Abraham – who twice saves his life at the risk of her virtue by the quasi-incestuous expedient of claiming she is his sister – she takes her place on the first throne of legitimate motherhood. For a second time we see her cut herself off from other women by casting out Hagar and Ishmael so that Isaac should not have to share his inheritance. Against Abraham's wishes, but approved by God who repeats that the lineage must go down through Sarah's son, she insists on their departure, aligning herself exclusively within the triadic male chain. It is soon after this that God tempts Abraham and demands that he sacrifice his beloved son.

The love-test is made between men. With good reason commentators have called this a version of the Oedipus complex. As Ruth Kartun-Blum has shown, almost all male Israeli poets of recent years (and no female ones) have written a version of the binding of Isaac, so urgently and elliptically does it restate the conflict and tension between father and son. [15] The father takes his obedient boy (whose age may well be over thirty, if we judge by Sarah's age at her death) up the mountain with the knife and the kindling but no lamb. Both son and father dazzle by their appalling submissiveness; jointly accepting that 'God will see to it that he has a lamb for the burnt offering . . . they [go on] the two of them together' (Genesis 22: 8). What few of the poets point out, taking here the viewpoint of the heartlessly sublime patriarch, there that of the innocent, benighted son, is what really makes this scene oedipal. The inner struggle of each man, and the more violently suppressed mutual murder of their conflict, are both swallowed up by the repeated unity of their agreement upon the gesture of sacrifice to their greater maker, the Lord. Thus in the structure, parricide is replaced by filicide all down the line. They deserve the reward of the ram caught patiently in a thicket, a fit victim for the common motion of partnership they have willingly offered the deity. The final blessing and multiplication of the patrilineage follows immediately upon the burning of the ram.

In the next chapter, Sarah dies in Kiryat-arba (the city of the four) and Abraham mourns and buries her. Touchingly, it is said, she cannot outlive the shock of realising her husband almost murdered their child: this is understood as the poignantly human reaction to the excessive sublimity shared by the men in whom no movement of rebellion to divine ordinance is perceived. Thus male readers find her death apt and moving, while women may feel her utter subordination to the patrilinear chain as somehow distasteful. But I think there is something else to find in Sarah's death. The binding kills not so much the son as the mother, not because the son almost died but because he did not die. In unbinding Isaac and offering up the ram in his place, Abraham gives life to his son a second and more important time. Exactly as in the Oedipus, where the boy dances gracefully into his father's embrace on the joint understanding that, after all, in all that matters the male lineage reproduces itself without significant intervention of the woman (for her desire is not what really counts, since the mutual murder of father and son is more surely productive than the lonely labour of the mother) here their triumph makes her entirely redundant. The princess is not on the throne after all, her beauty offered up to Pharaoh and Abimelech as a sibling-exchange to keep the men from each other's throats, her body required to start the generations, but not needed once the four – God, father, son and male animal – have come together to exclude her.

The story of Naomi appears much more tangentially in the biblical text, in the final section, the Writings. It is usually read as the triumphant tale of Ruth's motherhood as a reward for her loyalty as much to God's people as to her beloved mother-in-law, but I want to look most closely at the fate of Naomi, from declared barrenness to what can be read as a miraculous lactation sealing an indirect fertility. Naomi is the inverse of Sarah in several ways. As opposed to Abraham, who from the start is destined for plenty and fruitfulness, her husband takes his family out of their native land by reason of famine. Wife and mother of two sons, she has everything she wants until the famine brings the death of all her menfolk within ten years. Only 'the woman was left, out of her two sons and her husband' (Ruth 1: 5): here the woman becomes protagonist by an almost scandalous default, and the order of the bereavements stresses not only the later loss of the young men but perhaps also the greater disappointment to her to be left without hope of grandchildren.[16]

Naomi has failed after all to do what was the source of Sarah's pride: despite her fertility she has not passed on her husband's seed as a mother should because her sons have died. She is alone in the foreign land of Moab and decides to return now that (precisely in the hour of her bereavement) the famine is lifted in her own country. Her two daughters-in-law follow her. She instructs them to return to their families, since widowhood releases them from the genealogy of their husbands: unlike her they have no obligation to Elimelech's line. Rather, it would be incumbent on her to produce more sons for them to marry if she could, but as she says:

> have I any more sons in my womb who could be your husbands? Go back, my daughters, go. I am too old to be with a husband. Even if I said, there is still hope for me to be with a husband at night and I gave birth to sons, would you wait for them until they grew up, would you remain widows for their sake without taking husbands? No, my daughters, I feel very bitter on your account that the Lord's hand has gone out against me. (Ruth 1: 11–13)[17]

In this speech Naomi begins her move towards a matrilinear position. Left without menfolk, she stands central in a triad of women, and what she says to the two younger ones shows a lively consciousness of the obligations women bear to each other. She realises, first of all, that she has only had them on loan: they belong not just to their people and the second husbands that may be found for them but more precisely 'each woman to her mother's house' (Ruth 1: 8). She perceives her duty to compensate their widowhood with almost comic literalness, but in portraying her inability to make men for them a second time she is doing two most impressive things. Firstly, she is seeing herself as their double, her motherhood provoked imaginatively by their need for motherhood; secondly, what she is (extraordinarily) offering is to bear sons *to give to them*. Naomi is wishing to put Orpah and Ruth in the position of husband to her: she would secure their lineage if she could.

Naomi's doubling of the young women's needs is a nice reply to the cross-generational bonding of Abraham and Isaac: it differs by being a matter of choice or gift to women with whom she has no blood-tie, only an analogy of loss. The reproduction of sons becomes a homage to other women, another kind of surrogacy which does not involve replacement.

Both Orpah and Ruth are moved by Naomi's speech, but while Orpah reluctantly agrees to leave, 'Ruth stuck close to her' (Ruth 1: 4). Ruth's famous plea of loyalty repeatedly stresses that the social and religious 'conversion' undertaken is above all personal in motive: 'do not implore me to leave you or to turn back from following you, for where you go, I shall go, and where you lodge, I shall lodge; your people are my people and your God is my God. In the place where you die, I shall die and there I shall be buried. May God do such things to me and more, for [only] death can bring a parting between me and you' (Ruth 1: 16–7). While this passionate declaration has the ring of love and its final terms especially are reminiscent of what became the Christian wedding-vows, Ruth is offering Naomi not so much a kind of marriage, a complementary pair, as the tie of mother and daughter. For her sake she is replacing her 'mother's house' with migration and an unknown grave.

From this point on Naomi habitually calls Ruth 'my daughter', though the narrator is careful to stress at every opportunity her foreign origin and their in-law relationship, as if to draw attention to the voluntary nature of their attachment. Ruth is first characterised to Boaz in terms of her loyalty to Naomi and when the latter sends her to him she describes him with an ambiguous possessive: 'this man is a kinsman of ours, one of our redeemers' (Ruth 2: 20).[18] The arrangement is initiated by Naomi and the levirate redemption, carefully detailed as the required negotiation by which Boaz can lay claim to Ruth, is the way for the man to '[buy] all that belonged to Elimelech, and all that belonged to Chilion and Mahlon, from the hand of Naomi' (Ruth 4: 9). Thus when Boaz takes up the genealogical duty to continue the line of Elimelech, he is the link by which Naomi fulfils her promise to give Ruth a husband.

Ruth re-enters the male genealogy and is celebrated by the (male) elders as worthy to take her place alongside the matriarchs Rachel and Leah, but unlike them and Rebecca (and Sarah, if we recall the pretence of siblinghood made by Abraham) she is attached to her husband by no preceding blood-tie. She marries and bears a son, the ancester of King David. The child is received by 'the women' who declare to Naomi: 'blessed be the Lord, who has not left you without a redeemer today; his name will be cried aloud in Israel. He will be a restorer of your spirits and will support you in your old age, for your daughter-in-law, who loved you, gave birth to him – she who was more good to you than seven sons' (Ruth 4: 14–15). Here the female chorus (heard almost nowhere else in the Bible) mitigates the reward of a male child, though not negatively: for the pleasure of a son can be surpassed by the love of a daughter by choice; and the gifts promised through him to Naomi are realised by another startling reversal. 'Naomi took the boy and laid him in her bosom and became his nurse' (Ruth 4: 16). The terms here do not specify, but can be understood to hint at, a miracle of lactation. Naomi takes the place of mother to him, restoring a kind of fertility that replaces all she had lost. Not only does she become, in this way, a mother to Ruth's child, who bears no direct kinship to herself, but by another remarkable reversal she is also described in the formula of paternity: 'a son is born to Naomi' (Ruth 4: 17).[19] Motherhood and fatherhood came to rest in her. Genealogy becomes maternity, and the patriarchal line is replaced by a mutuality of women.[20]

Ruth is the eponym of this Book (one of the only two in the Bible named after female protagonists) but as a variant of the annunciation topos, it is really the tale of Naomi's reversed barrenness. In the end it is rather Ruth than her mother-in-law who is the surrogate mother: she is the bearer of the child, but it is really Naomi's. The mystery of daughterly passion is embodied in acts that are both courageous and modest: Ruth's initiatives are bold but take the form of replies, obedience. We can see her original move of attachment to Naomi as being an emotional reply to the latter's offer of bearing a son for her sake. At the end she performs the ultimate courtesy: recompensing with fine exactitude the offer of Naomi, Ruth passes her motherhood to her. The first promise of exchange is answered by a choice of filiation, and on the basis of this mother–daughter bond, they twice exchange a man between them – first Boaz, then his son – keeping intact the primary pairing of women across generations that marks the matrilinear contract.

Something else emerges from the comparison between Sarah and Naomi. The two figures are distinguished in addition to the differences of patrilinearity and matrilinearity by an opposition between endogamy and exogamy. When the two sexes mate, we observe, blood-kinship is a repeated adjunct, more or less pre-empting choice: like royalty, Isaac or Jacob are just lucky if they also manage to fall in love with the predestined cousin. Where this topos is missing, Abraham twice creates it by his lie that Sarah is his sister, thus familiarly linking heterosexual desire (it is because Sarah is so beautiful in other men's eyes that she can be both a danger and a sop) to incest. But in the story of Naomi and Ruth, a mating of the same sex, stress is constantly laid on the foreignness of Ruth and, as a direct and implicitly essential link, the extent of her choice. Ruth acts knowingly and voluntarily in choosing Naomi and Naomi only slightly less so in accepting Ruth. The exchange of Boaz is a like gift, a moment when the older woman offers and the younger woman takes up the masculine mysteries of the Hebrew legal system. Ostensibly the objects of exchange, they have pre-empted the structure by choice and desire. Finally, culture is crowned by nature when the infant is shared by them, one giving birth, the other nurturing so that the 'restoration of life and nourishment in old age' predicted as the boy's future gifts to Naomi are similarly pre-empted and shared. In these terms, the baby boy is almost feminised. Or rather, he resembles the Judaic God, whose defining privileges – creation and providence – are so patently displaced from those of the female body. Both male figures are miraculous precisely insofar as they appropriate women's gifts and offer them back when women no longer have them: to the old woman the child will give life and nourishment, just as God may restore gestation and lactation.

The miracle of the annunciation, with all its variants, can be understood, as Fuchs suggests, as a sign of God's utter control and men's superiority – 'the implication is that Yahweh violates nature's rules and gives the barren woman a child because of her husband's magnanimity and despite her pettiness' (p. 121) – since those faculties that define the female remain in God's hand and are allocated only according to patrilinear needs.[21] But it could also be read as hiding another motive. Barren women are aberrations, fit objects for the intervention of a mutant God. Before the end of fertility, or in the massive majority of women, the functions here donated as a reward are simply there. Miracles distort and reroute nature: they must do so in order to illustrate the *extremis* of the principle of masculine providence, for the mythic male parthenogenesis that is the base structure of monotheistic patriarchy is a drastic compensation for the fear of expendability. The most deeply repressed fact of the whole structure (which, like all repressed facts, returns in dreams or texts to haunt us) is that women are not always or only links in the passing-on of a male line. They give birth to daughters, can love them and be loved by them, and this can be a matter not of the 'sterile narcissism' of like to like, but of choice, knowledge and desire.

NOTES

This essay is largely based on the introductory chapter of my *Mothers and Daughters and Sons* (forthcoming, Cambridge: Polity Press, 1992). All translations from French and Hebrew, unless otherwise attributed, are my own, and reference is given to the original text. Further references to a cited text will appear after quotations; passages without page-reference are from the last-cited page. Unless otherwise stated, all italics are the author's and all ellipses mine.

1. Roy Pascal, *The Dual Voice* (Manchester: Manchester University Press, 1977), pp. 45–6.
2. Julia Kristeva, *Pouvoirs de l'horreur*, (Paris: Seuil, 1980), p. 43.
3. John Forrester, 'The Untold Pleasures of Psychoanalysis: Freud, Dora and the Madonna', *The Seductions of Psychoanalysis* (Cambridge: Cambridge University Press, 1990), p. 61. See also Charles Bernheimer and Claire Kahane (eds), *In Dora's Case* (London: Virago, 1985).
4. Judith Arcana, *Our Mothers' Daughters* (London, 1979), p. 34.
5. She does, of course, though in far smaller quantity. Such collections as Karen Payne's *Between Ourselves* (London: Picador, 1983), and Tillie Olsen's *Mother to Daughter, Daughter to Mother* (London: Virago, 1984), present writings that go in both directions, and other examples are the article by Sara Maitland in Stephanie Dowrick and Sibyl Grundberg (eds.), *Why Children?* (London: Women's Press, 1980), pp. 78–103, and Marianne Grabrucker, *There's a Good Girl*, translated by Wendy Philipson (Frankfurt and London: Women's Press, 1988).
6. Nancy Chodorow, *The Reproduction of Mothering* (Berkeley, Los Angeles and London: University of California Press, 1978).
7. Carol Gilligan, *In a Different Voice* (Cambridge, Mass., and London: Harvard University Press, 1982).
8. Dorothy Dinnerstein, *The Rocking of the Cradle and the Ruling of the World* (elsewhere entitled *The Mermaid and the Minotaur*) (London: Women's Press, 1987), p. 68; Luise Eichenbaum and Susie Orbach, *Understanding Women* (Harmondsworth: Penguin, 1983), p. 57; Rosalind Coward, *Female Desire* (London: Routledge and Kegan Paul, 1984), p. 228.
9. Luce Irigaray, *Sexes et parentés* (Paris: Editions de Minuit, 1987), p. 15.
10. Verity Bargate, *No Mama No* (London: Fontana, 1979), p. 112. The protagonist embraces her infant son whom she has dressed in girls' clothing and temporarily renamed: 'I picked Rainbow up and held her hard, as Joy had done, to see what she might have felt but she was all softness, nothing male about that sweet pliable body.'

11. All the examples that follow are developed at length in *Mothers and Daughters and Sons*. For a similar discussion of the confessional *récit* in French, see my *Narcissus and Echo* (Manchester: Manchester University Press, 1988).

12. See Chris Knight, 'Lévi-Strauss and the dragon: *Mythologiques* reconsidered in the light of an Australian aboriginal myth', *Man*, no. 18, pp. 21–50; and Irene Elia, 'The dragon-slayers must have babies', unpublished paper delivered to the Women's Study Group, Cambridge on 19 April 1988.

13. Esther Fuchs, 'The literary characterization of mothers and sexual politics in the Hebrew Bible', in Adela Yarbro Collins (ed.), *Feminist Perspectives on Biblical Scholarship* (Chico, Cal.: Scholar's Press, 1985), p. 119. I am indebted for help on the Hebrew and midrashic sources to Ruth Kartun-Blum and Nicholas de Lange.

14. The language used in Ruth 4: 16 does not explicitly say that Naomi becomes the child's wetnurse, though the usual translations into English have the ambiguous 'nurse'. The Hebrew 'omenet' has the main meaning of 'childminder' or educator, but can also have the broader and more ambiguous sense of 'foster-mother'. See F. Brown, S. R. Driver and C. A. Briggs, *A Hebrew and English Lexicon of the Old Testament* (Oxford: Clarendon, 1959), p. 52. See also Phyllis Trible, *God and the Rhetoric of Sexuality* (Philadelphia: Philadelphia Fortress, 1978), p. 69. Despite various disagreements, I have found the chapters on Ruth in this book and in Mieke Bal, *Lethal Love* (Bloomington, Ind.: Indiana University Press, 1987), illuminating.

15. Ruth Kartun-Blum, '"Where does this wood come from?": The binding of Isaac as a test-case in modern Hebrew poetry', *Prooftexts* no. 8 (1988), 293–310.

16. L. Rabinowitz, in H. Freedman and M. Simon, *Midrash Rabbah VIII: Ruth, Ecclesiastes* (London: Soncino, 1961), pp. vii–viii, shows that this midrash concentrates at great length on the figures of Ruth, Boaz and Elimelech – the latter being the oddest, since the Scroll says more or less nothing about him. The centrality of Naomi is generally ignored.

17. Curiously, the two pronominal phrases here ('for them/for their sake' and 'on your account') are reversed in gender, the daughters-in-law being addressed in the masculine, the putative sons referred to in the feminine.

18. The Authorized Version tautologously has: 'the man is near of kin unto us, one of our next kinsmen', but the Hebrew 'go'el' means 'redeemer', both in the sense of a close relative entitled to 'redeem' the widow by whom his family line must be continued, and also in the general sense of saviour, as it may be used of God. The term reappears in Ruth 4: 14, where the baby is both a 'kinsman' (Authorized Version) and – as forefather of David, elided with him – a saviour of the people.

19. The passive formula 'yulad le-' according to F. Brown, S. R. Driver and C. A. Briggs, is used exclusively of the relation of paternity, except in this instance (where I think we can take it as the sub-text) and in Isaiah where similarly it is implicit: 'unto us a son is born'.

20. The Scroll ends with a patrilineal genealogy from Phares to David; A. Jones, *The Jerusalem Bible* (London: Wharton, Longman & Todd, 1968), argues in a footnote that since the narrator identifies Obed as legally Naomi's and Elimelech's child, the last four verses must have been added by a different author.

21. H. Freedman and M. Simon, *Midrash Rabbah I: Genesis* (London: Soncino, 1961), p. 381, quote a rabbinic view that the matriarchs were barren because 'the Holy One, blessed be He, yearns for their prayers and supplications'. But see also Trible, *op. cit.*, p. 34: 'in the Hebrew scriptures the wombs of women belong to God', and pp. 31–71 for a study of images of God as mother.

Chapter 11

Women's *Mauvaise foi* in Simone de Beauvoir's *The Second Sex*

Terry Keefe

In the Introduction to *The Second Sex* Simone de Beauvoir explains that the philosophical framework within which she is writing is that of existentialist ethics (28; I,31).[1] The central place occupied in that framework by the notion of *mauvaise foi* (which for present purposes we may regard as synonymous with 'bad faith', 'self-deception' or 'inauthenticity') is fairly well understood, but the application of this notion to women in *The Second Sex* is a rather neglected topic, in spite of the fact that it is one of very considerable importance for a full understanding of Beauvoir's major text, and possibly for many broader feminist inquiries and debates.

The matter is complex, both by virtue of the different uses to which Beauvoir puts the concept of *mauvaise foi* in her book and, above all, because of the intrinsically paradoxical and elusive nature of the phenomenon of self-deception itself. Perhaps the best general model of *mauvaise foi* to bear in mind is that of lying to oneself, but although there is no theoretical restriction upon the range of subjects about which individuals may be self-deceived, the precise topic at issue here is somewhat limited by the point that within French existentialism virtually all cases of *mauvaise foi* are ultimately reducible to the following pattern: knowing that one is free, but simultaneously persuading oneself that one is not.

Needless to say, Beauvoir has no inclination to assume that people are either wholly self-deceived or completely lucid: certain kinds of mixtures of the two states are recognised as perfectly possible. Moreover, although in many of her works she is concerned with cases at the extreme end of the spectrum, where *mauvaise foi* can lead to psychological disorder or madness, the central argument of *The Second Sex* refers, in general, to women's self-deception in more ordinary cases, more normal circumstances. Many men, as well as women, are charged with *mauvaise foi*, but because the book is centrally about women there are far more detailed descriptions of women in bad faith than of men. If this is an uncomfortable

147

fact about *The Second Sex*, it would be rash to react to it by denying the existence of female self-deception altogether. The best working hypothesis is that both *some* men and *some* women are indeed guilty of the various kinds of bad faith that Beauvoir describes.

The starting-point for an investigation of this theme is the section in the Introduction where Beauvoir explains her general perspective in *The Second Sex*:

> The perspective that we are adopting is that of existentialist morality. Every subject asserts itself concretely as a transcendent being through chosen projects, and realises its freedom only by continually surpassing itself towards other freedoms. There is no justification for earthly existence other than its outward expansion towards an indefinitely open future. Whenever transcendence descends into immanence, it is a case of existence being degraded into being in-itself, freedom being degraded into facticity. This debasement is a moral fault if the subject consents to it: it takes the form of frustration and oppression if it is inflicted upon the subject. In either case, it is an absolute evil. Every individual concerned to justify his/her existence experiences that existence as an indefinite need to transcend himself/herself.
>
> Now, what marks off a woman's situation in a special way is that, although like any human being she is free and autonomous, she discovers herself and chooses herself in a world where men compel her to assume the role of the Other. They want to make her an object and doom her to immanence, since her own transcendence will be perpetually transcended by another consciousness that is essential and sovereign. Women's drama lies in the conflict between the fundamental claims of any subject, which always asserts itself as essential, and the demands of a situation that makes her inessential. (28–9; I,31)[2]

Some of the binary oppositions established or implied in this sequence can easily be tabulated and, faced with Hélène Cixous' question, 'Where is she?', no one would have difficulty in placing women in one of the columns that result and men in the other:

trancendence	*immanence*
pour-soi	*en-soi*
freedom	facticity
Subject	Object
essential	inessential
sovereign	(subordinate)
fundamental claim	demands of a situation
?	Other

But the key point, of course, is that Beauvoir is arguing that women are associated with the right-hand column only because of the male dominance that has prevailed since the dawn of history. She wants them to pass from the right-hand to the left-hand column, although the usual difficulty of finding a term to contrast with, and oppose to, 'Other' already raises one of the most controversial questions about *The Second Sex*: do we simply replace the question mark with 'man', in which case we prejudge the issue of whether Beauvoir really does want women to become more like men; or, if not, what exactly do we replace the question mark with?

For the moment, however, since all human beings are said to start in the left-hand column, it is the *movement* from left to right that should concern us. This movement is expressed in terms of another two polarities: if it is inflicted upon women it produces frustration or oppression, but if women agree to it they are morally at fault. Beauvoir's broad picture, then, is that of men trying to force women from left-hand to right-hand column, and of women being morally in the wrong if they *consent* to this pressure.

Nevertheless, there are different forms of consent and Beauvoir is not nearly clear enough on this point. It can easily be shown that both she and Sartre are often rather careless in this area, in that they frequently confuse and conflate *mauvaise foi* with cynicism.[3] She does say, at a number of points in *The Second Sex*, that one reason why women consent to being pushed into the right-hand column is that this enables them to go on enjoying certain privileges or securities that male dominance affords them. Whatever one may think of this view, the fact is that such an attitude on the part of a woman may be adopted *either* on a cynical/prudential basis, *or* in a state of self-deception. That is to say, women may go along with male dominance in two markedly different ways, according to whether they are claiming: 'Whether it's right or wrong, it suits *me*'; or telling themselves: 'I have no option'. Beauvoir's contention is that to the extent that women think the latter they are in bad faith, but *The Second Sex* would have been a good deal sharper if she had explicitly drawn and developed this contrast, which she does not. Yet, in any case, it remains true that in *The Second Sex* bad faith is said to be at least one of the principal processes whereby women give their morally deplorable consent to the move from the left-hand to the right-hand column, and indeed to remaining there.

Earlier in her Introduction, in fact, Beauvoir has already asserted unequivocally not only that women's profound complicitly in men's aims and arrangements is one of the main reasons for their continuing sub-jugation, but also that this renouncing of their transcendence rests upon a tendency deeply rooted in *all* human beings, male or female – the tendency to flee from freedom, to try to become an object or thing, the temptation of inauthenticity (21; I,21). She comes back to this at numerous stages of *The Second Sex*, also using phrases like 'the subject's tendency towards *alienation*' (79; I,88); 'inauthentic flight' (83; I,94); 'the temptations of convenience' (168; I,228); 'longing for oblivion, for sleep, for ecstasy, for death' (296; II,14); 'resignation is tempting' (321; II,43); 'an inauthentic longing for resignation and escape' (325; II,47); 'the snares of bad faith'

(639; II,455); etc. Thus not only are both sexes said to be subject to, and guilty of, *mauvaise foi* as a matter of established fact: both sexes apparently have a deep-rooted tendency to give up or alienate their freedom. This must, of course, be set alongside each individual's equally basic drive to use his or her freedom as a means of genuine transcendence, and it has to be said that the former, negative tendency to inauthenticity is by no means wholly unproblematic within the Sartrean system in *Being and Nothingness*, where it is more fully explained. But what is of particular interest here is Beauvoir's account of *differences* in the ways in which the fundamental tendency to bad faith is relevant to the cases of men and of women.

The key notion is that of 'situation'. Although, in principle, both sexes are subject to the same basic temptation of *mauvaise foi*, Beauvoir's frequent claim in her text seems to be that, because of male dominance, women's situation in the world is such that the temptation of bad faith is *greater* in their case than in the case of men. This is because the role of Other is actually offered to women from the first; because they are invited, encouraged, expected to consider themselves as objects, to abandon their freedom and transcendence; because it is *easier* for them to take the 'escape routes' of *mauvaise foi* than to do otherwise. Or, to put the matter the other way round, as there is a 'tradition of resignation and submission' on the part of women (146; I,194), it is *harder* for women to choose the route to independence or freedom; a greater moral effort is required of them than is required of men (169; I,228).

This second version of the point, of course, takes us very close to a view that is likely to be accepted by virtually everyone with feminist sympathies. But, in any case, it is effectively this general thrust in Beauvoir's argument that dominates the second volume of *The Second Sex* and has made the book so influential. For one thing, the very *range* of directions in which she pursues her point is impressive by any standard.

In the section called 'The Formative Years', she stresses that from the age of 3 or 4 onwards more is expected of boys, because they are *valued* more highly, and that girls are encouraged to become passive, to see themselves as objects. Yet it is important to recognise that Beauvoir already attributes some degree of choice, of responsibility to the young girl: 'she is a human being before becoming a woman; and she knows already that to accept her feminine role is to abdicate and to mutilate herself; and though abdication is tempting, mutilation is odious' (321; II,43). She also goes on to say that adolescence is an especially difficult and decisive moment for girls, but that most consent to a feminine role (359–60; II,89–90). Then in 'Situation' Beauvoir describes the corresponding temptations that are later held out to married women and mothers in particular, arguing that, although the pitfalls of *mauvaise foi* await men and women alike, the only freedom women enjoy is an abstract and empty one, so that they can achieve authenticity only through *revolt*. Giving in to the limitations imposed upon their situation in the world by men is morally wrong: it is the specific form of bad faith that is most obviously open to women, but they must resist it, refuse these limitations and work for their liberation.

By this stage, Beauvoir's view is that liberation is necessarily a *collective* matter for women. Hence her intriguing but somewhat odd section, 'Justifications', in which she describes three types of women – the narcissist, the woman in love, the mystic – who are trying to go it alone, who accept their immanent situation as individuals and try to justify themselves, try to find transcendence *within* immanence. This, of course, is doomed to failure and is therefore another fertile source of examples of women's *mauvaise foi*. Even towards the end of the book, when she is describing women who have to some extent overcome their situation and attained a certain degree of independence, Beauvoir talks of the great difficulties involved, of the almost irresistible temptations they face.

Yet if we take this general feature of Beauvoir's argument in *The Second Sex* – the claim that women's situation more or less throughout their lives encourages complicity with male dominance – and if we isolate within it the idea that the temptation of *mauvaise foi* is therefore greater for women than for men, then an examination of the philosophical positions involved produces some complex results. Three types of comment immediately impose themselves.

Firstly, we cannot simply ignore the fact that there are two or three stages in *The Second Sex* where Beauvoir implies that women's situation – or perhaps the situation of certain women, at certain points in their lives – makes them *less* inclined to bad faith and inauthenticity than men. She argues, for instance, that 'Masculine pride hides from men all that is equivocal in the drama of eroticism. They lie to themselves spontaneously, whereas women, who are more easily humiliated, more susceptible, are also more lucid; they manage to pull the wool over their own eyes only by means of a more subtle kind of bad faith' (697; II,530; cf 636; II,452; and 638; II,454). In other words, women find it *harder* to deceive themselves than men do! (It is interesting to note, in passing, that this appears to have been Sartre's view: he was inclined to suggest, in a rather sexist way, that women are more fun to be with than men, that they are less self-important, more genuine, and their conversation more enjoyable.) It is difficult to be sure of the significance of the apparent contradiction in Beauvoir's views in this precise area.

Secondly, it is not clear whether either her 'main' view on this issue *or* its contrary can be justified within the general Sartrean, existentialist frame-work that Beauvoir claims to have adopted. It may be doubted whether, in the philosophical scheme of things in *Being and Nothingness*, the notion of one choice being easier to make than another, of one temptation being stronger than another, could be defended – indeed, whether the concept of temptation figures at all in *Being and Nothingness*. One might well say, 'So much the worse for *Being and Nothingness*', but some of the interest of the point would then reside in the fact – and it is now emerging as a fact in other areas – that Beauvoir is not working strictly within the Sartrean framework in the way that she claims to be. Increasingly, critics are en-gaging with the task of sorting out those points in Beauvoir's philosophical writings that are taken directly and openly from Sartre, and those con-tributions that are Beauvoir's own. And of course the further task of deciding whether her own contributions are wholly consistent with the borrowed Sartrean foundations, or in some sense in contradiction with them.

The third comment relates, precisely, to such possible contradiction. On the common-sense level, it may seem perfectly reasonable to suggest that there is a greater temptation for women to abdicate their freedom than for men to do so. But in the context of belief in the absolute metaphysical freedom of every individual, what exactly can this mean? At the end of her long section on 'Situation', Beauvoir says the following:

> If one compares these situations in themselves, it is obvious that man's is infinitely preferable; that is, he has many more concrete possibilities of exercising his freedom in the world. The inevitable result is that men's achievements are far greater than those of women. Women are more or less forbidden to *do* anything. However, to compare the use which, within their limits, men and women make of their freedom is *a priori* a senseless undertaking, since, precisely, they use it freely. In various forms, the pitfalls of bad faith, the mystifications of taking oneself too seriously lie in wait for both sexes: freedom is complete in everyone. (638–9; II,455)

As already indicated, Beauvoir goes on to argue that, since freedom remains an abstract and empty notion for women, the only authentic reaction to their situation is revolt, but it is noticeable that her prescriptive line of argument – from the complete freedom of everyone to the moral need for revolt in the case of women – now dispenses with the notions of temptation and difficulty altogether, with the emphasis falling, rather, on women's lack of opportunities. In any case, *how* exactly, could temptation and difficulty have been said to impinge on women's choices – that is, by what mechanism? The answer could not possibly be by any causal process, for determinism is precisely what is rejected in the existentialist doctrine of 'complete' freedom. Nor is there any point in thinking that mere mention of the term 'conditioning' resolves the matter, since it simply displaces the problem by generating the need for an account of this particular concept that at one and the same time has some substance and is itself compatible with the doctrine of freedom.

There is a very grave philosophical difficulty for Beauvoir at the heart of these matters and it would not be difficult to demonstrate that an unease over her position manifests itself in the use of a whole series of words, phrases and concepts calculated to suggest that, although women are free, somehow their situation impels them more towards *mauvaise foi* than men's does. We have already mentioned 'temptation' (sometimes 'almost irresistible temptation') and 'taking the easy way', and the term 'conditioning' is one that Beauvoir does actually use in *The Second Sex*, at least once, though probably not much more. But there are more obviously worrying terms: she sometimes says that women are 'disposed' (or even, astonishingly, 'predisposed') to a particular sort of choice; she says that they are 'led' to certain attitudes, 'obliged' to make certain responses, etc. The list is not endless, but a first count suggests that around forty such expressions can be listed with no difficulty.

Yet, starting from the basic existentialist belief in the metaphysical freedom of all, how can one possibly justify philosophically *any* differential remarks about *mauvaise foi* in men and in women? We need constantly to bear in mind, in the first place, that the central point of *The Second Sex* is that there is no pre-determined feminine (or masculine) nature; and, in the second place, that no *causal* chain between a particular situation and particular human conduct is acceptable within existentialism. There is, of course, absolutely no reason why Beauvoir should not acknowledge empirical or statistical differences in the behaviour of men and women. If one could do the count, it might indeed turn out that more women are self-deceived than men; or, for that matter, the other way round. But the point to be stressed is that Beauvoir has no sound philosophical apparatus whatever for elucidating any such differences, no legitimate means of forging an explanatory link between women's situation on the one hand and any patterns of conduct they may display on the other. There is a crucial gap or discontinuity in her theory at this point, albeit one that she attempts, consciously or otherwise, to paper over.

It is perhaps no surprise, therefore, that quotations can be found to support *three* different views in *The Second Sex*: 1. that men and women are equally susceptible to *mauvaise foi*; 2. that it is much more of a temptation for women than for men; and 3. that women are *less* inclined to deceive themselves than men. Whether or not the second of these theses – that women's situation makes them *more* liable to bad faith than men – can be taken to be Beauvoir's main contention in *The Second Sex*, for very good philosophical reasons she is uneasy about this position, never justifies it satisfactorily, and quite often undermines it in one way or another.

In the light of all of this it is particularly instructive to examine the Conclusion to *The Second Sex*. It has not been emphasised nearly enough that in a book so enormously influential and incalculably valuable in its attack on male dominance, Beauvoir's considered view is that the responsibility and blame for the present situation must be shared equally between the two sexes. One of the epigraphs to the second volume (omitted from the translation) is a quotation from Sartre, 'Half victims, half accomplices, like everyone else', and in the course of the Conclusion Beauvoir also quotes Montaigne: 'It is easier to accuse one of the sexes than to excuse the other' (728; II,563). This last quotation, used in the Introduction as part of her argument that men's comments on women never rise above the partial and the prejudiced (22; I,23), is now taken to illustrate the point that both sexes bear responsibility for the conflict between them. And, in general, it is clear that the war between the sexes is as much the centre of focus in the Conclusion as male dominance.

In a number of ways Beauvoir's precise argument in her Conclusion, even in this single dimension of *mauvaise foi* with which we are principally concerned, is more complicated than anything explicitly formulated earlier in the book:

> If this vicious circle is so difficult to break, it is because each sex is at one and the same time its own victim and the victim of the other sex. Between the two opponents, confronting each other in their pure freedom, an agreement could easily be arrived at, all the more so as this battle benefits no one. But the complexity of the whole business arises because each party is in complicity with the enemy. Woman pursues a dream of abdication, man a dream of alienation. Inauthenticity does not pay. Therefore, each takes it out on the other for the misfortune he/she has brought upon himself/herself by giving in to the temptations of the easy way. What men and women hate in each other is the obvious failure brought about by their own bad faith and cowardice. (728; II,563)

This quotation reinforces the view implicit in the epigraph already mentioned: it is not only women who are half victims and half accomplices, but men too ('like everyone else'). It is by no means the first time in *The Second Sex* that Beauvoir has suggested that women oppress men, albeit in different ways from the ways in which men oppress women. It is probably not even the first time that she has implied that most men consent to this oppression, as most women consent to theirs. But it is certainly the first point in the book at which she has brought out the symmetry in the situation so clearly and sharply. And the symmetry is now marked by considerable complexity, for if we were to go back to our original two columns of polarised concepts, we would find that their original significance has been wholly subsumed in a much more elaborate analysis of men–women relations.

For one thing, Beauvoir now appears to be *contrasting* 'alienation' and 'abdication', the first being the temptation faced by men and the second that faced by women, whereas earlier in the text she was content to see these as more or less synonymous expressions flagging *mauvaise foi*. The suggestion now seems to be that a 'temptation to take the easy way', faces men too, and this really amounts to acknowledging that there are gender roles and gender models that *men* are expected to conform to, just as there are for women. In commenting on *The Second Sex* more than twenty years after its publication Beauvoir was to say, after all, that while she still accepted her assertion that 'One is not born a woman: one *becomes* a woman', she would want to add to it that 'One is not born a man: one *becomes* a man'.[4]

However, in saying in the Conclusion that both men and women have their obvious temptations and that both give in to them in bad faith, she is primarily concerned to add another layer to this base. *Mauvaise foi* does not work, she argues, so that the consequences of giving in to gender roles are unsatisfactory for both sexes. Each sex sees that it has brought misfortune upon itself by giving in, but then each sex blames the other for the situation and this clearly constitutes a *second* layer of self-deception. The first layer consists in accepting a gender role to begin with, convincing oneself that there is no alternative; and the second layer consists in persuading oneself that someone *else* – namely the other sex – is responsible for the resulting failure.[5]

Beauvoir's final account of *mauvaise foi* in *The Second Sex*, then, is an infinitely more complicated and a much richer one than was discernible earlier in her text. It can still accommodate any of the cases of women's bad faith that she originally had in mind, but is now also capable of explaining a much wider range of phenomena concerning men–women relations. What is more, insofar as the account in the Conclusion does not depend upon any claim that *mauvaise foi* is somehow commoner in women than in men, it will avoid some of the philosophical difficulties mentioned above. The only question is, of course, whether the view expressed in the Conclusion, or at least the emphasis given to it, is entirely compatible with all of the affirmations made in the preceding parts of the book.

It is not that Beauvoir in any way abandons the idea of male dominance in her Conclusion – far from it. But she does now place the phenomenon in a markedly different context. Broadly speaking, there is an added element in the form of a certain kind of attempt to excuse men for oppressing women. She describes man as 'guilty in spite of himself and oppressed by this fault that he himself has not committed' (732; II,568). Fascinatingly, Beauvoir now brings the wheel full circle, for just as she had argued in the Introduction that women commit a moral fault in consenting to male oppression, so she now suggests that men are morally in the wrong only if *they* consent to the oppression and the injustices that it generates (*ibid.*).

In some respects this may seem, in itself, a quite unremarkable and even rather obvious point, although it is far from clear that it will be acceptable to all feminists. But, in any case, it has to be seen as representing a development in Beauvoir's views as expressed in the course of *The Second Sex*. The development may well have taken place while she was in the process of writing the second volume, either as a result of reflections associated with the writing itself, or because of general movements in her own views and those of Sartre during this period. Certainly, this was precisely the time at which they were beginning to shift their focus from individual morality as such to the influence of social forces. The idea that both sexes are locked into an unjust situation, within which it is impossible to act justly – 'one can never create justice within injustice' (732; II,568) – is strongly echoed and expanded in *The Mandarins*, which Beauvoir began writing in 1951, yet it is not an obvious feature of *The Ethics of Ambiguity*, the work that Beauvoir completed just before beginning *The Second Sex*.

But whatever conclusion one may draw on these matters, the general importance of the topic of *mauvaise foi* in *The Second Sex* can now be seen to lie in the fact that Beauvoir is the type of feminist who never lays all of the blame for male dominance on men.[6] It has recently been remarked, perhaps with a touch of irony, that '*The Second Sex* does not err on the side of over-indulgence towards women'.[7] And many years ago a substantial article was published under the challenging title, 'Simone de Beauvoir: Feminism's friend or foe?'.[8] The specific issue of bad faith is bound to re-raise that question for many feminists and, indeed, a great proportion of the work currently being carried out on Beauvoir's life and works revolves around the question in one way or another. My own intention was to do no more than begin to map out one narrow, but fertile strip of territory on which the debate can take place.

NOTES

1. Bracketed references in the text are, firstly, to *Simone de Beauvoir: The Second Sex*, translated and edited by H. M. Parshley (Harmondsworth: Penguin Books, 1972); and, secondly, to the original two-volume edition of *Le Deuxième Sexe* (Paris: Gallimard, 1949).

2. In this and all other quotations, I have preserved as much of Parshley's translation as possible, but have had to make many modifications in the interests of both accuracy and comprehensibility.
3. See my 'Simone de Beauvoir and Sartre on *mauvaise foi*', *French Studies* XXXIV, July 1980, pp. 300–14.
4. *Tout compte fait* (Paris: Gallimard, 1972), p. 497.
5. One is irresistibly reminded, at this point, of the convoluted tangles in men–women relations traced by R. D. Laing in *Knots* (London: Tavistock, 1970).
6. Since we have been considering only a theoretical work by Beauvoir, it would be especially interesting to know how the particular patterns that we have discerned in relation to *mauvaise foi* apply to her fiction. I myself have gone some way in this direction in 'Simone de Beauvoir's *La Femme rompue*: Studies in self-deception', *Essays in French Literature*, no. 13, November 1976, pp. 77–97.
7. Elizabeth Fallaize, *The Novels of Simone de Beauvoir* (London: Routledge, 1988), p. 14.
8. C. B. Radford: 'Simone de Beauvoir: Feminism's friend or foe?', *Nottingham French Studies*, no. VI, October 1967, pp. 87–102, and no. VII, May 1968, pp. 39–53.

Chapter 12

Childhood Reading and Role Models in Simone de Beauvoir

*Notes towards the making of the heroines in
Simone de Beauvoir's fiction*

Penny McWatters

In *Les Mémoirs d'une jeune fille rangée*, the reader is presented with a closely written analysis of Simone de Beauvoir's first twenty-one years as a dependent female member of a middle-class family. We are taken from her birth to the intoxicating independence which came with the completion of her studies. We remember that *The Second Sex* was published in 1949 and that therefore this first volume of her autobiography, appearing in 1958 when she was 50 years old, was written from the viewpoint of successful maturity, in the light of her thinking about women and with the knowledge that she had attained her literary ambitions. Her autobiography illustrates Simone de Beauvoir's attitude to the power which she believed was an intrinsic quality of the written word. At the age of 15 she thought all artists were admirable, they justified and endowed with unique qualities the life of the individual, forming a necessary pattern from what would otherwise remain as random existence. The supremacy amongst creators she reserved for authors, and particularly novelists. Literature for Simone de Beauvoir was for long a source of powerful experience which she integrated into her own life and which she called upon when, in her own turn, she came to write. The aim of this short paper is to study what she read when young, to suggest what she derived from her childhood and adolescent reading, and to ask what these experiences reveal about her earliest literary education, and whether any links are retained with the women she was later to describe in her own novels.

It is evident that Simone de Beauvoir considered she received an unusually thorough literary grounding. In 1972 she wrote:

> Reduced to a sort of poverty my parents went in for cultural values rather than for the ostentatious spending which my father would have preferred. The principal

158

amusement which they offered me was reading, a pastime which cost little. I loved books with passion.[1]

In France, even in 1920 by which time Simone was about 12 years old, many middle-class parents still felt that it was part of their duty as educators to exercise the closest supervision over their children's reading, especially if those children were girls. Madame de Beauvoir, her daughter tells us, believed firmly in her responsibilities as a Catholic mother and she consulted frequently with Church associations when she wished for help or guidance with her task. She was so aware of her role as mistress of the home and guardian of its purity that she had once snatched Colette's novel *Claudine at School* from the maid and confiscated it. For her daughter, certain books were banned altogether, others were censored, being handed over with pages pinned together. This censorship was justified by the teachings of the Church, and the school which Simone attended. The danger to faith and even to life itself provoked by unsupervised reading on the part of the young formed the subject of a sermon she heard during the retreat made immediately before her First Communion. The preacher illustrated his argument with the frightening example of a little girl whose bad reading habits led to loss of faith and suicide. By censoring her daughter's reading, then, Madame de Beauvoir was protecting her from the occasion of sin and was thus safeguarding her immortal soul.

Madame de Beauvoir therefore supervised her daughter's overall education. She provided her with respectable books suitable for young people, many of which she herself had read when young. One such author, the trace of whom Simone de Beauvoir confesses subsisted in her own early fiction, was Delly.

Delly – in fact a brother and sister writing team, Marie Petit-Jean de la Rosière (1875–1949) and her brother Frédéric (1876–1949) – composed pious and romantic love stories, intended for a young public. Their novels were published from the early years of this century onwards. Many titles were re-issued in the 1920s in the series *La Bibliothèque de ma fille* or in *La Bibliothèque de Suzette*, which were regarded by Catholic authorities as suitable reading for the young. One example is *L'Exilée* (*The Girl Exile*): Myrtô, an orphan of aristocratic and Catholic birth, is beautiful, 18 and penniless. She is invited as a poor relation into the distant household of rich cousins among whom is a mysterious, powerful and misanthropic prince. He is divorced and has lost his faith, he is cruel and embittered by the sufferings caused by his ex-wife, who has died in a fire at a theatre in America. A type of smallpox epidemic comes to the area, the prince's son catches the disease, Myrtô alone remains to nurse him, the child dies.

After various melodramatic devices, Myrtô brings the prince back to his religious faith, and they marry. The last words of the novel belong to the prince who is addressing his bride:

> You continue to be for me the beloved, the radiant flower fairy for it is because of the influence of your virtue that repentance, faith and charity, these celestial flowers have blossomed in the soul which previously was hardened and in revolt, in the poor sick soul of prince Milcza.[2]

In this novel, love is described as spiritual not sexual and the heroine acts in conventionally submissive feminine ways, showing values of service and devotion rather than initiative or independence. The supreme achievement of a woman's life is the redemption of a strong and superior male. This novel was typical. Literature proposed by her mother was thus either censored or revoltingly virtuous and conventional. It did not contain role models which appealed overtly to the demanding young Simone, although its influence and its values continued to exist – does not Françoise in *L'Invitée* share these ideas?

Although initially it was Simone de Beauvoir's mother and school teachers who encouraged her to read, when it became clear to her father that she was intellectually gifted he decided to assume much of the responsibility for his clever elder daughter's literary education, while of course leaving all other aspects of the upbringing of the children to his wife. So while Madame de Beauvoir was finding suitable books for the young Simone and her teachers were beginning to instil in the earnest schoolgirl a solid knowledge of seventeenth-century French literature, Monsieur de Beauvoir was introducing his daughter to the authors he himself prized.

This process seems to have commenced when Simone was about 8 years old. First, he helped her to express herself correctly. He carefully checked the accuracy of her written French, sending back to her with all mistakes indicated the letters which she wrote to him while he was at the front, and he made her do difficult dictation exercises during the school holidays. The pedagogic aspect of his attitude to Simone did not upset her, as one might have expected. On the contrary, the relationship seemed enhanced; being intelligent she easily learned to avoid the grammatical traps he set for her and thus made few errors; the father was proud of the daughter; she gained prestige and basked in his esteem. His ruling passion was the theatre, so he assembled for her a small anthology of poetry which he taught her to recite effectively. Finally, he introduced her to those of his favourite authors he deemed suitable for her age.

Monsieur de Beauvoir was an atheist, he moved in a wider world, he valued ideas and he revered literature; he had even expressed disapproval of the blinkered viewpoint of his daughters' school. Nevertheless, he was at one with his wife over the issue of censorship. For him, the reasons were social and sexual: the youthful innocence of daughters had to be protected from corruption, certain worldly knowledge was for married ladies only. Therefore, he too exercised censorship: 'Even in *l'Aiglon* my father made cuts'.[3]

The close supervision of a child who by training and inclination turned to literature in search of experience had three weak points: the books officially on offer were dull; the parents trusted their daughter's obedience; and her father's library was available. In spite of parental confidence in her, curiosity and greed for printed matter united to overcome all scruples, and, after initial experiments reading forbidden books did not seem to result in harm, Simone de Beauvoir abandoned herself whenever she could to the delights of clandestine uncensored reading of adult masculine literature, 'masculine' in the sense that the collection was assembled by a man. In the account we are given of the wide reading of her youth she talks very little, however, of enjoyment of content – the activity of reading was blissful in that it provided the escape and sexual information she was seeking but what she read did not, on the whole, excite. We are explicitly told in the *Memoirs of a Dutiful Daughter* that 'no author succeeded in moving me.'[4]

Are the reasons for this hard to find? An analysis of those names and titles mentioned by Simone de Beauvoir as being in her father's library reveals many playwrights, among whom one group, Sacha Guitry, Capus and Tristan Bernard, had much in common. They produced amusing comedies which were sometimes sophisticated or even satirical but were often superficial and light-weight. An interest in psychology, particularly in the dramatic presentation of extremes of passion and even the abnormal, explains the presence of works by Bernstein, Bataille or Paul Bourget. Monsieur de Beauvoir belonged to a class which was officially most respectful of women but in his private reading he showed his liking for writers whose works had the effect of denigrating women by showing what was felt to be female irrationality and lack of self-control, or even scandalous and sometimes aberrant female sexuality. Bataille's *Maman Colibri* of 1904, for instance, has as its theme the study of a middle-aged woman's shocking passion for her son's friend. The society novels of Marcel Prévost, whose *Les Demi-vierges* of 1894 Simone de Beauvoir tells us she read in secret, or the entertaining adulteries of Sacha Guitry, take for granted the continuation of existing values. The books preferred by her father amuse but do not disturb the reader or even question existing society. The depiction of women in them was, on the whole, displeasing to his daughter.

To summarise then, Simone de Beauvoir mainly read the books of a certain social class and discovered that she did not really appreciate what pleased that class. She found little inspiration in the French literature which she was offered openly or which she read secretly. She despised her teachers and does not seem to have shown any enthusiasm for the classical authors on the school syllabus. She found the virtuous idylls offered by her mother were too tame and her father's books did not satisfy her either; she uses words such as indignation or scorn to describe her response to most of them.

Certain authors, certain novels, did, however, supply the young Simone de Beauvoir with what she was craving: a possibility of identification with the imaginary world of the book; a recognition of her self or of her own situation which could both stimulate her ambitions and reassure her that she was not the only person to think as she did. When she read Louisa May Alcott's *Little Women* series, or when she slowly deciphered George Eliot's *The Mill on the Floss* (both in the original English), the miracle of recognition occurred. Comparing herself with the heroines, Jo March and Maggie Tulliver, she was able both to envisage a future where she would be successful and independent and to come to terms with a present which she found increasingly uncomfortable. It is perhaps inevitable that the books which played such a significant part in her adolescence should belong to other literary cultures. In her memoirs we are told that she was coming to detest the values of her family and class and to reject the role models proposed to her in their literatures. In these books which she felt she was conquering for herself – literature which was not mediated by her elders – she found solace and encouragement. She was about 10 when she read, in English in the Tauschnitz edition, *Little Women*. This book profoundly affected her both immediately and in the long term. What she gained from this novel was a durable inspiration; it was, she wrote thirty years later, 'a book in which I recognised myself and my destiny'.[5] When Simone de Beauvoir approved of a fictional character she strongly identified with it and even appropriated it; this time she became Jo, who she felt was the particular favourite of the author. This character provided a positive image of the woman she was to become, which gave value to her present life as a child. She was then all the more convinced that hers was a privileged consciousness charged with a particular mission, which marked her out from the ordinary people and raised her above the level of more attractive and 'feminine', if less clever, girls.

When we look more closely at the novel we find a variety of choices or models offered to the young girl reader by means of the four heroines. Jo, Simone de Beauvoir's favourite, is the most active of the four girls. It is significant that she has taken a boy's name for she rebels against the restrictions, such as those forbidding running or whistling, which her more lady-like and conventional sisters accept. She does not care much for girls or for girlish gossip, is forceful in expression, indeed her temper is fiery and she has trouble controlling it, and she disdains elegance of dress. Although these characteristics might have attracted the young Simone de Beauvoir, perhaps what is most admirable about Jo and which appealed at a deeper level is her ambition. She wants to 'do something splendid' with her life. Apart from her family, her main love is literature: the library is 'a region of bliss' and her ambition is to be fulfilled through writing. Jo says: 'I think I shall write books and get rich and famous: that would suit me so *that* is my favourite dream'.[6] Here we have a sympathetic heroine guaranteed to appeal to a girl already drawn to the world of literature and who had tried to write. Jo's ambition encouraged Simone de Beauvoir to think of herself and her own ambitions with approval, and emulating Jo she composed two or three stories immediately after reading the book. Nevertheless, in spite of her enthusiastic identification with the outgoing and energetic Jo, she did not notice that this character is shown as possessing a well-developed maternal instinct: she is Beth's 'little mother', for example, and in the course of the novel her 'boyish' qualities are perceived as defects which she is encouraged to eliminate. In one of the final scenes she is congratulated by her father for no longer being the 'son Jo' of the previous year. In early adolescence Simone de Beauvoir read the sequel, *Good Wives*, and was horrified to discover that the author had betrayed her by marrying the charming Laurie to the unworthy Amy, who was pretty, vain and frivolous, rather than to the intellectual Jo. When Jo finally chose to marry a learned teacher many years older than herself, Simone de Beauvoir's feelings were mixed. She tells us that she came to approve of the idea of Jo choosing a 'superior' man as his prestige endowed his partner with additional value. Doubtless, she shared to some extent the prevalent view that the male partner in a marriage should be more knowledgeable and wiser than the female, and have the role of initiator. Can one invoke here the 'Delly' aspect of Simone de Beauvoir's reading?

As a girl Simone de Beauvoir read several English writers: in translation, for example, *Gulliver's Travels*, some H. G. Wells, *The War of the Worlds* with certain of the pages pinned together, and some Dickens, including *David Copperfield*, which does not seem to have made a great impression on her. Possibly the fact that the hero was a boy was the reason she was not touched emotionally or imaginatively by his story: she was in search of models with whom she could identify and female characters in books written by women could best supply these.

She read George Eliot's *The Mill on the Floss* at a crucial period in her spiritual and personal development. Although she had lost her faith she still went to Mass and took Communion and so had extreme feelings of guilt, which made her feel cut off from and isolated within her family. Confronted with Eliot's heroine, the magic act of identification once more took place: 'Maggie Tulliver was, as I was, divided between others and herself: I recognised myself in her'.[7]

The points of contact were many, beginning with a shared love of Nature, a key element in this novel. First, Simone de Beauvoir's own most intense feelings of joy had always been associated with the countryside, and she responded to this novel at a very deep level. Second, given the heroine's plain appearance and unacceptable behaviour as a child, Simone could in the externals of her life identify with the frequently scolded Maggie. Maggie's love of books and her dislike of girls' pastimes were further elements which encouraged recognition.

It was not just the outer characteristics of the heroine that reflected back to Simone de Beauvoir her own vision of herself. More important was the tension in the girl's life which came from her parents' attitude to her. Simone now resented her mother's close and narrow supervision and still to a certain extent admired her father, associating him with a wider and more intellectual world. In the *Mill on the Floss*, Maggie's mother and her family were critical of the girl while her father and his family admired and cherished her. It must have been reassuring to read about a heroine whose mother was so demonstrably narrow-minded and stupid and could thus be despised in a satisfying way and whose father kept a special place in his heart for his daughter.

And yet Simone de Beauvoir's early admiration for the superior intellect of her father was becoming complicated in adolescence by the fact that he no longer seemed to delight, as he had once done, in her superior intelligence and intellectual achievements. Like Maggie, she had always loved books and learning and storytelling; reading about Maggie's father and his mixture of pride and irritation towards his daughter's capacities helped clarify her own ideas with respect to her father.

Perhaps the most telling point about George Eliot's heroine was her emotional and spiritual isolation. Her deepest needs were not understood by those around her, value her as they might, and when she chose to remain true to her own conscience her spiritual isolation is echoed in the social abandonment which she suffers. At this period in her own life, as we have seen, Simone de Beauvoir bitterly felt herself alone within the family unit.

Yet this identification with the heroine was not complete or final. There came a moment when Simone de Beauvoir, already strongly confident of her own capacities in spite of momentary hesitations, separated herself from the destiny of George Eliot's heroine. Although she wept sincerely over Maggie's defeat and death and burned with tenderness for the heroine in her abandonment, it is clear that Simone de Beauvoir felt that she herself gained personal strength through this vicarious experience of defeat.

The young Simone de Beauvoir, having sobbed over Maggie's fate, was able to determine that although she and Maggie were both superior beings and thus alike, her own future would be unlike that of Maggie. She would not merely survive but would triumphantly impose herself both on those around her and in a wider world. In fact, she transferred her identification from the heroine to the author of the novel and derived from the *Mill on the Floss* a positive encouragement to concentrate on the intellectual and creative life, She said: 'By means of the heroine I identified myself with the author: one day an adolescent girl, a copy of myself, would weep over a novel in which I had related my own story'.[8] We thus owe a debt of gratitude for Simone de Beauvoir's early reading of these novels in English.

To conclude, therefore, Simone's mother's literature provided her with traditional feminine role models which she quickly rejected, whilst retaining certain influences; at a later age she came to disdain her father's literature, but the effect of those childhood lessons when she had gained the approval of Monsieur de Beauvoir, who was the intellectual parent, by means of her unfeminine intelligence ('"what a pity that Simone isn't a boy, she could have gone to Polytechnique"'[9]) remained. Within the family, then, we have a girl for whom the feminine literary experience as mediated by her parents was ultimately of little value, who seized on the non-feminine aspects of heroines from other cultures as role models. Yet these role models involve values ultimately derived from her father and suggest a subduing of certain feminine qualities within her; a devaluation prefigured by her not noticing or cutting herself off from them when they are associated with the heroines with whom she identified. At the same time there is a persistence, as she herself said when commenting on the first drafts of her novels, of 'un petit côté Delly'. The heroines she was later to describe in her novels retain aspects of the passive femininity associated with her mother's reading-matter. Truly we are more influenced than we know by the ideas which we try to combat.

NOTES

All translations are my own. I supply here the original text and source.

1. 'Réduits à une demi-gêne, mes parents ont misé sur les valeurs culturelles plus que sur la "dépense ostentatoire" à laquelle mon père aurait été enclin. Ils m'ont proposé comme principale distraction la lecture, divertissement peu coûteux. J'ai aimé passionnément les livres.' Simone de Beauvoir *Tout compte fait* (Paris: Gallimard, 1972) p. 17.

2. 'Vous continuez à être pour moi la chère, la radieuse fée aux fleurs . . . car c'est sous l'influence de vos vertus que le repentir, la foi et la charité, ces fleurs célestes se sont épanouies dans l'âme autrefois révoltée et endurcie, dans la pauvre âme malade du prince Milcza.' Delly *L'Exilée* (Paris: Gautier et Languereau, La Bibliothéque de ma fille, 1925) p. 319 (original publication, 1908).

3. 'dans *L'Aiglon* même, mon père faisait des coupures' Simone de Beauvoir *Mémoires d'une jeune fille rangée*, hereafter abbreviated as *MJFR*, (Paris: Gallimard, 1958) p. 110.

4. 'aucun auteur ne réussit à m'émouvoir' *MJFR*, p. 110.

5. 'un livre où je crus reconnaître mon visage et mon destin' *MJFR*, p. 89.

6. L. M. Alcott *Little Women* (London: Associated Newspapers, n.d.) pp. 188–9.

7. 'Maggie Tulliver était comme moi divisée entre les autres et elle-même: je me reconnus en elle' *MJFR*, p. 141.

8. 'A travers son héroine, je m'identifiai à l'auteur: un jour une adolescente, une autre moi-même, tremperait de ses larmes un roman où j'aurais raconté ma propre histoire.' *MJFR*, p. 141.

9. '"Quel dommage que Simone ne soit pas un garçon: elle aurait fait Polytechnique!"' *MJFR*, p. 177.

Chapter 13

Rabelais and Obscenity

A woman's view

Carol Bellard-Thomson

At the outset I must explain that, as it was and is language that fascinates me rather than that restricted group of texts known as 'literature', it is almost against my will that I have found myself moving – fighting every step of the way – from the study of language into the study of literature as a manifestation of language in use. I have become that strange hybrid creature, the 'literary stylistician', and I do the unforgiveable to texts: I tear them apart in fine detail, examine the fragments I have in my hand and then – because texts can, happily, be torn apart and left whole at the same time – I marvel at the fact that the whole is, always, more than the sum of the parts.

The hand that forced me to this repeated desecration is that of François Rabelais (?1483–1553). He encouraged me to it by creating a text which visibly and consciously tears itself apart, only to re-embody itself, endlessly. This chapter is based in part on my M.Phil. dissertation; 'Parallelism and Persuasion: Structuring principles in Rabelais's *Pantagruel*' (unpublished, Lancaster University, 1987). It is also based on thoughts I have had since completing this research; those thoughts relate mainly to the nature of persuasion in language. Questions that arose for me were many. How did a text four hundred years old, from a culture and in a language not my own, persuade me to spend four years of my life in studying it? Why did this text, written by a man whom some have labelled misogynist, have so great an influence on my thinking about the question of what language is and how it works in a literary text? From thinking about persuasion, I have moved outwards in several directions, one of which I demonstrate here.

As a linguist and stylistician, rather than a student of the feminist debate, I have wondered much about that particular brand of thinking that says women and men write differently from each other, and that, accordingly, it is women who should read and criticise women's writing.[1] To fulfil this requirement is difficult, to say the least, as much women's writing is not

167

available to be criticised. But the aspect of this attitude which I find worrying is that, if taken to its logical limits, it necessarily excludes women from
studying and evaluating many centuries of thought and writing: and the
further back in time one goes, the more difficult it is to find women's texts
still extant – with notable exceptions such as Marie de France, Marguerite
de Navarre and Louise Labé. It is neither logical nor productive to suggest
that the absence of women's writing can be compensated for by ignoring
men's writing. Only a vacuum would remain. I therefore have to join in
with the chorus of women's voices that refuses to be excluded from
intellectual exchange simply because that exchange has for the most part
survived over time only if produced by men.

I have also wondered about the reason why (as the daughter of a former
Methodist lay-preacher, with all the intellectual freedom that entails) I
was able not only to accept the obscenity in the Rabelaisian text, but to
enjoy it and to find it profoundly significant. And the reason why I wonder
about that attitude is closely related to the fact that I am a woman.
Somewhere in my mind runs a thought that says, because I am a woman, I
should find obscenity, particularly of a sexual nature, upsetting or, at the
very least, unacceptable. This paper is an attempt to characterise the
reasons why I do not have the responses that are dictated by that line of
thought, and why the Rabelaisian text, in particular, is responsible for that
situation.

First, as a compensation to a more traditional outlook, there follows a
brief biography of Rabelais for those who are not already familiar with him
and his work.

François Rabelais was born at an uncertain date, some time between
1483 and 1496, and he died in 1553. His background was a comparatively
comfortable one: his father was a lawyer in Chinon. We have no knowledge at all about his mother, but his family were well-connected and had
friends in high places. (Perhaps, speculation runs, his mother died in
childbirth: this is occasionally given as a possible explanation as to why
some of the women in Rabelais' comic saga, Pantagruel, do likewise.)

As a young man, Rabelais took holy orders as a Franciscan priest. He
studied languages, including Classical Greek and Hebrew (which at the
time was considered a subversive act), and was said by other Christian-
humanist thinkers of the time to be learned beyond his years. In spite of his
vows, he had three children, two to an unnamed woman who later pursued
him through the Papal Courts for rights of inheritance for her children, and
a third child, born much later, who died in infancy: there is no information at
all about who this child's mother was. He was obliged to flee the Franciscan
abbey because of his reading of forbidden texts, and became a Benedictine

priest. Eventually, his apostasy (and the children) were overlooked when he, along with his abbey, was secularised. He seems to have had a considerable knowledge of law, presumably from his father, and as a priest he also studied medicine. He became a doctor of medicine, belatedly, in 1537. He was well known as a man of letters as well as being a physician of some standing. He was charged with obscenity several times, and his works were proscribed by the Sorbonne. He was, fortunately, under the protection of the powerful Du Bellay family, but on one or two occasions he was nevertheless obliged to take up a rather sudden residence in Italy, for safety's sake. He is remembered not for his medical and other writings but for the comic *Pantagruel* series.

The work consists of four, or arguably five, books, which centre on the comic adventures of a giant, Pantagruel, and on his father, Gargantua.[2] Less well-known than either of these is Pantagruel's alter ego, Panurge. Especially in the later works, Pantagruel is the ideal Christian Prince, and Panurge, a demonic windbag, is his lifelong companion.

My own work has concentrated on the first book in the series, 'Les horribles et espouventables FAICTZ & PROUESSES du très-renommé PANTAGRUEL Roy des Dipsodes, filz du grand géant Gargantua – composez nouvellement par maistre Alcofrybas Nasier' (this being an anagram of François Rabelais). One of the most obvious features of the whole work is its 'obscenity', of which the following is an example:

The anecdote of the walls of Paris

– Je leur enseigneray une manière bien nouvelle, comment ilz pourront bastir à bon marché.
– Et comment? dist Pantagruel . . .
– . . . Je voy que les callibistrys des femmes de ce pays sont à meilleur marché que les pierres. D'iceulx fauldroit bastir les murailles, en les arrangeant en bonne symmétrye d'architecture, et mettant les plus grans au premiers rangs, et puis, en taluant à doz d'asne, arranger les moyens, et finablement les petitz. Et puis faire ung bon petit entrelardement à poinctes de diamens comme la grosse tour de Bourges, de tant de vitz qu'on couppa en ceste ville ès pouvres Italiens, à l'Entrée de la Reyne.
– Quel diable defferoit une telle muraille? Il n'y a métal qui tant résistast aux coups. Et puis, que les couillevrines se y vinssent froter, vous en verriez, par Dieu, incontinent distiller de ce benoist fruict de grosse vérolle, menu comme pluye: sec, au nom des diables. Davantaige, la fouldre ne tomberoit jamais dessus. Car pourquoy? ilz sont tous bénist ou sacrez. Je n'y voy qu'ung inconvénient.
– Ho ho ha ha ha! dist Pantagruel. Et quel?
– C'est que les mouches en sont tant friandes que merveilles, et se y cueilleroient facilement, et y feroient leur ordure: et voylà l'ouvrage gasté et diffame. Mais voicy comment l'on y remédiroit. Il fauldraoit tresbien les esmoucheter avecques belles queues de renards, ou bon gros vietz d'azes de Provence . . .
(83–4)[3]

As for the enormous expense, which you say would be needful for undertaking the great work of walling this city about, if the gentlemen of the town will be pleased to give me a good rough cup of wine, I will show them a pretty, strange, and new way, how they may build them good cheap. How? said Pantagruel. Do not speak of it, then, answered Panurge, and I will tell it you. I see that the sine qua nons, callibistris, or contrapunctums of the women of this country are cheaper than stones. Of them should the walls be built, ranging them in good symmetry by the rules of architecture, and placing the largest in the first ranks, then sloping downwards ridgeways, like the back of an ass. The middle-sized ones must be ranked next, and last of all the least and smallest. This done, there must be a fine little interlacing of them, like points of diamonds, as is to be seen in the great tower of Bourges, with a like number of the nudinnudos, nilnisistandos, and stiff brac-mards, that dwell in amongst the claustral cod-pieces. What devil were able to overthrow such walls? There is no metal like it to resist blows, in so far that, if culverin-shot should come to graze upon it, you would incontinently see distil from thence the blessed fruit of the great pox, as small as rain. Beware, in the name of the devils, and hold off. Furthermore, no thunderbolt or lightning would fall upon it. For, why? They are all either blest or consecrated. I see but one inconveniency in it. Ho, ho, ha, ha, ha, said Pantagruel, and what is that? It is, that the flies would be so liquorish of them, that you would wonder, and they would quickly gather there together, and there leave their ordure and excretions, and so all the work would be spoiled. But see how that might be remedied; they must be wiped and made rid of the flies with fair fox-tails, or good great viedazes, which are ass-pizzles, of Provence.[4]

There immediately follows another anecdote, this time concerning an old woman and a fox, which is at least as obscene as the anecdote of the walls of Paris.

This, then, is the kind of sexually obscene material under discussion. So offensive is it to some students that it is not unknown for some to refuse to read the text, or to leave the seminar when it is being discussed. This reaction is, typically, a reaction of women students rather than of men.

However, it could be said that there are other kinds of 'obscenity' involved in reading Rabelais: for example, it is said that there is a near-absence of women in the text, and there is the fact that those women who do appear either die in childbirth (Gargantua's mother, Gargamelle, and Pantagruel's mother, Badebec) or are abused in other ways; or are figures of fun. Additionally, there is frequent 'disembodiment' of women, as already illustrated.

As a result of these observations and many like them, there is a compara-tively longstanding critical tradition that has seen Rabelais as a misogynist. So far, I have given some of the most frequently quoted reasons for seeing Rabelais' work as obscene, or, at the very least, sexist. Now for the other side of the coin.

First, that obscenity.

It must be understood that, though 'obscenity' was the given grounds for the proscription of Rabelais' work by the Sorbonne, at the time the word referred to doubts about the religious implications of the text rather than to its expression of sexuality or physicality. These days, we are less aware of religious matters and more strongly aware of sexual ones. Though, clearly, sexual and scatalogical elements do occur in Rabelais, the Sorbonne was much more concerned by the challenge provided to the status of the Church, especially by Rabelais' second book, *Garantua*. The Church, be it said, was trying hard to hold on to the powers it had had, not least by means of the Inquisition: this was not a period in which challenge to the Church was insignificant. It is only in the nineteenth century that 'obscenity' came to refer to matters connected with sexuality, and it is with that definition of obscenity that we are still coming to terms. The definition of obscenity is both chronologically and culturally variable, and so naive imposition of the word on this text as a judgement of it is somewhat unwise.

If the work is not simply classifiable as obscene, then, is it possible to consider as non-sexist a text in which women scarcely feature, except as mothers dying in childbirth, as old hags, as caricatures of soothsayers – always as object of comic ridicule? This question has two answers.

The first is historical. Women's roles and status in the sixteenth century were not what they are now. Women did not change their names on marriage, they often 'married' unofficially whomever they wished to marry, and their wealth did not become their husband's on marriage. Until the 1560s a widow, particularly, was free to marry whomever she wished. Women frequently worked beside their husbands in trade: when Rabelais' publisher died, the business automatically continued under the direction of his widow. At the Hôtel-Dieu in Lyons, girls as well as boys were fed, clothed, (minimally) educated and put to apprenticeships.[5] However, women were liable to be allocated 'functional' rather than fully functioning standards of literacy. In the 1560s in Lyons, only 28 per cent of the women could write their names. Nevertheless, many women took an active part in the religious reform movements and the Counter-Reformation. On the other hand, the continuing *querelle des femmes* had been feeding a steady debate, more or less well-informed, as to what women were and how they functioned, both physically and spiritually, since the late middle ages, and from that debate women were in general excluded.

Women were, however, active both economically and in the realm of religion – and therefore of politics, for the two were inseparable at that period – though less so, for the most part, than men. So the question of sexism is rather difficult to define: the expectations of large sections of the population were very different from those of today, in all spheres, and their world-view was very differently constituted. I would not like to give a judgement as to what a woman in the sixteenth century would find 'sexist', had the term been available to her. However, I must observe that, in *Pantagruel*, the working women are there, the great ladies are there, the women giving birth and dying are there. Women intellectualising and writing are not. This was, as far as I am able to judge, as much a reflection of the state of the world as a deliberate attempt to exclude women from the text.

The second answer to the question of whether or not this text is sexist is to do with the presentation of the 'obscene' parts of the text. Importantly, obscene episodes are often produced by or related to the presence in the text of Panurge. Further, the comedy and the obscenity aim at the male as well as the female of the species, and all the characters are objects of ridicule, except, most significantly, Pantagruel himself. Additionally, not all the ridicule is of a sexual nature. There is as much satirical comedy in the presentation of a filthy old academic, coughing and spewing his way through a speech interlarded with bad Latin, as there is in the sight of a proud and fickle woman being pursued through the streets by packs of dogs, following the scent of a bitch with which her gown has been sprinkled. However, I must add that there have been other difficulties with interpretation, which cannot be laid at Rabelais' door.

First, Panurge suggests rebuilding the walls of Paris out of an interlaced stack of vulvas because, he claims, these will resist any degree of pounding to break down the walls; he then adds that they could interweave penises for extra strength. But I have looked in vain for critical discussion which mentions the interweaving of male members, not just the stacking up of female ones.

Secondly, I cannot be the only researcher to have noticed that, though Rabelais was a physician and therefore familiar with the frequent deaths of women in and after childbirth, there is no critical speculation that his presentation of giant mothers who die in childbirth might be more a reflection of reality than a decisive way of removing women from his text for less sensible reasons.

Thirdly, I have been unable to find comment that would allow of the presence of comic obscenity as being related to the 'cartoon-like' nature of his characters: indeed, as they are hardly characters at all, but more akin to medieval 'types'; it is not logical to see the antisocial elements of their behaviour as in any way being condoned. It is also worth remarking that, whenever obscenity occurs, there are marked distancing devices in the text, which ensure that the reader picks up the full ironic or satirical impact of the events.

Finally, what do I make of all this, as a woman? I make of it a great deal. I also do not make of it a great deal.

I do not make of it that Rabelais was a misogynist; I do not make of it that he considered women somehow incapable of thought; I do not make of it that I should, as a twentieth-century woman, resent his explicitness about the human body. What I do make of it is that I can and do enjoy this obscene comedy. This is, I believe, likely to be the case for many women; especially, perhaps, those who, like me, are from a working-class background, where 'rude' and crude jokes are not only acceptable but are almost the norm in women's conversation in the absence of men. I make of it that I am unwilling to pretend to be offended by these texts. But I have been and am offended by the two-edged moralising which suggests that I 'must', as a woman, be offended.

In his seminal work, Mikhail Bakhtin discusses orality and anality in Rabelais in a very full manner, and observes particularly a strong tendency to 'downward movement' in the text.[6] But he fails to see what I consider to be the female characteristics of this text. First, for a woman, the obvious observation is that what is internal becomes external in the act of birth. Rabelais' text has both births and acts of excretion as part of its 'downward movement'. But acts of excretion, like obscene events, are frequently connected with the presence of Panurge in the text, while acts of giving birth are not. Birth is related only to the two giant 'heroes' of the text, Pantagruel and his father Gargantua. Both of these characters embody what is the best in human beings. Women giving birth therefore produce human beings capable of the highest functioning. Panurge, and the acts of excretion, on the other hand, are related to the physicality of the human being, the human body without the human spirit.

In many critiques, there is a continuous searching after a way of characterising the relationship between Pantagruel and Panurge, for they are the centre of the whole Rabelaisian text. It has been observed that Pantagruel constitutes the higher functions of a human being – intellect, spirituality, love – while Panurge constitutes the lower or 'demonic' functions of the human being – sex, sexuality, bodily functions of all kinds, including the production of speech and excretion. Therefore, Panurge is not simply Pantagruel's 'alter ego'. They are each a representation of half of the human condition. That is why Panurge is Pantagruel's friend, 'lequel il aymoit toute sa vie'.

The Rabelaisian text may therefore be seen as a coming to terms with the extremes of being human. The text was and is subversive in that it takes a satirical and comic perspective on the complexity of life itself. But the text does not forge a false reconciliation of the two parts of the human being, for neither concedes any aspect of its sovereignty to the other. Instead it presents a paradoxical combining of unlikely companions in a permanent and continuously fluctuating relationship. It is my opinion that until women can become that paradox, it is not likely that women's writing will achieve its full potential.

I see the subversiveness of the Rabelaisian text as its most important feature. It challenges the Church and the law; it does not challenge patriarchy because that was not the controlling power. I maintain that a subversive text cannot be obscene, however much it may shock accepted morality, for subversiveness is the nature of female writing.

In conclusion, I have learned two things from the thoughts that Rabelais's texts have prompted. First, that female 'modesty', far from being a basic trait, is an imposition required by a society unwilling to accept female sexuality, and that, had I been discouraged from reading a male-written text because of some supposed feminist principles, I would have missed what has been a life-transforming experience.

NOTES

1. I use 'linguist' to mean one who studies language as a phenomenon rather than one who learns languages – though the former often involves the latter.
2. The edition of *Pantagruel* I refer to in this paper is that edited by V. L. Saulnier for Droz (1946). However, this reproduces the earliest extant version of the text. For the definitive version of *Pantagruel* and the later books, see *Oeuvres complètes*, edited by P. Jourda (Paris: Garnier, 1962).
3. The spelling and grammar of the extract are archaic, and some aspects of it were intentionally archaic even at the time it was produced.
4. English translation by Sir Thomas Urquhart, from the Everyman edition of *Gargantua and Pantagruel* (London: Dent, 1980), vol. I, p. 188.
5. For full and fascinating information about this period, I cannot do better than refer the reader to N. Z. Davies, *Society and Culture in Early Modern France*, (Cambridge: Polity Press in association with Basil Blackwell, 1987).
6. M. Bakhtin, *The World of Rabelais*, (Cambridge, Massachusetts: MIT Press, 1986).

Chapter 14

Absent from Home

Female voices and male reading, in Aphra Behn, Rochester and Elizabeth Malet

Edward Burns

I am confident I shall never sleepe agen, and twere noe great matter if it did nott make mee looke thin, for naturally I hate to be soe long absent from my self as one is in a manner those seav'n dull how'rs hee snores away, and yet methinks not to sleepe till the sun rise is an odd effect of my disease, and makes the night tedious with out a woman, reading would relieve me, but bookes treate of other men's affaires and to me that's ever tiresome, beside I seldome have candle, but I am resolv'd to write some love passages of my own life, they will make a pritty Novell, and when my boy buy's a linke, it shall burne by mee when I goe to bedd, while I divert myself wth reading my owne story, wch will be pleasant enough.[1]

So says one Mr Daynty, in the opening speech of a comedy, scribbled by Rochester when perhaps in a state not all that remote from that of his protagonist. Woman figures as a commodity, a diversion from the tedium which is itself the only alternative to an absence from the self that he dreads more. The calculated casualness of Rochester's misogynistic discourse is not, however, what my paper is about. Rather, I want to consider two aspects of his writing and its context which may seem to go athwart his (more often discussed) relation to a misogynistic tradition. First, Rochester periodically sets out to construct female voices in his texts and these voices tend to be in conflict with misogynistic voices, and with the presentation of a 'masculinised' authority in reading and writing elsewhere in his work. Late seventeenth-century English writing, in almost all genres, tends to foreground gender, not simply in the depiction of social forms, but as the condition of writing, reading and speaking. Gender difference is 'in play' in a lyric or a letter as much as it is in a restoration comedy or in a public polemic.

The second aspect of Rochester's work I want to address is the appropriation of his voice, his texts, or, in a sense, of Rochester as text (the cultural text created by 'fame' and gossip) in the work of women writers; of his wife Elizabeth Malet, his mother Ann Wilmot, and his niece Anne

175

Wharton, as well as in the writing of Aphra Behn. Again, 'misogyny' may seem to present a problem here. Rochester acts as a kind of locus for women writing, both in his own family circle, and for the professional women writers, of whom Behn is still the most famous, who tend to be labelled 'the female wits'.[2] I want to examine some traces of Rochester in texts by women, as well as looking at his use of the idea of the woman writer as a vehicle of his own concern with the disruptive and transgressive voice.

'SHUT UP AT HOME'

In the same collection of papers as the play fragment is another unfinished dramatic monologue:

> What vain, unnecessary things are men!
> How well we do without 'em! Tell me, then,
> Whence comes that mean submissiveness we find
> This ill-bred age has wrought on women-kind?

The speaker does not reflect on herself as writer, but she does tell us how she reads:

> Ere bear this scorn, I'd be shut up at home,
> Content with humoring myself alone;
> Force back the humble love of former days
> In pensive madrigals and ends of plays . . .[3]

Like Mr Daynty's, her practice is narcissistic, a reading that gives her back herself. It could be seen also as a kind of retreat into delusion – how can she 'force back . . . humble love' by means of this solitary activity? Writing from the country to the town, the anonymous speaker seems to be a counterpart to the better-known Artemisia, who writes from the town to her friend Chloe in the country:

> Chloe,
>   In verse by your command I write.
> Shortly you'll bid me ride astride, and fight:
> These talents better with our sex agree
> Than lofty flights of dangerous poetry . . .
> Amongst the men, I mean the men of wit
> (At least they passed for such before they writ),
> How many bold adventurers for the bays,
> Proudly designing large returns of praise,
> Who durst that stormy, pathless world explore,
> Were soon dashed back, and wrecked on the dull shore,
> Broke of that little stock they had before!
> How would a woman's tottering bark be tossed

Where stoutest ships, the men of wit, are lost?
When I reflect on this, I straight grow wise,
And my own self thus gravely I advise:
     Dear Artemisia, poetry's a snare;
Bedlam has many mansions; have a care.
Your muse diverts you, makes the reader sad:
You fancy you're inspired; he thinks you mad.
. . . Thus, like an arrant woman as I am,
No sooner well convinced writing's a shame'
That whore is scarce a more reproachful name
Than poetess –
Like men that marry, or like maids that woo,
'Cause 'tis the very worse thing they can do,
Pleased with the contradiction and the sin,
Methinks I stand on thorns till I begin.[4]

'Bedlam has many mansions; have a care.' In the gospel according to St John, Jesus tells the apostles that his father's house, meaning heaven, has 'many mansions'.[5] Male reading – 'you fancy you're inspired, he thinks you're mad' – imprisons Artemisia in the father's house, a mad-house, the denial of her voice. It is a typical Restoration device to use a flippant liturgical or scriptural parody to destroy the authority of the religious text (in the largest sense the word of the father) and thus to offer the reader a key to alternative ways of constructing meaning.

The envisaged male reader is threatened by Artemisia's claim to literary 'fame', to 'lofty flights' which imply an Amazonian role, an assumption to herself of the 'heroic', 'adventuring' model of the male writer that Artemisia (and Rochester) parody at the beginning of the poem. But within the fiction of the poem male reading amounts to a misappropriation of a letter written not for that reader, but for a female reader. A text that exists solely between female writer and female reader is more typically a non-literary text. The frame of Rochester's address to a male *and* female readership propels Artemisia into the hazardous masculine world of 'the literary'. So there are two models for a woman writing; transgression – public writing is a contradiction and a sin, a sin, to return to the religious parody, against the father but a transgression also in the more literal sense of a lawless adventurous movement, of a kind seen in men as heroic – or the solitariness of the house that is also a mad-house, a bedlam. Only the fact that the female voice here is a fiction, Rochester writing as a woman usurping a male practice in writing, allows the choice to be held in poise.

It is precisely as transgression, as contradiction, that female voice interests Rochester. The female voices in his satirical squibs are defiant and disrespectful – 'Quoth the duchess of Cleveland to counselor Knight/ "I'd fain have a prick, knew I how to come by't"'.[6] Other voices are rendered inarticulate, as in the unthreatening baby language with which the woman in 'The Imperfect Enjoyment' responds to the speaker's sexual embarrassment – 'smiling she chides in a kind murmuring noise',[7] a wordless liquidity of sound that seems associated with the beneficently feminine, like the Venus of the Lucretius fragment.[8] But it is in the transgressive/disruptive voice that Rochester's women find words, and this I think links him to the 'female wits', the first English school of professional women writers, whose style and concerns seem continuous with those of male writers themselves equally capable of misogyny. The authoritarian male reader is often presented in Rochester's male-voiced poems as attempting to contain or halt the defiant intellectual individualism, the libertinism, that constructs Rochester for us as a disruptive voice. The 'Rochester' of these poems tries to pre-empt such an attack – from the 'wiser men' in 'The Mistress',[9] and the 'formal beard and band' in the 'Satire on Reason and Mankind',[10] an attack which takes the form of a rationalist or deist attempt to fix the meaning of a wandering and transgressive text. Rochester, like Artemisia, like Aphra, escapes and defies – but what happens to those shut up at home?

The collection of papers in which Rochester wrote the rough and sometimes the only draft of these writings (kept at the University of Nottingham as Portland MS PWV 31) also contains poems by his wife Elizabeth Malet, and pairs of poems in which they answer each other. Elizabeth Malet was a wealthy heiress who acquired a kind of independence in London by playing suitors off against each other, and was then kidnapped by Rochester. For this he was imprisoned in the Tower of London. A few years later she agreed to marry him, apparently of her own free will. She spent most of her time apart from him in the country, often with his mother, with whom she did not get on. The terms 'home', 'absence', 'fugitive', 'freedom', 'humble', 'tyrant', are the key-words in her lyrics, as in his:

> Phillis misfortunes that can be exprest
> Admit some gentle hours of peace and rest
> But from loves empire I hope noe release
> For though dispairing still my flames increase
> And dull complaint can never ease a care
> Thats caused by absence nourished by despair.

In poems like 'Absent from thee I languish still' or 'The Mistress', Rochester presents equivalent ideas as elegant, if anguished, paradoxes of feeling, explored by the 'fugitive' male. Malet, too, explores these paradoxes, but seems conversely kept in place by them. Though she starts the poem as an address to a conventionally named pastoral heroine, the situation the poem presents comes to focus on a self-accusing female complainant:

Such conquering charms contribute to my chain
And ade fresh torments to my lingerin pain
That could kind love judge of my faithful flame
He would return the fugitive with shame
for haveing bin insenceble to love
That does by constancy its merrit prove.

But I that can thus slavishly complain
Of tedious absence and injust disdain
Merit the scorn with which I am repayn
For she that calls not reason to her aid
Deserves the punishment of Thersis hate
The utmost rigor of relentless fate.[11]

In other poems, Malet, like the speaker of 'What vain unnecessary things', works through the old fashioned Petrarchan discourse of power and submission. A lyric by Rochester complains:

But alas against my will
I must be your captive still
Ah be kinder then for I
Cannot change and would not die.[12]

A companion piece by Malet reasserts the power ascribed to the addressee of the poem – to herself, if this is how we read this private (unpublished) dialogue of poems. But at the same time she disavows such 'power' as 'feign'd', as an 'art' that conditions the relationship of the subjects presented in the poems:

thinke not thersis I will ere
By my love my Empire loose
you growe constant through dispare
kindness you would soon abuse
Though you still possess my hart,
Scorn and rigor I must fain
there remains noe other art
Your love fond fugitive to gain.[13]

The dialogue form, and an implied pastoral context for it, provides her with the material of other exercises in the exposure of the power manoeuvres informing such a language. The most complex and obsessively worked on of her poems is a pastoral dialogue. A shepherd tries to coerce Armilla by accusing her of a 'self concepted ignorance/ which furst inclind you to delight in hate/ that enemy to love and comon sence.' Armilla turns the ploy against him; 'your arguements/ appear so vain, so empty of true Sence', as she puts it in a first draft. But in the final version the shepherdess refers to another superior shepherd, Strephon, 'whom you so much adore'. Strephon can

> preserve his Empire or inlarge his power
> Without insulting o'er our innocence
> In pitty your vain arguments I hear
> But nothing can be said in its defence
> Since opposit to reason and I fear
> to vertue; since now you know my thoughts of love
> be henceforth so discreet never to name
> that hated passion. For nothing can remove
> My firm resolve near to admite his flame.[14]

It is easy to see from the manuscript which lines Malet was most anxious to get right. 'Your arguements so empty of true sense'; 'so opposit to vertue and to sense', are other versions of the fifth and sixth lines quoted. In this poem, more explicitly than in those in which she turns the Petrarchan language back on itself, she articulates a refusal by hitting back at the male speaker with his own tactic – a refusal to allow reason, sense or meaning to the other's utterance. The effect of breaking away, on Malet's part as well as on Armilla's, is there in the breaking of the couplet by its running on into the next half line. The effect is almost unique in Malet's work, and is used by Rochester for emphatically disruptive effect (by Artemisia, for example). And yet . . . who is Strephon? Strephon was Rochester's own pastoral nickname, used by Behn among others. Malet assents to, rather than disrupts, her husband's cultural eminence.

'RUNN AWAY LIKE A RASCAL'

As a summation of libertine styles, Rochester becomes himself a kind of text, a text constructed in gossip and surmise, confirmed and extended by his writings and those of his circle. The importance of this for Aphra Behn was that the 'fugitive', the 'Rover' Rochester (to cite in that last instance the name of her best-known play) acts as the emblem of a style that escapes enclosure in the father's house, even, in her memorial poems for him, in the tomb. In a poem written in response to a poem by Rochester's niece Anne Wharton, itself a response to a poem by Behn on Rochester's death – so Rochester roves across a web of female texts that are both letters and literary 'flights' – Rochester 'appears' to Behn. Aphra is ill and despondent, 'scarce thought a subject found'. But he appears as an 'it', ungendered because the 'medium' of this inventive use of the 'ghost-visitation' convention is Wharton's text. In this form he/it ('he' in remembered life, 'it' in his current trace on a woman's writing) enters into and orders Behn's poem:

> Careful of the Fame himself first rais'd,
> Obligingly it School'd my loose Neglect . . .[15]

Wharton in her poem exempts Behn from the process Rochester seems to have gone through in moving from the gendered historical 'himself' to the appropriable and neutered 'it' of textuality. She assures Behn that:

> Fame, Pheonix like, still rises from a Tomb
> But bravely you this Custom have o'ercome. [16]

Behn defies the tomb in that her living self and her text are continuous. This avowal in Wharton's poem seems to renew Behn, cured of her illness, even reborn within her own poem, and, after the textual apparition of the ungendered Rochester, able to find a subject. Rochester revives in her the sense of creative, transgressive adventure of which he is almost a personification, but Wharton's text transforms 'him', makes him/it present in Behn's own writing. Behn compares herself to a shepherd suddenly in touch with the music of the spheres:

> He starts and in a transport cries, – '*Tis there!* [17]

Behn's metaphors for writing habitually situates her outdoors. She sees writing as membership of a pastoral community. Her writing cheats both home and tomb. Wharton's model of writing similarly extends beyond the domestic – 'ruin'd temples try to build again' she exhorts Behn, but Behn isn't really interested in temples. Her response to the Rochester she extrapolates from Wharton's text may be corrective of Wharton's poem, or at least evasive of Wharton's wishes for her. Wharton exhorts:

> May yours excel the matchless *Sappho's* Name;
> May you have all her Wit without her Shame . . .
> Scorn meaner Theams, declining low desire
> And bid your Muse maintain a Vestal Fire. [18]

Behn's writing of herself is more mobile, more fugitive than this, more into wrecking temples than rebuilding them. The transgression, the ironic sin, lies in declining to decline.

> Runn away like a rascal without taking leave, deare wife, it is an upolish't way of proceeding wch a modest man ought to be ashamed of, I have left you a prey to your owne immaginations, amongst my Relations, the worst of damnations, but there will come an hower of deliverance, till when, may my mother be merciful unto you, soe I committ you to what shall ensue, woman to woman, wife to mother, in hopes of a future appearance in glory. [19]

So writes Rochester, leaving Elizabeth at home. As in the lyric 'Absent from thee I languish still', absence is death and death absence – he dies to rise again in glory, a parody of the Easter service – but death is also home, the home that in the poem becomes his 'everlasting rest', and in the letter the ashes to ashes and dust to dust of wife and mother. The controversy surrounding Rochester's own death provides an ironic coda to the opposition of enclosure and transgression, to the rebellion against entrapment in the Father's word. Rochester's mother Ann survived all her family but for five granddaughters. She lived on into her eighties. A religious woman, from a parliamentarian background, she authorised the publication of five letters to her friend Lady St John, written while her son was dying, in order to contribute to the controversy as to whether or not Rochester had repented on his death-bed.

> Last night, the very expression you have made in your good wishes for his soul, he made to God in the conclusion of his prayer last night, that he might enjoy that unspeakable bliss of a place in heaven, though he were but a door-keeper, to sing praises to the Lord with the heavenly host. I do believe if any has reported that he should speak ridiculous, it has been the popish physician, who one day listened at the door whilst my son was discoursing with a divine. But my son spoke so low that he could hear but half words, and so he might take it for nonsense, because he had a mind to do so.[20]

So we leave Rochester on the threshhold of the father's house. At the door of his own death chamber different parties compete for the right to read his last utterances. For his mother his voice disappears into a religious discourse already voiced by her friend; a final attempt to fix the fugitive text of Rochester's fame, the text that for Behn continues to abet her own absence from the father's house.

NOTES

1. From Portland MS PWV 31, in the collection of the University of Nottingham, folio 11r. Thanks to the University library for their permission to publish this material, and to the staff of the manuscript department for their help.
2. A label popularised recently by Fidelis Morgan's anthology of plays of the period written by women, *The Female Wits* (London, 1981).
3. *The Complete Poems of John Wilmot, Earl of Rochester*, edited by David M. Vieth (New Haven and London: Yale University Press, 1968), pp. 102, 111–14, 21–4.
4. *ibid.*, pp. 104–5, 111–31.
5. John, 14.1.
6. Vieth, pp. 48, 111–12.
7. *ibid.*, p. 38, l.19.
8. Also in PW V 31. Vieth, pp. 34–5.
9. Vieth, p. 87, l.13.
10. *ibid.*, p. 96, l.46.
11. PW V 31, 13r. V. de Sola Pinto reprinted this and the other poems I ascribe to Malet as either by Rochester or Lady Rochester – in Lady Rochester's hand. *Poems by John Wilmot, Earl of Rochester* (London: Routledge and Kegan Paul, 1953), pp. 143–7.
12. Vieth, p. 10, ll. 5–8.
13. PW V 31, 12r. Vieth publishes this poem in a modern-spelling text, to accompany the Rochester piece, p. 10.

14. *ibid.*, 19r + v.
15. From Germaine Greer *et al.*, *Kissing the Rod: An anthology of seventeenth-century women's verse* (London: Virago, 1988), p. 250, ll. 37–8.
16. *ibid.*, p. 251 (no line numbers).
17. *ibid.*, p. 250.
18. *ibid.*, p. 251 (no line numbers).
19. *The Letters of John Wilmot, Earl of Rochester*, edited by Jeremy Treglown (Oxford: Blackwell, 1980), p. 73.
20. *ibid.*, p. 251.

Part IV

Teaching after Cixous

Introduction

In one of the 'Conversations' transcribed in the final section of *Writing Differences*, Hélène Cixous remarks:

> Everything begins with love. If we work on a text we don't love, we are automatically at the wrong distance. This happens in many institutions where, in general, one works on a text as if it were an object, using theoretical instruments.[1]

Cixous herself works in an institution, albeit one of an unconventional kind: in the aftermath of the events of 1968, she founded the Centre d'Etudes Féminines as part of the experimental University of Paris VIII–Vincennes. Her seminar there is committed to a 'feminine' pedagogy as well as to 'feminine' writing and research, but is it possible to practise a 'feminine' pedagogy within other, more traditional academic institutions, and if so what would it be like? The three essays in this section address these questions, drawing on a range of experiences in Britain, France, Norway and Scotland.

Susan Sellers begins her essay with an account of her own experience of studying English literature at a British university in the early 1970s, an experience which was disappointing and unsatisfactory because of the distance she felt between herself and the texts she read, and because of the pressure to get good marks by regurgitating other people's opinions. For her, the first importance of Cixous' seminar was the discovery of a non-judgemental, non-competitive approach to texts in which the reader opens herself to what may have motivated the writer to produce a particular text as well as to the sorts of life-experiences with which the text deals. This 'open' mode of reading is characterised as 'feminine' and is very similar to what Judith Still describes as 'reading in a motherly, creative fashion' in her essay in Part I of this book and which privileges 'the reconstructive over the critical, the generous over the calculated' (page 57 above). One of its implications is indeed to break down the distinction between 'critical' and 'creative' writing by acknowledging the collaborative role of the reader.

In her pedagogic practice, teaching French literature at the University of Trondheim, the Norwegian writer and teacher Sissel Lie engineers precisely this breakdown in order to encourage her students to 'fall in love with [Cixous'] texts, to rediscover themselves as they do when they're in love, to change and never be the same again, because of what they've read'. They learn to read by learning to write, using the non-intimidating method of process-oriented writing, and sharing both their writing and the experiences they describe in relation to the text. They keep diaries of their reading and they write short papers which their teacher treats as 'letters', responding to them personally and positively, without corrections or criticisms. In this way, they recover the pleasure of their earliest writing experiences at the same time as they are 'reborn' to reading.

'This is fun', say the Norwegian students, 'but will it lead us to a university exam?' Lie acknowledges the comparative luxury of being able to teach her modern French literature course in this very unusual way, and of being able to spend a whole term studying a single text. As Susan Sellers also points out, to adopt the *Etudes Féminines* approach is to mount a radical challenge to conventional methods of organising and teaching literature courses. It means providing more opportunities for creative work, and pooling our resources as readers instead of competing with each other. It also means rethinking the relationship between the teacher and the student 'in ways which neither negate the experience a teacher has to offer students nor fall back onto the convenient and oppressive hierarchy by which the teacher's position is comfortably assured'. And finally it means allowing for greater flexibility for students to choose not only which texts they will work on but also how and when they will present their own work – the implication being that this kind of learning cannot be assessed by traditional grading and examination systems.

All these points are recognised by Jennifer Birkett, who, while valuing the radical *potential* of *Etudes Féminines*, cautions that, if we are to realise this utopia somewhere other than in language, we shall have to confront 'real institutional practices'. She asks whether, given the constraints of working in an institution such as her own (the University of Strathclyde), and the larger political and economic pressure on higher education in Britain today, the career and example of Hélène Cixous might suggest that 'in order to write anything meaningful, honest, truthful you have to move out of the academy'. Within the academy (at least within most academies) we are not free to choose what we teach, how we teach it or how our students are assessed. We have to make decisions about how much 'theory' needs to be taught and when, how significant gender difference is at specific historical and geographical moments, how we cope with students' ignorance, students' anxieties, and with men. While we can rejoice that Women's Studies are acquiring academic respectability, we should also see the dangers they face of losing touch with their radical roots on the one hand and seeming to enforce a new orthodoxy on the other. It is implied here that most of us will need to be pragmatic about how much of the methodology of the Cixous seminars we can import into our own practice, and that we shall probably need to be pluralist about adopting the 'feminine' approach as one that can be complemented by others.

These three papers were given at very different points during the conference in Liverpool: Susan Sellers opened the very first session with her wide-ranging but also very personal introduction to *Etudes Féminines*, Sissel Lie gave her paper in the middle of the programme in a session which concentrated on Hélène Cixous' own writing, while Jennifer Birkett's paper was the focus of the final, plenary discussion. Those who were present will recall the special resonances of all three occasions while, we hope, appreciating the logic of presenting the papers together in the current context.

A.T.

NOTE

1. *Writing Differences: Readings from the seminar of Hélène Cixous* edited by Susan Sellers (Milton Keynes: Open University Press, 1988), p. 147.

Chapter 15

Learning to Read the Feminine

Susan Sellers

This paper, which was originally written to follow the paper by Sarah Cornell (see Part I, pages 31–4 above), explores some of the implications of *Etudes Féminines* for the way we read, write about and teach works of literature. I have divided the paper into three parts. In the first part, I explore some of the implications of *Etudes Féminines* for the way we read texts. In the second part, I consider briefly the implications of *Etudes Féminines* for the way we write about texts, concluding, in the third and final part, with some brief remarks on the implications of *Etudes Féminines* for the way we organise and teach literature 'courses'.

A FEMININE READING

In this first section, I explore some of the implications of *Etudes Fémines* for reading. This can be summarised by three questions: 1. why do we read? 2. how do we read? and 3. what difference does it make if it is I, Susan Sellers, reading, and if I, Susan Sellers, am a woman?

Why do we read? What do we read for?
I would like to explore this first question by describing my own experience as a reader. I was a student of English in Britain in the early 1970s, and whilst the university I went to had all kinds of riveting course descriptions in its prospectus, promising radical new approaches, I feel now, looking back on my three years as an undergraduate, as if I spent the entire time drifting from course to course, becoming increasingly despairing in my efforts to find out exactly what it was I was supposed to do with a text in order to get good marks in my essays: and getting good marks, for a number of reasons, to do with wanting to prove myself, and still please 'Daddy', was definitely my priority at the time. Looking back on those three years now

I'm not sure I ever did find out. I accumulated great heaps of lecture notes, most of which I shamelessly regurgitated in my exams, and which mainly seemed to concern the lecturer's opinion of other people's opinion of (somewhere very far down the line) the text. There were occasional insights, occasional glimpses of . . . something else, when the activity of reading Shakespeare or Virginia Woolf suddenly seemed to connect with something, but on the whole my three privileged years as an English undergraduate rarely included me as reader, or even took account of the – admittedly hazy – notions I had had that literature was somehow important, was about extending one's experience, and encountering another's point of view, that had led me to choose literature, and not history or politics or sociology, as a degree.

I eventually acquired my BA, and went on to do postgraduate work. Here, I encountered for the first time feminist critics like Kate Millett, Ellen Moers, Elaine Showalter, Mary Ellman, Sandra Gilbert, Susan Gubar and Tillie Olsen, working to expose instances of sexism and misogyny in texts by male writers – at last these things had names – questioning the authority of the traditional male canon, and bringing centre-stage the various ways in which women are perceived and represented in our culture. Coming to this work was a release after three years as an undergraduate, in which, insofar as I was ever able to formulate what the required approach was, the vestiges of Leavisite 'close-reading' and the need to assert oneself as critic had left no space – no words or form – in which to express the vague sense of unease I had felt reading D. H. Lawrence – or even Henry James. After having no scope to develop the notion I had that there was so much more to say about *Wuthering Heights* or *Jane Eyre* than an examination of the chronological structure of narration, or whether Charlotte Brontë had, in fact, succeeded in creating Mr Rochester a 'real' man – whatever that was – the encounter with their texts was both liberating and enabling.

In 1983 I heard about and began attending Hélène Cixous' research seminar at the Centre d'Etudes Féminines in Paris. Here, unlike anything I had yet experienced, either as an undergraduate or even in my encounter with the Anglo-American feminist critics of the late 1970s and early 1980s whose work ultimately depends on a conservative view of both text and reader[1], was a place where texts were read not to demolish another's theory in order to replace it with one's own, nor to appropriate the text by listing all its flower or blood metaphors – nor even to explore all the various ways in which men and women are represented – but which focused on the text itself, on the author's motivations for writing and our own role in reading, on the processes by which meaning is created and the life-experiences with which the text deals.

*How do we, as readers, engage with and contribute to the processes
of meaning in the text?*
As I have suggested, the mode of 'feminine' reading pioneered by Hélène
Cixous at the Centre d'Etudes Féminines is radically different to the type of
critical practice I had come up against as an undergraduate, which, insofar
as I was ever able to discover what this practice was, mostly seemed to
consist of negotiating a way through others' theories and opinions. I do not
mean to imply by this that a 'feminine' reading is anti- or non-theoretical,
but simply that its goal is not that of producing 'a' theory, and making it 'fit'
a text, with all the 'finishing the jigsaw' feelings of satisfaction that
experience gives, once every piece has been sorted and slotted into place,
and each paragraph read to prove, or disprove that such and such a text is,
or is not, an example of such and such a movement or school: triumphantly
proclaiming, of course, the identity of the critic as master of his text in the
process. In fact, as I hope will become clear from the range of readings
collected here, *Etudes Féminines* uses a number of theoretical 'methods' and
insights, such as Freudian psychoanalysis, post-structural theories of
language, and Derrida's work on deconstruction, as a means of approaching
the text.

Perhaps the best way to describe a 'feminine' reading is to say that it
implies 'opening' the self to what it is the text is saying, even if this is
puzzling or painful or problematic. It entails reading to see how a text is
made, by exploring all the various resources for meaning a writer has
at their disposal: the writer's intended meaning, as well as the 'other'
meanings that contradict, complement, unsettle or dislodge this meaning.
It involves standing back from the text and looking at its overall construction; it entails reading at the level of the words themselves, at the level of
the syntax, the syllables and letter-patterns, the rhythm and punctuation.
It means asking who and what produced this text: and why? It means
acknowledging that I as reader participate in the ongoing process of the
text's creation; it means recognizing that my reading is itself a product of
certain questions, blind-spots, needs and desires, and that these motivations are constantly changing.

The question of how we read includes the question of what we read, and
Hélène Cixous' seminar in *Etudes Fémines* has worked on texts in a number
of languages, by a range of writers, from many different periods and genres.
The criterion for choosing texts has not been, as is so often the case,
because they embody a specific historical period or exemplify a particular
genre – or even because they are written by one sex rather than the other –
but because they address the issues and experiences that confront us as

human beings, and which it is the particular province of literature to explore.

Reading as a woman
I'd like to say something now about sexuality and gender in their relation to reading. I have mentioned my discovery, as a postgraduate student, of what is now often referred to as the 'first-wave' of Anglo-American feminist critics, and I think *Etudes Féminines* fills two gaps in connection with their work on sexuality and gender which I had found absent in their writing. First, I had often been struck, even as a much younger reader, how, reading books like *Jane Eyre* or *The Adventures of Huckleberry Finn*, it is possible to be constructed as both 'masculine' and 'feminine' by a text, sometimes identifying with, and at other times alienated from, the 'hero' or 'heroine'; and I want to suggest that Hélène Cixous' work on the fluctuating nature of gender, on the way we all take up different 'gender' positions, of mastery or openness, when confronted by different attitudes and situations, offers a useful context in which to explore the various ways we as readers collude with, merge with, resist or appropriate the 'gender' positions proposed by a text. At the same time, and without in any way diminishing the things that join us as human beings rather than divide us through sexual differences, *Etudes Féminines* offered itself as a place where it is possible to explore what it means if I, the reader, am also a woman.

Hélène Cixous has talked about the relationship between biological sex and one's 'gender' identity in terms of the way patriarchy has laid down the law for men and women according to biological sex.[2] This question, of how much being a woman has to do with having a biologically female body, and how much with the way women have been taught to behave, has long been a battle-ground for feminism; my own response to this question is to see the fact of having been brought up a woman in a society which privileges men *and* the fact of having a biologically female body as areas I want to explore. Like many women, I feel I could say a great deal about the ways in which I have stuggled (and am still struggling) to throw off all the negative constraints that have been imposed on me, but perhaps there is something positive – and perhaps something revolutionary – in the impetus a position on the margins can give. Perhaps because we do not, as women, feel we have everything to lose, but in fact have everything to gain, it is easier for us to be more radical, more daring in evisioning change, more 'feminine' than it is possible for men to be? In the 'Conversations' at the end of *Writing Differences*, Hélène Cixous describes the different experiences of a male or female body as entailing different sensations and perceptions, and offering different sources of metaphor for understanding these.[3] She suggests, for instance, that the female potential to conceive, nurture and give birth to another human being may contain the blueprint for a different type of self–other relations to the one that has created patriarchy.

A FEMININE WRITING

I would like to say something briefly about the implications of *Etudes Féminines* for the way we write about texts. As I have suggested, a 'feminine' reading means refusing the ego-comfortable positions of traditional criticism and acknowledging our participation as readers, and this has implications for the way we write. Blurring the rigid and, to me, absurd distinction between 'critical' and 'creative' writing, a 'feminine' writing entails relinquishing the pseudo-objectivity of conventional critical discourse and implicating ourselves as writers, accepting our role in the signifying process as well as the way language itself works on and shapes what we write.

A FEMININE TEACHING

Finally, I would like to say something very briefly about the implications of *Etudes Féminines* for the way we organise and teach literature courses.[4]

I believe *Etudes Féminines* has implications for the way we organise literature courses, for the way we define ourselves as 'teachers' or 'students', for the way we work, for the way we examine and assess work, and for the texts we work on. I believe it implies creating more opportunities for collective work, in order for us to pool our resources as readers, so that differences between our readings re-creates all the various meanings of a text. I believe it entails exploring the relationship between 'teacher' and 'student' in ways which neither negate the experience a 'teacher' has to offer 'students' nor automatically elevates the 'teacher' to a position of God. I think we need to create more opportunity for the participants on literature courses to choose what they will work on, and to be more actively involved in encouraging individual work-programmes, including how and when participants decide to present their work. Finally, and this may be the hardest one of all to negotiate in the present climate, I believe *Etudes Féminines* implies a radical reassessment of the way we comment on and judge others' work. A number of women's studies courses are now experimenting with alternatives to traditional examination formats, and I think *Etudes Féminines* offers an example of another way of working that could further this endeavour and help to create a fairer, more flexible, more 'feminine' form of education.

NOTES

1. For an account of the way I see the early mainstream of Anglo-American feminist criticism depending on a 'fixed' view of the text and reader see Susan Sellers, *Language and Sexual Difference: Feminist writing in France* (Basingstoke: Macmillan, forthcoming).
2. See my 'Introduction' to *Writing Differences: Readings from the seminar of Hélène Cixous*, edited by Susan Sellers (Milton Keynes: Open University Press; and New York: St Martin's Press, 1988), p. 1.
3. *ibid.*, p. 151.
4. For a more detailed account of the implications of *Etudes Féminines* for teaching literature see my 'Biting the teacher's apple: Opening doors for women in Higher Education', in *Teaching Women: Feminism and English studies*, edited by Ann Thompson and Helen Wilcox (Manchester: Manchester University Press, 1989), pp. 23–33.

Chapter 16

Pour une Lecture Féminine?

Sissel Lie

I've called this paper 'Pour une Lecture féminine', to relate my method of teaching a 'feminine' way of reading to the openness and generosity of the *écriture féminine*. Hélène Cixous' texts and readings of texts inspired me and gave me ideas as to how to read her novel *La Bataille d'arcachon* with a group of students.[1]

My first meeting with Hélène Cixous' texts was one of surprise and incomprehension. When I later understood that I had to give something of myself in the reading, had to read with my head and my body, to mobilise feeling and memories in order to meet her texts, I could understand what she says and let it change me. And I answer her books with my own witchcraft as she tells me to, writing short stories and novels. Although I never talk about her texts in my books, I still engage in dialogue with what I've read all the time. In 'Le dernier tableau ou le portrait de Dieu' she talks about how writer and reader must meet to make a text:

> Je suis la sorcière maladroite de l'invisible: ma sorcellerie est impuissante à évoquer, sans le secours de ta sorcellerie. Tout ce que j'évoque dépend de toi, dépend de ta confiance, de ta foi.
> Je rassemble des mots pour faire un grand feu jaune paille mais si tu n'y mets pas ta propre flamme, mon feu ne prendra pas, mes mots n'éclateront pas en étincelles jaune pâle. Mes mots resteront mots morts. Sans ton souffle sur mes mots, il n'y aura pas de mimosas.[2]

> (I am the awkward sorceress of the invisible: my sorcery lacks power to evoke, without the help of your sorcery. Everything I evoke depends on you, depends on your confidence, on your faith.
> I gather words to make a great straw-yellow fire but if you do not put in your own flame, my fire will not start, my words will not burst into pale yellow sparks. My words will remain dead words. Without your breath on my words, there will not be any mimosa.) (English translations in this chapter by Sarah Cornell and Susan Sellers.)

I was in a consciousness raising group in the 1970s. When we were fed up with talking, we started writing. That was in 1977, and to write my first texts was torture. I knew neither what to say, nor how to write. But the

196

other women in the group were waiting for whatever I could put down on paper. Step by step I came to feel that I had something to say about being a woman, especially being a woman wanting to create in a society where nothing was done to encourage me. And when I met Hélène Cixous for the first time in 1986, I was publishing my first book of short stories. Her lectures and later her texts encouraged me to open up to whatever is to be found inside me, and to consider more closely questions of passion, creativity and feminine writing.

I ended up writing a novel about the French Renaissance poet Louise Labé. She meets a woman from the 1980s, and the Renaissance and our own time enter into a dialogue about creativity and love. Now the time has come for women to compete with men in science and literature, Louise Labé said in the 1550s, and wrote about the close relationship between physical passion and poetic writing, between love and creativity.

Inspired by Hélène Cixous' texts, I opened up to more spontaneous ways of writing and established more contact with my 'inner voices'. My own dreams and bizarre waking ideas answered what my heroine from the Renaissance told me in her poems. And things happened to my writing that I had never dreamt of when I began, a beginning so painfully and totally despairing in front of my own incapacities. I discovered myself as a well; if I threw a bucket into my dark waters, it came up filled up with strange and interesting knowledge. And little by little I became more aware of my unknown readers, because I wanted them to listen to the important things I could tell them.

I'm not only an author, I'm also a teacher. When I write novels, I have something to share with my readers, a fascination, a truth, some important knowledge, a way of saying. But my first profession is to teach French literature at university. And I wanted very strongly to share with my students what Hélène Cixous had given me, but how could I teach them to open up to her texts? I wanted them to fall in love with her texts, to rediscover themselves as they do when they're in love, to change and never be the same again, because of what they've read. In Le Livre de Promethea[3] Hélène Cixous says that the story of Promethea is written on the heart of the narrator: I wanted the words of the book to be written on the heart of the readers. But how do you get young students that far? It is not as easy as just handing out a book and telling them to love it.

Could I find a method for a lecture féminine? I wanted to let 'the text talk', as I was told in Hélène Cixous' seminar in Paris, but how could I provoke the required openness to the texts? My students are mostly very young women, they often come straight from secondary school. They don't have any knowledge of the theories of the 1970s and the 1980s. They are mostly used to realistic novels, when they read fiction at all. They don't read poetry if they don't have to, and some have to be lured into the world of literature, because they have two years to learn French language with me and never beforehand believed they had to read fiction.

If I start with the theories, they will write down all I say and be impressed, but not touched, not changed. They will be taking notes, not making notes. If they read Hélène Cixous' texts, most of them will find them too different from what they know already and therefore too difficult. They will give up before having even tried. So where could I start? I got some ideas from a text in *La Bataille d'Arcachon* where Cixous talks about how difficult it is to capture the voices of creativity in yourself. There are so many things to disturb you when you want to write, your own thoughts and feelings, what goes on around you, people who demand your attention, cars in the street . . . How can we create an inner landscape, a desert, with silence and space enough to hear our own inner voices when it is as difficult as to hear God's heart beating?

> C'est pour ses poèmes que H a besoin de désert. Elle a besoin d'un désert intérieur délicat et bien protégé. Les poèmes de H, comme la plupart des poèmes d'ailleurs, s'effraient et fuient à la moindre brusquerie. Or comme H et Promethea habitent avenue Gambetta, H a le plus grand mal à protéger son propre désert intérieur. D'une part les poèmes ne se laissent attirer que rarement. D'autre part à Paris H a du mal à entendre ce qu'ils disent. Réussir à recueillir et élever une page d'écriture 21 bis avenue Gambetta, est aussi précaire que d'entendre battre le cœur de Dieu: le jour c'est impossible, il faut se lever vers deux heures du matin et entre les roulements des derniers camions et les roulements des premiers camions, espérer.[4]

> (H needs the desert for her poems. She needs a delicate and well-protected inner desert. H's poems, like most poems for that matter, take fright and flee at the least brusqueness. Now as H and Promethea live in Avenue Gambetta, H has the greatest difficulty in protecting her own inner desert. On the one hand the poems only rarely let themselves be enticed. On the other in Paris H has difficulty hearing what they say. To succeed in gathering and raising a page of writing at 21a Avenue Gambetta, is as precarious as listening to the beating of God's heart: by day it is impossible, it is necessary to get up towards two o'clock in the morning and between the rumblings of the last lorries and the rumblings of the first lorries, hope.)

I read this text as a text about creative reading, about the difficulty of hearing what a text says, of creating a receptivity towards the text. The question will then be, how do you create this kind of receptivity, how do you create silence and space enough to hear the voices of the text? Do the students have to read early in the morning when the outside world doesn't interrupt their reading? Of course not, even if I wanted them not only to hear the voices of *La Bataille d'Arcachon*, but also to let their own inner voices mingle with them.

I had been working for some time on what is called process-oriented writing. It is a theory of writing developed in the United States and in Great Britain, and most teachers use process-oriented writing to make students write in a more personal, engaged way – the theory being that you can learn to write better texts in dialogue with other writers and with literary texts.[5] Writing is seen as a process whereby teacher and students can engage in an exchange all the way to the finished product. Students are encouraged to write spontaneously, to submit their first efforts to the teacher and the other students at an early stage and discuss and rewrite many times before they consider the text finished. A secondary product of this method is that the students learn to think with their pencils, and perhaps even more important, they learn to feel with their pencils.

Let's return to *La Bataille d'Arcachon*. I could make the students use spontaneous writing to reflect on their own memories, their own feelings, their own writing, in relation to Cixous' novel. It relates a story of separation and togetherness, and is most of all about the power love has to change our lives and let us be born again. The book talks about the love relationship as a series of first times, of discovery, and of liberation from old constraint. It is also a reflection on writing, on how you cannot live and write at the same time, and, nevertheless, how you cannot write if you're not really in the midst of life. For creativity, and writing which is so closely related to and dependent on passion, also needs its own space, and seems to be contrary to the longing for a kind of osmosis in love.

La Bataille d'Arcachon steers us into the lives of the two heroines who don't want to be apart. But one of them, the poet H, feels that she must be alone for some time to be able to write. The needs of creativity trigger off the drama of separation; she leaves, and in the end we wouldn't know if she could write in her anxiety and loneliness if we didn't have in our hands a book relating the story of the separation and the reunion of the two lovers, told by an 'I' who is and is not H.

One of my main ideas is that the students have relevant experiences to bring to the text. Or as one of them wrote about *La Bataille d'Arcachon*: 'L'interprétation du texte demande un engagement émotionnel de la part du lecteur.' They should meet the novel, not only with their heads, but also with their bodies, and with the openness that Cixous' books require. This would be the *lecture féminine* – when it works.

When the book speaks about creativity and writing, the students know a lot about this from their own experience. We all have something to report about creativity, about writing, successes, failures and dreams, about how we could have written if only . . . But these memories have to be mobilised to motivate our reading and open us up to this kind of question. The students are asked for instance (there are many ways to do this) to write spontaneously for some minutes a list of what kind of writing they have done (car numbers, compositions, letters, the latest hits), and I always write with them. Afterwards we let the others hear one or two of the items on the list. We are all encouraged to steal ideas, and everybody takes another three to five minutes to write of the first things that they remember about writing at school. Afterwards we read aloud one or two sentences for the others.

Surprisingly enough, most first memories of writing are positive, even if the decorations on the pages are often remembered better and with more pleasure, than the writing itself. Later on in school, writing is considered difficult and tedious, and most of us forget the pleasures connected with it. But as the memories pop up under our pencils, we feel the pleasure of remembering and also a new pleasure in writing. And that's where we can start reading about writing and creativity, because we've been motivated to reflect on these questions by our own writing. My citation from *La Bataille d'Arcachon* about the inner voices can be the subject of a new three minutes of spontaneous writing, perhaps more, when students write what comes into their minds about the possibilities of hearing their inner voices, the possibility to create.

I shall give you another example of my reading with the students. This is related to the lists of 'the first times' in the book and is closer to their immediate experience, because it describes what can happen to you when you fall in love. In *La Bataille d'Arcachon* H is reborn to new ways of living and feeling. We could start by reading one of the texts talking about 'the first times' and write spontaneously about the ideas that come into our heads when we read the text before we discuss what we've written. Then we could try to write something about our experiences of falling in love and the feeling of being reborn to life. We can make lists of our 'first times' experiences as Hélène Cixous does, exchange these with each other and continue to develop the subject with a series of very short writing sessions and discussions. Or we could do it the other way around: start with our own experiences and then meet the novel. And we do not always discuss what we write with everybody, sometimes we go into smaller groups, sometimes we talk to our neighbours in the room; we're 'buzzing'.

It is not only the themes of the book that you can open up to and discuss in this way, but also the ways of writing, the style, the metaphors, etc. As the students become more conscious of the way they write, how they can express things differently, they want to study this more closely. Even if the narrator of *La Bataille d'Arcachon* says that a good sentence should be transparent, that does not mean that it can't be poetic. This book is so poetic you can keep the words in your mouth for a long time to savour their flavour. And the more conscious the students become about the qualities of the book, the more interested they are in finding out why the words give them such pleasure. So they go from a spontaneous reaction to the texts to a more analytic attitude.

They can, for instance, write and talk about the passage discussing how to write sentences in *La Bataille d'Arcachon*. The narrator here seems to discard the form and be interested in the words only insofar as they tell exactly what she wants to tell. The students can feel that the book they are reading is not transparent and *éphémère* at all, but a book where the words have a quality of their own and keep lingering in their heads for a long time because of their poetic quality.

> Qu'est-ce que je voulais dire?
> Ah oui – Je voulais dire que la vérité, on ne peut pas la dire. On peut seulement la transmettre d'un corps à l'autre. Et les phrases alors? Les phrases dont nous autres conteurs, poètes, parleurs, nous nous servons? C'est pour quoi faire? Je ne sais pas bien. Je crois que les phrases, qui sont nos instruments toujours improvisés, doivent être des petites boîtes en peau très souples et transparentes, qui laissent passer la lumière, et les battements de cœur. Pour moi, une bonne phrase ce serait une enveloppe éphémère et elle fondrait une fois le message transmis. Vraiment, pour les phrases, je ne trouve rien dans mon panier.
> Tout ce que je sais, par expérience, c'est qu'il y a des bonnes phrases et des mauvaises phrases. Les mauvaises sont épaisses, opaques et elles agissent comme des escrocs: elles détournent l'attention sur elles-mêmes. Elles font miroir. Je les abhorre (c'est le mot exact).[6]

> (What did I want to say?
> Oh yes – I wanted to say that one cannot say the truth. One can only transmit it from one body to the other. And what about phrases then? The phrases which we other story-tellers, poets, speakers use? What are they for? I do not know exactly. I believe phrases, which are our ever-improvised instruments, must be small very supple and transparent skin boxes, which let light and the heartbeats through. For me, a good phrase would be an ephemeral envelope and would dissolve once the message was transmitted. Really, as for phrases, I find nothing in my basket.
> All I know, from experience, is that there are good phrases and bad phrases. The bad ones are thick, opaque and they behave like crooks: they divert attention towards themselves. They mirror. I abhor them (this is the exact word).)

With this passage we can also start discussing what truth the narrator wants to tell, what truth is for us and if there is a truth in poetic writing that you can't approach in a university lecture. We can go to other texts by Hélène Cixous and to other writers and philosophers to find more material for our discussions. We have prepared our way and are ready to learn something about theory, about aesthetics and literature. Throughout the term the students are supposed to keep 'reading diaries' where they note whatever they can come up with concerning their reading of the book. This is not read in the group, but can be useful when, at the end of the term, they write an essay on their reading of *La Bataille d'Arcachon*.

You may ask if the first steps are not felt to be too personal, a kind of 'peeping-Tom activity'. First, the students are not forced to answer and second, every time we meet they write a short paper for me at the end of the lesson with commentaries. They ask me questions, they tell me what they liked and disliked, and I answer as though they had written me letters; no corrections, no criticisms! This permits me to change and adapt my strategies to what the students want, to explain what I want more clearly, to discuss further things they didn't understand, or were especially interested in. And of course, you can't be too personal in your first reading of fiction – afterwards you can decide what you want to do with what you've read, but it's my opinion that you have to build a commentary on literature on strong likes and dislikes to have something interesting to say. What do the students tell me in their 'letters'? They are at first very surprised, coming to the University with ideas of reading that don't correspond with what we're about to do. 'This is fun', some of them say, 'but will this lead us to a university exam?'. Is serious university work supposed to make you happy? Can you learn anything about French modern literature when talking about yourself? They all liked the book very much, funny and serious as it is at the same time. Many of them stressed the feeling of having enough time – we used the whole term, one hour a week, to read *La Bataille d'Arcachon*. The importance of having enough time can't be stressed enough. They also expressed their pleasure at taking an active part in the teaching, to try to put their feelings and thoughts into words, and they felt that they had learned how writing can help you think. They also felt that exchanging opinions, memories and feelings was a way of getting to know their fellow students – and their teacher – better. They thus established a secure situation that made learning, opening up, changing, possible. Some had decided before going to university that they hated literature, they were fed up with the analysis of literature by their teachers at school. But at the same time they were so happy to discover that their experience was valued, and the pleasure of writing got stronger and stronger as the book opened up before them. The reading itself became a story of a 'first time', of being reborn to reading, of having an experience that changes you for ever. This is what Hélène Cixous' *La Bataille d'Arcachon* can do for you if you fly into the text, and let it fly away with you.

NOTES

1. Hélène Cixous, *La Bataille d'Arcachon* (Quebec: Editions Trois, 1986).
2. Hélène Cixous, *Entre l'ecriture* (Paris: Editions des Femmes, 1986), p. 175.
3. Hélène Cixous, *Le Livre de Promethea* (Paris: Gallimard, 1983), p. 112.
4. *La Bataille d'Arcachon*, p. 17.
5. For example, Martin Lightfoot and Nancy Martin (editors), *The Word for Teaching is Learning* (London: Heinemann Educational Books, 1988).
6. *La Bataille d'Arcachon*, p. 71.

Chapter 17

The Implications of *Etudes Féminines* for Teaching

Jennifer Birkett

I am going to start with something that is somewhat inappropriate in the context of this book: a definition. In fact, I shall start with two. First, I have to define my subject, since Women's Writing and *Etudes Féminines*, which are the subjects of concern here, can imply very different things. The first is very wide, involving a range of texts and approaches; the second I take to be the particular approach to Hélène Cixous' seminar at the Centre d'Etudes Féminines in Paris. It is the second that has been the distinctive feature of this collection, and which I intend to focus on now. But that in no way rules out for us the wider subject of women's writing, and Women's Studies in general.

Second, I ought to define my particular perspective on the subject. I lecture in French at Strathclyde University. I teach in most areas. My research is in eighteenth- and nineteenth-century prose fiction, and its historical and cultural matrix. The women I study are mostly very much caught up in their contemporary patriarchal discourse, and what I read most of the time are the limiting effects of that discourse. I find that the approach of the Cixous seminar throws into relief how limiting it is, by establishing the possibility of a radically different kind of writing. I study the existing relations between self and other history: that is, imbalances of power. Hélène Cixous' work sketches the possibility of very different relations: exchanges on a basis of equal power. It provides a useful alternative perspective.

My present aim is to start off a discussion on what difference *Etudes Féminines* makes not for research but for teaching practice. I will assume an agreement on the importance of the research–teaching link. The purpose of teaching is to hand on the best you know. For me, the best of the *Etudes Féminines* approach is its considerable radical potential, which needs to be made generally available. But I do stress radical 'potential', because the approach is a two-edged enterprise. One thing that this discussion might do is sort out some of its contradictions and difficulties. Many of them are inevitable contradictions, arising directly from the decision to work in an academy with a methodology that goes against the academic grain.

A major contradiction is the one spelt out in, for example, *La Jeune née*.[1] On the one hand, *Etudes Féminines* presents itself as an instrument of disruption in the primacy it gives to feminine discourse. Another very simple definition might be helpful here. Masculine – propositional – discourse brings everything back to itself. Feminine discourse is self-effacing, self-giving, receptive to the infinite variations of the real. Masculine relations with the world seek to expropriate; feminine, to 'depropriate' (the word is borrowed from 'Sorties', p. 96). Feminine discourse challenges the binary oppositions by which patriarchal discourse functions. It challenges particularly the basic binary of the all-powerful father, set against the passive, or non-existent mother. The challenge of feminine discourse, fed into academic institutions, shakes the rigid assumptions of the whole hierarchy. It announces the return of the repressed:

> Woman, who has run her tongue ten thousand times seven times around her mouth before not speaking, either dies of it or knows her tongue and her mouth better than anyone. Now, I–woman am going to blow up the Law: a possible and inescapable explosion from now on; let it happen, right now, in language.
>
> When 'The Repressed' of their culture and society come back, it is an explosive return, which is *absolutely* shattering, staggering, overturning, with a force never let loose before, on the scale of the most tremendous repressions. (p. 95)

On the other hand, this hyperbolic disruption is only a language effect. Another account in 'Sorties' of the radical transformation effected by feminine discourse has as its keyword 'imagination'. As you read it, the account implies new powers for the imagination, and hints at its magic possibilities ('Let us simultaneously imagine a general change in a¹l the structures of training, education, supervision – hence in the structures of reproduction of ideological results . . . Imagine!'). But there is nothing beyond that hint to indicate how anyone passes from imagination to reality. The transformations all happen in writing:

> Nothing allows us to rule out the possibility of radical transformation of behaviours, mentalities, roles, political economy – whose effects on libidinal economy are unthinkable – today. Let us simultaneously imagine a general change in all the structures of training, education, supervision – hence in the structures of reproduction of ideological results. And let us imagine a real liberation of sexuality, that is to say, a transformation of each one's relationship to his or her body (and to the other body), an approximation to the vast, material, organic sensuous universe that we are. This cannot be accomplished, of course, without political transformations that are equally radical. (Imagine!) Then 'femininity' and 'masculinity' would inscribe quite differently their effects of difference, their

> economy, their relationship to expenditure, to lack, to the gift. What today appears to be 'feminine' or 'masculine' would no longer amount to the same thing. No longer would the common logic of difference be organized with the opposition that remains dominant. Difference would be a bunch of new differences. (p. 83)

The value of imagination is something to be reinstated in institutions that are sold out to utilitarian, functionalist politics. But we need to keep an eye open for the conservative force of imagination, with all its Romantic pre-emptions. Resolutions in writing, in theory, and in language cannot make up for continuing contradictions in lived reality. Utopia should not be a place of retreat, but a way of remaking the present. Turning the discursive practices of *Etudes Féminines* into pedagogic practice could be one way to do this.

As Susan Sellers' new book shows, Hélène Cixous' seminar already has a worked-out pedagogy.[2] The following summary of key principles and practices derives from the last section of Susan Sellers' text: 'Conversations with Hélène Cixous and members of the Centre d'Etudes Féminines' (two conversations, held in April 1986). Many of the points that arise are reminders of just how much has been lost from the British academic tradition over the last ten years.

We can begin with what modern management practice, now lodged at the centre of our institutions, has taught us to call the 'mission statement' of the seminar. Each seminar member is an active 'guardian' of the text, a Promethean 'fosterer of the vital flame' (p. 141). This is teaching practice that puts as central the personal relationships of text and reader – a re-humanisation of the critical process.

The group is the main unit of organisation. The seminar is *international* in its membership and commitments: 'a country floating above all the countries in the world' (p. 142).[3] That is of some significance for us: the seminar, I would say, affirms the internationalism of the intelligence, as against a commitment to the narrow interests of particular institutions. Members are mostly women, and all are volunteers; this is 'a country on the side of freedom' (p. 142). There is a common focus on what Hélène Cixous describes as 'the revelation which I believe to be the core of human experience: the nature of the relationship to the other' (p. 143). The common starting point is a collective study of questions of writing and sexual difference. From there, individuals branch off along their own paths, returning with presentations on their personal projects. This all adds up to a useful model for organised group work with a humane centre.

Turning to the intellectual principles on which the group works, we find that the relationship to theory is an important starting point. Here Hélène Cixous appears to be responding to a uniquely French teaching problem, created by the power struggles of the various theoretical schools: 'Some years ago there was such an inflation of theoretical discourse in France that whole generations of students were arriving at university already terrorized by the monster' (p. 144). Students need to know how to use theory without being used or 'terrorized' by it. Their thinking should begin with Freud and Derrida in order to go beyond them. Too much theory bars access to the living heart of the text:

> The text is always more than the author wants to express, or believes s/he expresses. As a result of fashionable theoretical practices, all this has been repressed. We have been in the phase of non-meaning, in the suspension, the exclusion of the message. (p. 144)

Psychoanalysis and philosophy cannot deal with the 'poetically beyond' qualities of the text. Preserving its 'strangeness' (p. 146), meeting the text on its own ground, rather than wrapping it up in another, alien discourse, is what matters.

At the heart of criticism is the relationship of reader and text: 'letting oneself be read' by the text, and in the process discovering one's own self and its evasions. 'Through recognition of my own differences, I might perceive something of you' (p. 146). This is a process that rescues the reader from her own ideological limits, as well as the text. I would see it as encouraging a critical self-consciousness that is vital for good academic practice.

There are very specific prescriptions for the ways in which the critic is to think and articulate her reading of the text. In critical thinking, poetry, not philosophy, is the paradigm: 'Philosophy proceeds in a manner which I find restrictive. I prefer thinking in a poetic overflowing' (p. 142). A student clarifies what 'poetry' involves:

> The poetry we are concerned with in the seminar could be described as the opposite of the lie. It's the act of 'stepping out' – a stepping out propelled by a childlike innocence, the sort of innocence which is capable of knowing and writing those moments of our genuine bedazzlement, the truths which are the most difficult to think and bring to life, the magnificent, vital, terrifying questions of life and death, so fundamental to our human condition and yet so consistently repressed. (pp. 142–3)

This seems to me one of the most difficult tenets of the seminar for the modern university to assimilate. Rhapsodic thought is alien to the rationalist logic of the academy. This rhapsody does not in theory involve the loss of reason, because this is an 'innocence capable of knowing' – it is not ignorance – and the bedazzlement it is interested in has to be 'genuine'. But real difficulties of discrimination do arise. Academic institutions have no criteria for assessing 'genuine' bedazzlement. And certainly, articulating a bedazzlement is not easy. The whole point about the dazzling otherness of the text is that it cannot be reduced to its reader's discourse. You need to find a 'corresponding' language, that is, a poetic language to model the text, that will not betray or expropriate it:

> I don't believe we can play with the facts. Someone who has not been in a con-centration camp cannot say what someone who has been imprisoned says. But one thing we who have escaped the camps can do is to make the effort to turn our thoughts towards those who are in captivity. The other thing is to try to find a language that corresponds to the reality of the camps. (p. 152)

Sometimes the only way to do that is by noting your impotence to speak at all. Hélène Cixous herself has dealt with the problem by moving from criticism to creative writing. Does that suggest that in order to write anything meaningful, honest, truthful, you have to move out of the academy? What kind of language, then, do we expect our students to write? The exchange with Catherine Clément on the discourse of the universi-ties, at the end of *La Jeune née*, finds a practical, if unsatisfactory, answer. Hélène Cixous states:

> I use rhetorical discourse, the discourse of mastery, orally, for example, with my students, and obviously I do it on purpose; it is a refusal on my part to leave organized discourse entirely in men's power. I never fell for that sort of bait. (p. 136)

Catherine Clément agrees. But it is a masculine discourse, and 'Woman doesn't enjoy herself in it' (p. 146). The italicised question, slapped in the middle of the text, gets no satisfactory response: '*What remains of me at the university, within the university?*'

Choosing a text to work on is important. Hélène Cixous works on the texts that 'touch' her (*Writing Differences*, p. 148), by which she seems to mean the humanly positive texts, ones that still have a residue of 'hope' in them. I find myself working on some fairly hopeless cases – decadents, and counter-revolutionaries, who interest me precisely because of their backsliding or selling-out to closure. I think it is vital to have both kinds of texts on the syllabus. But I fully agree with the fundamental point that her approach implies. No one should work on any text that isn't a provocation – whether it rouses to anger or delight.

The last point I want to raise here is one of the most important, and certainly for me at the moment, one of the most interesting that the seminar raises. This is the problem of how to handle the question of writing and sexual difference. Hélène Cixous starts from the presumption that the differences between men and women are basic, but are not in the long run as important as the ideal femininity that men and women are said to have in common: 'These differences are simply a small part of the entirety of a human being' (p. 151). My immediate response is that the presumption that these differencs are of minimal significance is not in fact true: or that it is more true for some than for others. For women who hold top academic posts in European institutions, it has some validity. For a university cleaner, it has much less. For women in Islamic countries, it has none. I have just finished reading Nawal el Sadaawi's short story, 'She has no place in Paradise', where the Islamic wife puts up patiently with all her husband's atrocities in the belief that all differences will be levelled out in Paradise. Paradise, in consequence, comes finally as something of a shock: Paradise too is the embodiment of phallocentric prejudice, this time written into eternity. Gender differences have significant historical implications, which can permanently obstruct the realisation of any ideal. Hélène Cixous seems to play these down, privileging the private body at the same time as she denies it its full place in public history:

> If I were to write a historical novel, what would it matter if I were a man or a woman? But if I write about love, then it does matter. I write differently. If I write letting something of my body come through, then this will be different, depending on whether I have experience of a feminine or masculine body. (p. 151)

At this point, the work of the seminar seems to me to fall into its place in the teaching practice of Women's Studies as one way of reading that needs to be complemented by others. There is radical potential in its emphasis on the body as the place where we engage with and understand the world. That potential is limited if the body is not granted its full historical rights. The historical novel is a bad example to choose here. Madame de Genlis, writing across the 1789 Revolution, adapting Walter Scott's historical novel, writes simultaneously about history and love, and writes as a female body with a specific class allegiance. In the interests of preserving aristocratic order against bourgeois claims, she makes her own patriarchal and misogynist version of women which sets them down as the naturally subordinate sex. Everything she writes is marked by her embodiment as a woman in a man's world. From the other end of the political spectrum, Elsa Morante's *History* is a brilliant evocation of what living history through a female body means.

Bodies exist in real, material history, and I see that as a fundamental point to teach. I am concerned that it may be missing from the practice of the seminar. I am, however, happy to admit that this is a point of Hélène Cixous' work that I have not as yet managed to think through to my own satisfaction. My next project is going to be an investigation of her play about Cambodia (*L'Histoire terrible mais inachevée de Norodom Sihanouk, roi du Cambodge*, staged in 1985), which should give me the chance to explore her idea of history more fully.

That last point aside, the pedagogic practice of *Etudes Féminines* remains of considerable value, not least in its potential, as Gayatri Spivak puts it, to be 'productively conflictual when used to expose the ruling discourse'.[4] If we turn now to the context of our own institutions, we can perhaps list the principal areas where conflict is likely to arise.

Women's Studies is entering a dangerous stage: it seems to have acquired a new respectability. There are eleven courses signalled in this year's United Kingdom postgraduate prospectus alone, to which we in Strathclyde University will next year be adding the first taught course in Scotland. Undergraduate programmes and courses in Continuing Education continue to expand. Negative responses are still forthcoming from the men of the *arrière-garde*, just like those described by Mary Evans at the beginning of the 1980s in her article in *Feminist Review*.[5] (Is the subject sufficiently developed? There is not enough literature in the area. What do you mean, you're writing it yourselves? What about library resources? There aren't enough women staff to teach a course. He's the specialist in that area; why isn't he down to teach it?) But there are fewer hostile voices, and even they fall silent in the end. This is still partly, as Mary Evans said, because it's too much trouble to keep up the opposition. It is also partly because other male colleagues are beginning to recognise the intrinsic academic value of the new work. But even more potent now is the argument from market forces. Women's Studies have a high potential for student recruitment. Publishing prospects are substantial; even the most recalcitrant men have noticed the new headings in the publishers' catalogues, the packed shelves in the bookshops, the special sections in the libraries. The problem is to find a way of living humanely in that marketplace, at a time when Government is cutting grants and fewer women stand a chance of finding the fees and the maintenance costs for their courses. Can we use our new position to keep alive the group ethos, the collective values, and the claim for freedom and accessibility with which Women's Studies began? The *Etudes Féminines* approach foregrounds all of these.

An initial cluster of questions relates to students. At what levels can we start teaching *Etudes Féminines* in particular, or Women's Studies in general? Are we limited to university and polytechnic undergraduates, or is there a chance of taking some areas of Women's Studies into schools, or *Etudes Féminines* into Continuing Education? What preliminary commitment and what qualifications can and should we require from students?

Hélène Cixous' students are all volunteers, already fired by the same enthusiasm. The average student's enthusiasm tends to fluctuate, and s/he is often conscript to courses. Could we generate enthusiasm for Women's

Studies if they were a compulsory part of a syllabus? One of the students who is currently following my undergraduate option on French women's writing is insistent that it must be volunteers only, because one's own experience is always being put into question. Some women, she thinks, couldn't 'stomach' the concepts we use. She also thinks that men haven't a hope of tackling the course, because they can't understand the break that women are always confronting, in life and in text, between self-image and reality. Should we invite men to be students on Women's Studies courses? Should we be forcing them to confront their difference, and think themselves into the feminine situation? The logic of the university teaching situation has to be followed through: the teacher has authority to require students to follow the courses she thinks will benefit them most, and we all agree that Women's Studies are an important area of study. Or are Gender Studies now more relevant than Women's Studies?

A preliminary course in theory is obviously invaluable. On most British syllabuses, theory appears only at Honours level, which is often too late. How do you explain to British students reared to distrust intellectualism, let alone theory, that theory can help in the discussion of the role of women? Women students who are enthusiastic at the idea of Women's Studies can be alienated by too much initial difficulty, and by technical language that can be dismissed as elitist and exclusive.

What do we do about the teacher–student relationship and the problem of authority? When we transmit knowledge from a position of power within the institution, we also transmit the values of the institution, which are the values of established culture. Mastery has repressive effects:

> Being able to organise or give order to a discourse and being able to make progress are absolutely indispensable, but there are opposite, negative effects as well. For example, controlling and censoring imagination, free production, other forms, et cetera.[6]

How can women avoid acting as masters? Hélène Cixous advocates that we should:

> Execute the master, kill him, eliminate him . . . The person who transmits has to be able to function on the level of knowledge without knowing . . . one should have the guts to occupy the position one has no right to occupy and show precisely how and why one occupies it. I set my sights high: I demand that love struggle within the master against the will for power.[7]

Time constraints, rigid syllabuses, and the fact that elsewhere in the institution deference systems are still operating makes non-authoritarian teaching difficult. Students at the beginning of their careers need more direction than graduates. How can they choose their own texts for project study, when they don't know what texts exist to be studied? Many students become very anxious when given free rein, and worry about being disadvantaged in final examinations. One last question as regards mastery. Should men be teaching on Women's Studies courses? Can they make the break with the discourse of mastery? Will the students let them?

Examinations raise substantial problems. A student enters the academy on a contract which supposes that there will be a grading at the end of the programme. Grading is done to assist learning, but also with an eye to what comes after the course, for the benefit of students and employers. We spend three or four years teaching students to be expressive and critical, but at the end of the day we have to set up hoops for them to jump through. What can we do about the final examination, that doesn't vitiate every principle of self-development? Is continuous assessment and project work a solution? If we are tied to a formal written examination, what kind of questions do we ask? How do we mark? In the specific context of *Etudes Féminines*, how do we grade someone's reading of text and self, their personal evaluation of the poetic beyond? What standards do we require? Do we fail people, and on what criteria? It is important to have an external examiner who is prepared to deviate, where necessary, from the usual examining criteria. Will such an examiner have the respect of the rest of academy? Will our courses have the respect of the rest of academy?

We do of course need respect – intellectual recognition – within the academy. We live in a real world of power relations, which it is in women's interest to change. The academy turns out people whose grades can qualify them for major policy-making and executive places in that world. Signing a contract for a post in the academy carries heavy responsibilities for determining who will and who will not be in a position to aspire to those places.

The existence of the Centre d'Etudes Féminines, as a prestigious unit of feminist research, has already made a difference within the academic system. Women's Studies are taking on new importance. But the process is still very slow. Women are still consumers rather than producers in education, under-represented in all positions of influence. New strategies are always coming into play to contain our work, as they do for any kind of work that goes against the grain. If change is to be more than imagined, if we are to realise utopia somewhere other than in language, then we have to confront real institutional practices. To acquire enough influence to change things without becoming incorporated into the discourse of institutions is a difficult balancing act, but one which now has to be attempted.

NOTES

1. Hélène Cixous and Catherine Clément, *La Jeune née* (Paris: Union Générale d'Editions, 1975), translated by Betsy Wing as *The Newly Born Woman* (Manchester: Manchester University Press, 1986). All following page references are to this translation, unless other sources cited.
2. Susan Sellers, *Writing Differences: Readings from the seminar of Hélène Cixous* (Milton Keynes: Open University Press, 1988). Susan Sellers' own summary of the pedagogic practice of the seminar is on page 7 of her Introduction.
3. In the discussion that followed this paper, other members of the Centre informed us that the internationalism of the seminar's membership reflected also the absence of sufficient postgraduate grants for home-based students, and the need to recruit heavily from self-funding overseas students. The situation is a familiar one.
4. Gayatri Chakravorty Spivak, *In Other Worlds: Essays in cultural politics* (New York and London: Methuen, 1987), p. 149. Spivak's comment here is applied to French feminism in general, but she has just been writing in detail about Hélène Cixous.
5. Mary Evans, 'In praise of theory: the case for Women's Studies', *Feminist Review*, 10, Spring 1982.
6. *The Newly Born Woman*, p. 146.
7. *ibid.*, p. 140.

Notes on Contributors

Carol Bellard-Thomson teaches literary stylistics in the Department of Linguistics and Modern English Language, and French language in the Department of French Studies, both at Lancaster University. She is an editorial member of PALA, the Poetics and Linguistics Association, and a founding editor of the Association's new journal, *Parlance*. Her recent postgraduate research was on Rabelais, and current research interests centre on literary stylistics as a pedagogical tool in the teaching of French literature at tertiary level.

Jennifer Birkett is Professor of French Studies at the University of Strathclyde, and convenor of the MLitt in Women's Studies at Strathclyde. She is the author of four books, most recently *Determined Women: Studies in the construction of the female subject 1900–1990* (1990), and of articles on English, American and French women writers. She is currently co-editing *The Macmillan Guide to French Literature* and researching books on feminist literary criticism and one titled *Sexuality, Politics and Fiction in the French Revolution*.

Edward Burns is a lecturer in English language and literature at the University of Liverpool. He has published *Restoration Comedy: Crises of desire and identity* (1987), *The Chester Mystery Plays: A modern staging text* (1987) and *Character: Acting and being on the pre-modern stage* (1990). He is currently editing a collection of essays on Rochester.

Hélène Cixous is Professor of Literature at the experimental University of Paris VIII – Vincennes, of which she was a founder member in 1968, and is director of the Centre d'Etudes Féminines which she founded in 1974. She is the author of numerous works of fiction, drama and criticism, including 'The Laugh of the Medusa' ('Le Rire de la Méduse') published in English in 1976, and *The Newly Born Woman* (with Catherine Clément, 1986), originally published as *La Jeune née* in 1975.

Sarah Cornell, born in Springfield, Ohio, United States, graduated with an MA from New York University. She is currently completing a doctoral thesis on Hélène Cixous for the Centre d'Etudes Féminines. She has been a member of the research centre since 1976.

Françoise Defromont is a senior lecturer and teaches at the University of Reims and at the University of Paris VIII, where she belongs to the Bureau de la filière Etudes Féminines. She has written articles and a book on

214

Virginia Woolf, *Vers la maison de lumière* (Editions des Femmes, 1985), and is finishing another one on Katherine Mansfield. Her main field of research is 'Women and Writing'.

Shirley Foster teaches English and American Literature at the University of Sheffield. Her particular areas of interest are nineteenth-century fiction and twentieth-century American literature, especially contemporary women poets. She has recently written a book on Victorian women travellers and plans more research on the language of female discourse. Her first book was a study of singleness and marriage in Victorian women's novels.

Anne Green is a lecturer in French at King's College, University of London. Her publications include *Flaubert and the Historical Novel: 'Salammbo' reassessed*, (1981), and she has a forthcoming book: *The Writings of Madame de Lafayette*.

Terry Keefe is currently Professor of French Studies and Head of Modern Languages at the University of Lancaster, and formerly Head of French and Dean of Arts at the University of Leicester. He has written articles on Descartes, Sartre, Camus, and de Beauvoir, and two books: *Simone de Beauvoir* and *French Existentialist Fiction*. He is co-editor of *Zola and the Craft of Fiction*, and is researching a monograph on *Le Deuxième Sexe*.

Sissel Lie has been Assistant Professor at the University of Trondheim, Norway since 1975, teaching French literature. She has published short stories and a novel *The Lion's Heart* (1988) which will be translated into English in 1990. She has also published articles and anthologies on women's cultural history and on French women authors of the eighteenth century.

Keith McWatters is Professor of French in the University of Liverpool. His main interest lies in Stendhal, whose work for English periodicals he is now editing. He has also written on Stendhal and English novelists, and is interested in George Sand.

Penny McWatters is Head of Modern Languages at Birkenhead High School, Girls' Public Day School Trust. Her doctoral thesis had as its subject Simone de Beauvoir's literary apprenticeship and dealt in particular with *L'Inviteé*. She has a further interest in Raymond Queneau.

Phil Powrie is a lecturer in French at the University of Newcastle upon Tyne. He has published a book on René Daumal and Roger Gilbert-Lecomte and articles on Daumal, André Breton, contemporary women writers in France, French films, and applied linguistics. He is currently co-editing a collection of essays with Margaret Atack entitled *Contemporary French Fiction by Women: Feminist perspectives.*

Naomi Segal teaches French and comparative literature at St John's College, Cambridge. She has published a number of articles and four books, most recently *The Unintended Reader: Feminism and 'Manon Lescaut'* (1986) and *Narcissus and Echo: Women in the French récit* (1988). She is now working on *Mothers and Daughters and Sons*, a study of women in the novel of adultery.

Susan Sellers has published on feminist theory, women's writing and women in education and is author of *Language and Sexual Difference: Feminist writing in France* (forthcoming). She has worked in association with the Centre d'Etudes Féminines in Paris since 1983.

Judith Still is a lecturer in Critical Theory at the University of Nottingham. She is a member of the editorial boards of *Nottingham French Studies* and *Paragraph*, and co-editor of *Intertextuality: Theories and practices* (1990). She has published articles on Jean-Jacques Rousseau, George Eliot and Djanet Lachmet and in the general areas of critical theory and of feminism, and has translated Lachmet's *Lallia* as well as articles by Hélène Cixous and Rodolphe Gasché. She is currently working on a book on Rousseau.

Ann Thompson is a reader in English at the University of Liverpool. She is co-editor of *Teaching Women: Feminism and English Studies* (1989) and author of a number of books and articles on Shakespeare, as well as editor of *The Taming of the Shrew* (1984). Current research is focused on feminist readings of Shakespeare's tragicomedies, editing *Cymbeline* and preparing a 'consumer guide to Shakespeare editions': *Which Shakespeare?*

Nicole Ward Jouve was born in Marseilles but has lived all her adult life in the United Kingdom. She writes fiction in French and criticism in English, and is interested in the practice of bilingual writing and in translation as a way of re-writing. Her books include a translation of her own short stories, *Shades of Grey* (1981), *Colette* (1987), *'The Streetcleaner': The Yorkshire Ripper case on trial* (1988) and a collection of essays, *White Woman Speaks with Forked Tongue: Criticism as autobiography* (1990).

Helen Wilcox lectures in English at Liverpool University. She is co-editor of *Teaching Women: Feminism and English studies* (1989) and *Her Own Life: Autobiographical writings by seventeenth-century Englishwomen* (1989), and editor of the poems of George Herbert. Her current research includes feminist readings of Shakespeare's tragicomedies, and a study of the seventeenth-century religious lyric.

Linda R. Williams is a lecturer in English at the University of Liverpool. She has taught at the Universities of Exeter, Manchester and Sussex, where she completed her doctoral research on gender and epistemology in D.H. Lawrence, Nietzsche, Freud and feminism.

Susan Wiseman is a lecturer in English at the University of Kent at Canterbury.

Index

219